JOHN'S GOSPEL AS WITNESS

This book defends the claims of historical-critical research into the New Testament as necessary for theological interpretation.

Presenting an interdisciplinary study about the nature of theological language, this book considers the modern debate in theological hermeneutics beginning with the Barth-Bultmann debate and moving towards a theory of language which brings together historical-critical and theological interpretation. These insights are then applied to the exegesis of theologically significant texts of the Gospel of John in the light of the hermeneutical discussion. Drawing together the German and Anglo-American hermeneutical traditions, and discussing issues related to postmodern hermeneutical theories, this book develops a view of the New Testament as the reflection of a struggle for language in which the early Church worked to bring about a language through which the new faith could be understood.

ASHGATE NEW CRITICAL THINKING IN RELIGION, THEOLOGY AND BIBLICAL STUDIES

The *Ashgate New Critical Thinking in Religion, Theology & Biblical Studies* series brings high quality research monograph publishing back into focus for authors, international libraries, and student, academic and research readers. Headed by an international editorial advisory board of acclaimed scholars spanning the breadth of religious studies, theology and biblical studies, this open-ended monograph series presents cutting-edge research from both established and new authors in the field. With specialist focus yet clear contextual presentation of contemporary research, books in the series take research into important new directions and open the field to new critical debate within the discipline, in areas of related study, and in key areas for contemporary society.

Other Titles in the Series:

The Ecclesiology of Stanley Hauerwas
A Christian Theology of Liberation
John B. Thomson

Swinburne's Hell and Hick's Universalism
Are We Free to Reject God?
Lindsey Hall

John's Gospel as Witness

The Development of the Early Christian Language of Faith

ALEXANDER S. JENSEN
Church of Ireland Theological College, Ireland

ASHGATE

Published by
Ashgate Publishing Limited
Gower House
Croft Road, Aldershot
Hampshire GU11 3HR
England

Ashgate Publishing Company
Suite 420
101 Cherry Street
Burlington, VT 05401–4405
USA

Ashgate website: http://www.ashgatepublishing.com

British Library Cataloguing in Publication Data
Jensen, Alexander S.
    John's Gospel as witness : the development of the early
    Christian language of faith. – (Ashgate new critical
    thinking in religion, theology and biblical studies)
    1. Bible. N.T. John–Criticism, interpretation, etc.
    2. Language and languages–Religious aspects–Christianity
    3. Language and languages–Religious aspects–History
    I. Title
    226.5'06

Library of Congress Cataloging-in-Publication Data
Jensen, Alexander S., 1968–
    John's Gospel as witness : the development of early Christian language
    of faith / Alexander S. Jensen.
        p. cm. – (Ashgate new critical thinking in religion, theology and
    biblical studies)
    Includes bibliographical references and index.
    ISBN 0–7546–3546–5 (alk. paper)
    1. Bible. N.T. John–Language, style. 2. Bible. N.T. John–Theology.
    I. Title. II. Series.
    BS2615.6.L3J46 2003
    226.5'06–dc22   2003057772

ISBN 0 7546 3546 5

Printed and bound in Great Britain by MPG Books Ltd, Bodmin, Cornwall

Sybille and Kathrin

Contents

Acknowledgements

This book is the result of many years of study. It is based on a doctoral thesis, which was accepted by the University of Durham 1997, and has undergone many changes and revisions since. A great number of people have influenced, assisted and aided my work during this long period of time, and I would like to take this opportunity to express my gratitude to them.

I would like to thank Dr Stephen C. Barton and Dr Loren T. Stuckenbruck, both of the Department of Theology at the University of Durham, who supervised the original thesis, for their friendship and support.

In addition, I would like to thank the members of the New Testament Seminar at Durham University at the time for all the stimulating discussions in the seminar and at other occasions.

I am deeply indebted to St. John's College, which not only became a home for me during my studies at Durham, but also enabled me to become part of English life and culture, and all my friends there.

I would also like to thank the people and clergy of the Parish of St. Michael and All Angels, Norton, for their patience with their curate while he rewrote the thesis into this book.

I am grateful to Prof. John Bartlett, formerly principal of the Church of Ireland Theological College, for his advice and help in preparing the final version of this book.

I dedicate this work to my mother Sibylle and my sister Kathrin in great gratitude for their love and support.

List of Abbreviations

CR Corpus Reformatorum, Halle et.al. 1834ff.

EWNT BALZ, Horst and SCHNEIDER, Gerhard (ed.); *Exegetisches Wörterbuch zum Neuen Testament*, Stuttgart, Berlin, Köln, (Kohlhammer) ²1992.

K&M BARTSCH, Hans-Werner (ed.); *Kerygma und Mythos. Ein theologisches Gespräch;* 6 vols. with supplements, Hamburg (Reich & Heidrich) 1948ff.

KD BARTH, Karl; *Die kirchliche Dogmatik*, 4 vols. 13 parts and Register, Zürich (TVZ) 1932-1970.

RGG³ GALLING, Kurt et.al. (eds.); *Die Religion in Geschichte und Gegenwart: Handwörterbuch für Theologie und Religionswissenschaft*, Tübingen (Mohr-Siebeck) ³1957ff.

THAT JENNI, Ernst, WESTERMANN, Claus; *Theologisches Handwörterbuch zum Alten Testament*, Gütersloh (Chr. Kaiser) ⁴1993.

ThWNT KITTEL, Gerhard, FRIEDRICH, Gerhard et.al. (ed.); *Theologisches Wörterbuch zum Neuen Testament*, Stuttgart (Kohlhammer) 1933ff.

WA LUTHER, Martin; *Kritische Gesamtausgabe*, Weimar 1883ff.

Periodicals are quoted by the abbreviations used by the *Journal of Biblical Literature*, except one journal that is not included in the instruction for contributors of the *JBL*:

NZSTh *Neue Zeitschrift für Systematische Theologie und Religionsphilosophie.*

Chapter 1

Language and Logos

Language is *logos*.

Language is *logos* as the meaningful interpretation of Being.

We find ourselves in an alien world. The world is full of other beings and manifold impressions. We are helpless against the rush of these other beings, unless we have language. Language is a powerful defence against the rush of the world. We name the other beings, as Adam named the animals in the Paradise-garden; being which is given a name can be set into relation, into meaningful relation to other beings and to the human self. Through language we can make sense of the world, understand and communicate what we encounter. Indeed, humanity can communicate!

Language is also based on convention within a group of people who share the same environment and experiences, and so one person can tell another the individual understanding of the world. As language develops, the interpretation of the world gets more and more complex. It starts with straightforward interpretations, like: 'I gather from the vibrations of the earth here, the trumpet-sound and the stomping we can hear that a mammoth will be here soon. As we are many and have our spears with us, we could hunt it' and proceeds to more complex ones like: 'Act only on that maxim through which you can at the same time will that it should become a universal law.' In both examples language is a meaningful interpretation of reality.

The two interpretations of reality I have taken as an example are connected by many thousand years of humanity trying to understand itself within the world in which it finds itself. All these interpretations, all this language, are is connected with and related to each other. Later interpretations refer to earlier ones, contemporary interpretations refer to each other, in both cases either in agreement or disagreement. Together they form the universe of the *logos*, which is pure discourse. Every interpretation of Being which has ever been formulated is a part of this universe of discourse. Every interpretation of the world being formulated comes from there and goes there. It comes from there, because if a human person understands his or her world, it always takes place in interaction with other interpretations which are already part of that universe. It goes there, because after the interpretation has been formulated and uttered, it is part of that universe and participates in the universal system of reference.

We humans are part of both worlds, of the natural, physical world and of the universe of *logos*. In the human person, both worlds meet. The human person, part of the universe of discourse, receives different possible interpretations of the world, which can be evaluated and applied to its physical world. The experiences one makes in the physical world then influence the interpretation of the world, which, in turn, becomes part of the universe of the *logos*. Through the human person, *logos* and *physis* interact. The *physis* is what is interpreted by the *logos*, without *physis* there would be no *logos*. And without *logos*, *physis* would be meaningless and dead.

Logos and *physis* are related to each other also in another, paradoxical way. *Logos* is never available without *physis*. Human understanding of the world is only possible in language, which, as we have seen above, is *logos*, and language is always physically bound. There is no language without the soundwaves which transmit the spoken language from mouth to ear, without ink and paper (or, in the contemporary environment, the hardware of the computer and the electromagnetic waves rushing through the computer-networks and the World Wide Web). Therefore, *logos* is mediated by *physis*, and *physis* is able to carry *logos*. All the interpretations of the world, of which the universe of the *logos* consists, have been oral or written utterings. Theoretically, they could all be written down and collected in a library. Even the understanding of texts, which consists of setting the text into meaningful relation to other texts, to the physical world and the human self, is a process which is expressed in language and thus can be written down. Therefore, *physis* is able to embody *logos*. Yet *physis* does not exhaust *logos*; they are not directly identical, but in a paradoxical unity. *Logos* transcends *physis* and *physis* embodies *logos*.

The universe of the *logos* is full of conflicting interpretations of the physical world. Yet only one interpretation can be meaningful at a time, and only one can be true. Absolute truth, in turn, is not yet visible or directly accessible. A central part of Christian faith is that truth will be visible in the *eschaton*; until then there is no possibility of seeing, only of believing. Every assumption of truth is a belief, for it means to prefer one interpretation of the world over against others. Even to say that there is no truth and to assert a radical relativism is to assume that the relativist interpretation of the world is the only valid interpretation. Therefore, in this world it is necessary to live within the conflict of interpretations and to accept that the final truth will never be found here. Knowing that absolute truth will never be seen in this world, discourse has to bear the multitude of interpretations. Theology, as any other academic discipline, has to accept that its authority is questioned and has to question the other authorities. Only in this context will opinions be tested and prejudices abandoned. To utter one's position, one's interpretation of the world, is always an act of authority, which needs to be responded to by criticism. Only according to this rule will discourse be relatively free from oppression in a communicative network of authority and critique.

Language is *logos*. Within this hermeneutical framework theology and biblical interpretation takes place. The Bible as a whole and its books individually are part of the universe of discourse. They offer a range of interpretations of the world which are the basis of Christian theology. Christian theology has to see the Bible and the biblical books in their place within the network of meaning which is the world of the *logos*. Having received Christian faith and Christian thought-patterns from discourse, they need to be tested in the worlds both of *logos* and *physis*. They have to be translated so that they may be comprehensible and plausible in discourse. Then they are handed on into the communicative universe of the *logos* again, from where they will be taken up again, criticised, transformed and passed on again. In this process of receiving and passing on theology has its place, and to explore the significance of biblical studies in this framework is the aim of the present study.

Chapter 2

Biblical Interpretation in Conflict

Especially in the Anglo-Saxon environment, theologians have embarked on a new hermeneutical debate. Owing to a certain frustration with the historical-critical approach to the New Testament, supposedly new approaches are discussed and find more and more acceptance. Neo-Barthian approaches like the 'canonical approach' and rediscovered 'biblical theology' are broadly discussed, not to mention the so-called post-modern approaches like reader-response, post-structuralism and deconstruction and whatever can be found in the theological marketplace. What all these approaches to the New Testament have in common is that they are in danger of not taking seriously Christianity as a historically conditioned religion. The New Testament itself emphasises that it originated from something that happened in history, in a certain place and at a certain time: so Matthew 2:1, Luke 2:1f. Early Christianity, too, was highly conscious of the historical condition of Christianity, as, e.g. the *under Pontius Pilate* in the creeds indicates. Therefore, to separate Christianity from its historical origin and development means seriously to misapprehend its very nature.

One may suspect that these misapprehensions of Christianity are grounded in an insufficient theory of language. It has been said that language refers to something outside itself, that its meaning is not contained in language itself but that language can only point at it. Post-modern approaches reject this very notion and thus abandon the concept of an identifiable meaning of language. Yet a critical discussion of this concept of reference and its presuppositions is urgently necessary and has, to my knowledge, not yet taken place in the Anglo-Saxon context. An integral part of this study is to challenge this perception of language and meaning and propose a view of language as *logos*, of language as bearer of meaning. Language, as I am going to argue, is able to contain meaning and to disclose it, rather than merely to point at it.

This is not to say that the text is a self-contained whole, because it was created in relation to the discourse of a particular time and place. Therefore, the text is part of a world. The world of the text consists not only of the world within the text, i.e. the narrative and the system of reference within it, but also of the world in which the text was written, for it was written in a language in which every word has not only a specific meaning but also manifold connotations and additional references. As Gadamer puts it, 'every word causes the whole language to which it belongs to resonate, and the whole of the perception of the world, that it is based upon, appear.'[1] Therefore, the text is meaningful within the world of which it is part and thus within the discourse, the network of meaning to which it belongs. To isolate the text from its world, i.e. its historical context, is to do great injustice to the text. I shall develop this theory of language in the first two chapters of this study and carry it out in the following chapters, where I interpret selected passages from John's Gospel.

The view of language as *logos* sets me in opposition to approaches which find the meaning of the text, in our case the New Testament or the Bible as a whole, behind the text. These approaches are represented, on the one hand, by scholars who reconstruct historical events or characters (especially the historical Jesus) and use this reconstruction of a reality behind the text as the basis of theology and faith. On the other hand, neo-Barthian scholars who see the Bible as a whole as referring to the Word of God, which is to be found behind the text rather than in it, also fall under this category. This matter certainly needs to be further explored, as I shall do in the chapter on the debate between Karl Barth and Rudolf Bultmann.[2] Yet the view of language as *logos* also challenges the basic assumption of postmodernism, i.e. that 'signification does not present or represent some original presence; the very notion of presence is *itself* an *effect* produced by signification.'[3] Or, in other words, in post-modernism

> There is no extratextual reality to which texts refer or which gives texts their meaning; meaning or reference are possible only to this network [i.e. texts referring to other texts], as functions of intertextuality.[4]

Thus, it is the very concept of meaning and text which I shall criticise in this study, which is also rejected by post-modernism by separating text and extratextual reality. The hermeneutics I am proposing in this study assume that the text has a distinct meaning which is to be found in the text rather than behind it. Therefore, the approach underlying this study has a thrust

---

1   Gadamer, Hans-Georg; *Wahrheit und Methode*, in: Gadamer, Hans-Georg; *Gesammelte Werke*, vol. 1: *Hermeneutik: Wahrheit und Methode: Grundzüge einer philosophischen Hermeneutik*, Tübingen (Mohr-Siebeck) [6]1990, 434 (English: *Truth and Method*, London (Sheed and Ward) 1979, 415f).

2   Cf. below, 'The Starting Point: Karl Barth and Rudolf Bultmann' pp.15ff.

3   Kearny, Richard; *Modern Movements in European Philosophy*, Manchester and New York (Manchester University Press) 1994, 116f.

4   The Bible and Culture Collective; *The Postmodern Bible*, New Haven and London (Yale University Press) 1995, 130.

critical of the post-modern separation of language and meaning. In consequence, we need to be aware that the way to post-modernism is actually
paved by the epistemology proposed by Karl Barth and his neo-Barthian
followers who are, in fact, open to post-modern criticism – if they are not,
wittingly or unwittingly, following post-modern presuppositions themselves.

This study is not the place for a comprehensive discussion of post-
modern epistemology (or, as ardent post-modernists might prefer,
tarachology), which would be a worthy subject of another study. However, I
should address two more points here. First, an important emphasis of post-
modernism is to identify power structures and hidden agendas in texts,
which then need to be unveiled and criticised. This is, in fact, an important
issue in hermeneutics in general as well as in biblical interpretation. However, one does not have to take a post-modern viewpoint in order to address this issue. In fact, the hermeneutical theory of Hans-Georg Gadamer,
which will be an important stage on the way to a theological theory of language, provides an alternative framework, in which the text can be taken
seriously as meaningful and yet be criticised for its ideological agenda.[5] If
the text is taken seriously as meaningful, then it must be accepted that it is
an authority, for it has to say something new, something the interpreter
would not know without this particular text. Authority, however, is not
something negative in itself (and, arguably, impossible to avoid anyway[6]),
but it must be non-oppressive and open to critique. Rather than pursuing
the (utopian) ideal of anti-authoritarian discourse I prefer to see discourse
as a network of authority and critique, receiving and passing on.[7]

Second, post-modernism stresses the important point that there is no
such thing as a neutral, innocent reading.[8] Although this perception is
right, it is not necessary to conclude that the reader creates the meaning
and imposes it upon the text, which, in turn, does not have any distinctive
meaning in itself. As I intend to show in this study, meaning is not created
by the reader; rather I propose a model of text and reader in which the text
has its own meaning or range of meanings within its world. The reader
approaches the text from his or her world and with his or her presuppositions, prejudices and expectations towards the subject matter and even
towards the text itself. In the tension between interpreter and text understanding takes place and meaning is unveiled. Not one dominates the
other, but understanding takes place in the dialogue between text and

---

5   Cf. below p.42.
6   Cf. *The Postmodern Bible*, 140f.
7   For the concept of authority and critique cf. Bayer, Oswald; *Autorität und Kritik:
     Zu Hermeneutik und Wissenschaftstheorie;* Tübingen (Mohr-Siebeck) 1991, 1-8.
8   Cf. *The Postmodern Bible*, 134f.

reader.[9] Oppressive reading, *eisegesis*, is certainly possible, but if taken as a principle it demonstrates an unwillingness to accept the text's integrity and otherness.

Neo-Barthian approaches to the New Testament represent a current in New Testament interpretation which is growing in interest and influence. Owing to a certain frustration with historical-critical scholarship, these approaches prefer interpreting the final form of the New Testament to understanding it in its historical shape. Among the main representatives of the application of Barthian hermeneutics to biblical interpretation are Brevard S. Childs, Hans W. Frei, and Francis Watson. All of them apply the hermeneutics of Karl Barth differently, yet their hermeneutical presuppositions are similar. Therefore, it shall be sufficient to enter into a discussion with one representative of neo-Barthian hermeneutics. I choose Francis Watson as partner in this discussion, for he has delivered the most recent major work on the theological foundation and methodology of this school of thought, interacting with and identifying the shortcomings of his forebears, especially Hans W. Frei and Brevard S. Childs.

The said frustration with historical-critical scholarship is mainly due to the perception that, in historical-critical scholarship, the New Testament is used as a historical source rather than as sacred scripture of Christianity.[10] Historical interpretation is seen as being committed to secularity rather than Christian faith,[11] so that private faith convictions cannot be made explicit in the theological discussion. 'A certain faith commitment [...] accompanies and motivates one's advocacy of the corresponding historical case; but the "faith commitment" itself is construed as a deeply personal orientation which it would be improper to parade in public.' Therefore, although the private faith commitments are governing the exegesis, 'the real theological concerns remain on the margin.'[12] This approach to biblical interpretation is rejected and replaced by an exegesis that takes seriously the Bible as a canon which belongs to the reading community of the Church, so that it has to be interpreted as canon and in the light of the creeds.[13]

Watson's analysis of the state of New Testament scholarship is indeed very depressing. It certainly applies to the resurrected quest for the historical Jesus, which Watson sees as an important opponent in the hermeneuti-

---

9   Cf. below, pp.39ff.
10 Cf. Watson, Francis; *Text, Church and World: Biblical Interpretation in Theological Perspective*, Edinburgh (T&T Clark) 1994, 2f and 46f.
11 Ibid. 12.
12 Ibid. 13
13 Ibid. 3-6.

cal debate,[14] yet, in my opinion, the rejection of these paradigms does not necessarily lead to 'theological exegesis'. There are other traditions of historical-critical scholarship which display a great sense of responsibility to the church. Rudolf Bultmann's demythologisation of the New Testament, for example, is controlled by his existentialist theology, and his hermeneutics were concerned to find truth relevant to the Church as well as to the individual believer. One may disagree with Bultmann's theology, but a statement like the famous 'In fact, *the radical demythologisation is paralleled by the Pauline-Lutheran doctrine of the justification without works of the law by faith alone. Or rather: it is the consistent application in the realm of knowledge'*[15] hardly points at a lack of theological interest. However, some scholars favouring 'theological exegesis' seem to overlook this element of his theology. Thus it is surprising when some Neo-Barthians accuse Bultmann of being a merely 'technical biblical scholar'.[16] The work of Harrisville and Sundberg spells out the theology behind the different historical critical approaches of exemplary New Testament scholars.[17] To neglect this means to do injustice to critical biblical scholars.

Francis Watson, however, has included a critical discussion of Rudolf Bultmann's theological agenda in his book *Text and Truth*,[18] focusing on Bultmann's use of the Old Testament. This particular question may not be directly relevant to this study, but I believe that a fresh discussion of Karl Barth's and Rudolph Bultmann's positions is necessary, for the original debate has actually never really come to a conclusion. Many questions remain still open, and it can only be fruitful in the theological arena to make the differences between the positions an issue once again.

Another important issue concerning the canonical readings of the New Testament is that these approaches apply a literary theory to the biblical text that is alien to it. Frei proposed to interpret the New Testament as realistic narrative, a concept that is taken from eighteenth and nineteenth

---

14   Ibid. 228f.
15   Bultmann, Rudolf; 'Zum Problem der Entmythologisierung' *K&M* II, 179-208, 207 (own translation, Bultmann's italics).
16   Cunningham, Mary Kathleen; *What is Theological Exegesis? Interpretation and use of Scripture in Barth's Doctrine of Election*, Valley Forge (Trinity Press) 1995, 71.
17   Cf. Harrisville, Roy A. and Sundberg, Walter; *The Bible in modern culture: theology and historical-critical method from Spinoza to Käsemann*, Grand Rapids (Eerdmans) 1995. In fact, it is not possible to speak of *the* historical-critical method for there are different approaches to the New Testament using historical-critical methods without a unifying paradigm.
18   Watson, Francis; *Text and Truth: Redefining Biblical Theology*, Edinburgh (T&T Clark) 1997, 153-169.

century novels.[19] Watson appropriates this concept critically and adopts it as 'intratextual realism'.[20] 'Intratextual realism' understands 'the biblical text as referring beyond itself to extra-textual reality, while at the same time regarding that reality as accessible to us only in textual form'[21] Consequently, Watson interprets the biblical texts in their final form, disregarding the significance of the text's prehistory. 'The present form of the text has erased its own prehistory, and the occasional trace of that prehistory that still shows through is simply a sign of the reality and comprehensiveness of that act of erasure.'[22] The logic of this statement itself deserves critical appreciation, yet, unfortunately, this would distract the focus of this study. It must suffice to note that Watson believes that the prehistory of the text is absolutely irrelevant for its interpretation.

However, this concept of realistic narrative is alien to an ancient text. It stems from modern literary theory and thus does not do sufficient justice to ancient texts like those of the Bible. The aim behind this approach is, certainly, to take seriously the literary dimension of the Bible, which is, in fact, an important and necessary task. Yet the Bible is not a nineteenth century novel, but a collection of ancient literature. Thus the devices for interpreting it must be chosen according to the nature of the literature, which in this case is ancient oriental and Hellenistic. To apply the methods of the interpretation of nineteenth century novels to the Bible is, as it were, like going to a dentist with a broken leg. In order to do justice to the New Testament we must understand it as literature within its contemporary environment, in which literature functioned quite differently from the way it does in modernity. For example, in ancient literature it was common to take up traditional themes and motifs and transform them in order to give them a different meaning. Yet the traditional and the new form of the traditional material were seen together, and the tension intended in the composition and contained in the work was perceived. To cite just one example, the Grammarian Aristophanes, director of the library of Alexandria (c.220 BC) notes in his preface to Sophocles' *Antigone* that, contrary to the version of the material presented by Sophocles, Euripides allows Antigone to survive, to be relieved from the tomb and to marry Haimon.[23] The whole A n t i - g o n e material is taken from the commonly known mythological tradition

---

19 Cf. Watson; *Text, Church and World*, 21.
20 Ibid. 224f.
21 Ibid.
22 Ibid. 55.
23 Cf. Sophocles; *Dramen*, Greek and German (ed. By Wilhelm Willige), Zürich (Artemis & Winkler) 1995, 190. Euripides' *Antigone* is, apart from some fragments, lost. Therefore we have to trust the testimony of Aristophanes the Grammarian.

of ancient Greece, which was transformed by Sophocles as well as by Euripides. This was seen as so significant, that even some centuries later, in the end of the fourth century AD, the Neo-Platonist Salustios finds it important to remark that there are different traditions about Antigone and her sister and includes this in his introduction to the drama.[24] This example demonstrates that even in antiquity traditions behind a text used to be recognised and played a part in understanding it. The approach I am proposing in the present study will attempt to take seriously the New Testament as *ancient* literature while not applying other, alien concepts to the text.

If the bible, as Watson suggests, is interpreted as one self-contained piece of intratextually-realistic literature, how can it then refer to something, to the subject of Christian faith? Watson states:

> The epistemological situation, that reality is textually mediated and that there is no independent access to it, is not reducible to the ontological claim that that there is nothing outside the text. In other words, one may envisage a hermeneutic guided by an intratextual, theological-exegetical *realism*: here, one would seek to identify and elaborate the *truth-claim* of a text, within a determinate contemporary situation, while acknowledging that this truth-claim comes not in the form of a pure transcript of reality but in an irreducibly textual form that necessitates an interpretation that will always itself be subject to contestation.[25]

However, Watson does not make clear how the Word of God as the reality beyond the text relates to the text; he supposes a 'truth-claim' of the text, which is only accessible through the 'irreducibly textual form', i.e. the text in its canonical form. In the passage 'Access to the reality of Jesus is textually mediated',[26] which is meant to clarify this question, Watson does not provide a differentiated explanation as to how the Word of God is textually mediated. Instead, Watson simply states again that the biblical texts refer to some reality beyond themselves, which is accessible to us only in textual form, and then he resorts to calling Karl Barth as witness for his intratextual realism, through Barth's concept of 'saga'. Watson interprets this concept as '[the] texts may or may not render faithfully the details of empirical history; but they do render faithfully the history of the relation of God and humankind, and it is in the light of this function that they must be interpreted.' Unfortunately, Watson does not clarify how the texts can render faithfully the relation between God and humankind if the history described in the texts was inaccurate and the prehistory of the texts is irrelevant. The only hint that can be found as to how the 'truth' may be found through the texts is that 'this is a claim that could only be justified by

---

24 Ibid. 190-192.
25 Cf. Watson; *Text, Church and World*, 152.
26 For this and the following, cf. ibid. 223-231.

the quality and the persuasiveness of the interpretative practice that proceeds from it.' Or, in other words, canonical exegesis is valid because the
results please the Church. One may be excused for asking whether this
justification is not somewhat uncritical.

In the final paragraph of *Text, Church and World*, Watson names the aim
of biblical interpretation as taking 'the more demanding but also more re-
warding way of *seeking to discern the truth* mediated in the texts of holy
scripture.'[27] The first paragraph of his book *Text and Truth* takes up the
same motif. He is more precise here, saying, 'The Spirit of truth bears witness to the grace and truth that are to be found in the enfleshed Word not
directly but through the Christian community – in and through its preaching, its worship and its canonical texts.'[28] Yet, as we have seen above, Watson has not offered a clear perspective as to how the texts actually mediate
this 'truth'. Although *Text and Truth* is meant to 'clarify and elaborate the
position outlined in [*Text, Church and World*]',[29] it does not contain any new
insights into this issue, except that to understand the literal meaning of the
text means to understand the authorial intention.[30] Similarly, his discussion
of Gadamer and Ricœur are not helpful in clarifying this point, for Watson
fails to recognise that neither of them supports his general hermeneutical
theory. For Gadamer, e.g., the process of distancing the text by understanding it within its historical context plays a crucial role. The reflections
on the classical text, which Watson uses,[31] need to be seen in this framework and cannot be read in isolation from it. The same way, Watson seems
to ignore that, for Ricœur, historical criticism, understood as a means of
'distanciation', is an integral part of interpretation[32] and that narrative is
interpretation of reality.[33] Thus, the two witnesses upon whom he calls for
support of his hermeneutical theory seem not to confirm his point at all.

However, if we take seriously that the New Testament consists of a variety of narratives, e.g. four distinct gospels, which all interpret Christianity
differently, then they must be interpreted bringing out their discreet
meaning rather than harmonising them into the framework of a 'canonical'

---

[27] Ibid. 293.

[28] Cf. Watson; *Text and Truth*, 1. More detailed also ibid. p. 27.

[29] Cf. Watson; *Text and Truth*, viii.

[30] Ibid. 123.

[31] Ibid. 49-54.

[32] Ricœur, Paul; *Interpretation Theory: Discourse and the Surplus of Meaning*, Fort
Worth (Texas University Press) 1976, 43f, 89-95.

[33] Ricœur, Paul; 'Erzählung, Metapher und Interpretationstheorie' *ZTK* 84 (1987),
232-253, 232-239. Cf. also Watson; *Text and Truth*, 54-57.

approach.[34] These different ways of interpreting the texts can only be explained by drawing attention to fundamental hermeneutical differences, which will be explored in the first chapter of this study. In fact, the contemporary argument between continental, historical-critical theology and the growing 'canonical' approaches in the Anglo-Saxon context are already prefigured by the argument between Rudolf Bultmann and Karl Barth.

Therefore, I begin this study by developing a methodology for interpreting the New Testament as both historical human document and holy scripture of Christianity, and by discussing the fundamental differences between the hermeneutical approaches of Karl Barth and Rudolf Bultmann. In the first chapter 'The Starting Point: Karl Barth and Rudolf Bultmann', I am establishing the implicit presuppositions, which lead Karl Barth to his 'theological' or 'christological' exegesis on the one hand, and Rudolf Bultmann to his 'existentialist' interpretation on the other. As we will see, Barth is building his hermeneutics upon the reformed *extra-Calvinisticum*, which is a christological statement of the reformed tradition, saying that the eternal and divine *logos* remains separated from the flesh and the flesh separated from the *logos* when the *logos* enters the flesh. Applied to biblical hermeneutics this implies that the Word of God remains separated from the human word and *vice versa*, i.e. human proclamation cannot contain the Word of God, it can only point to it. Bultmann, on the other hand, implicitly affirms the hermeneutical implications of the Lutheran position, which asserts the *genus maiestaticum* of the *communicatio idiomatum*, i.e. the doctrine that the divine attributes of Christ are also property of his human nature: For him the Word of God can be contained in the human words. On the ground of a critical discussion of this crucial issue of the Barth-Bultmann debate, I am going to follow Rudolf Bultmann's approach rather than Karl Barth's. However, it is impossible to follow Bultmann without further critical discussion and reference to the subsequent development to hermeneutical theory.

---

[34]   In this context it may be worth remarking that Watson seems to see the Bible as one narrative, beginning in Gen. 1 with the creation and ending with the new Jerusalem in Rev. 22. Yet, especially after the hermeneutical considerations in his first Chapter 'The Gospels as Narrated History' (Watson; *Text and Truth*, 33-69) this position seems hardly tenable. In fact, the Bible must be seen as a collection of individual narratives which are organised according to a meta-narrative, which can be seen as the history of salvation. Therefore, to see the meta-narrative as the narrative itself and not as the organising principle of individual narratives, which must be interpreted as such, confuses the categories and leads to the abandonment of the individual, distinct text and replacing it with a levelled, much shallower harmonisation.

This is going to take place in the second chapter 'On the Way to Language'. Here we will encounter and follow the later Heidegger on his 'Way to Language' in order to establish the relation between language and meaning. In this part of my study, the so-called New Hermeneutics as well as Hans-Georg Gadamer will be partners in discussion. This section leads naturally to the question of the historicality of understanding, which is discussed next in this chapter, mainly referring to the work of Hans-Georg Gadamer. The last stage on the path to language is the issue as to how language actually bears meaning, in which I am entering a conversation with Paul Ricœur in order to make his theory of metaphor and symbol fruitful for biblical interpretation.

In the next section, I am going to apply these insights to the interpretation of the New Testament, and to developing my view of the New Testament as *Struggle for Language*, i.e. the New Testament reflecting the attempts of early Christianity to develop a language through which it could understand and communicate the new faith. This approach to the New Testament will not separate the two essential aspects of its understanding, i.e. that it is a historical human document as well as the holy scripture of Christianity. This approach enables interaction with the New Testament on the basis of the interpreter's own tradition, yet it also facilitates the ecumenical and interdisciplinary discourse. It is meant to be an approach which takes account of the New Testament, today's church and the Christian tradition, which connects both and enables a critical reflection of all three elements.

The following chapters of this study apply the methodology which follows from the hermeneutical approach of the *Struggle for Language* to selected texts from John's Gospel. This is to demonstrate that this approach is useful to understanding the New Testament and doing justice to it as both sacred scripture and historical, human document. In the first chapter of the second part I am discussing various introductory questions in the light of the *Struggle for Language*, thus preparing the ground for the actual exegesis of the following chapters. It is important to note that my interpretation of John's Gospel does not attempt to be an authoritative interpretation, but an example of the way in which my hermeneutical insights can be put into action. Therefore, disagreement, even fundamental disagreement, with the historical presuppositions of my exegesis does not affect the main point of this study, which is the general hermeneutics and the methodology following the concept of the *Struggle for Language* rather than new insights into John's Gospel. I should be happy if anyone were to find interesting insights or interpretations of the Fourth Gospel in my work, yet this should not be much more than a bonus.

The first of the studies is the interpretation of the hymn underlying the prologue to John's Gospel. Here I am discussing issues of Johannine theology prior to the composition of the Gospel and identify the influences which lead to the foundation of Johannine Christianity. The second study contains an exegesis of the Nicodemus Discourse (John 3:1-21). In the course of these considerations I am highlighting the theology of the evangelist and the forces driving Johannine theology towards Gnosticism. In the third study I am discussing Jesus' final prayer in John 17 as an example of Johannine thought after the time of the evangelist and just before the 'Gnostic crisis' of the Johannine church. In the course of these studies I am highlighting how the development of Johannine theology can be made fruitful for our present understanding of Christianity and thus for our own participation in the Struggle for Language.

Through these studies I am demonstrating that a consistently historical-critical exegesis of the New Testament does not exclude theological reflection. In fact, it is necessary to develop a general hermeneutical approach which unites the main theological disciplines, biblical studies, church-history, including history of doctrine, and contemporary theology in the endeavour to formulate and understand the ancient Christian faith in the contemporary environment. Yet this will not take shape in the ruling of theology over interpretation but in a consistently hermeneutical theology.

Chapter 3

The Starting Point:
Karl Barth and Rudolf Bultmann

It is rather a commonplace to say that for the largest part of the 20th century, the debate between Karl Barth and Rudolf Bultmann dominated the hermeneutical discussion in theology. This debate, however, together with the discussion of Bultmann's demythologisation-programme, has never really come to a conclusion. It just subsided in the late sixties, being eclipsed by other questions that were able to raise more interest at the time.[35] Thus, the differences between these two theologians are far from being resolved and, all too often, underestimated. For example Werner Jeanrond suggests in his popular textbook *Theological Hermeneutics* that the difference consists of merely beginning at different starting points, i.e. Barth starting *extra nos* and Bultmann *intra nos*.[36] It is also not furthering the discussion simply to describe Barth's hermeneutics as 'theological' or 'christocentric' as opposed to Bultmann merely being a 'technical biblical scholar',[37] which underestimates Bultmann's theological and Barth's historical interest. Therefore, it is necessary to discuss the different presuppositions of their respective hermeneutical approaches, which bring about the 'christocentric' and the 'existentialist' exegesis. These commonly discussed differences are, however, only the surface of a deep-rooted disagreement. Behind the two theological approaches lie completely different epistemologies and understandings of the world. Therefore, Karl Barth is certainly right when he writes in 1952 that he did not believe that he and Bultmann could come to a mutual understanding in this life and that, therefore, those theologians who try to develop a viewpoint beyond Barth

---

[35] Cf. Körtner, Ulrich; 'Arbeit am Mythos? Zum Verhältnis von Christentum und mythischem Denken bei Rudolf Bultmann' *NZSTh* 34, 1992, 163-181, 164.

[36] Cf. Jeanrond, Werner; *Theological Hermeneutics: Development and significance,* London (SCM) 1991, 135.

[37] Cunningham; *What is Theological Exegesis?* 71.

and Bultmann should be advised to travel one of the two paths consistently to its end rather than to harmonise them.[38]

The deep-rooted differences between Barth and Bultmann are grounded in their completely different understanding of the task of theology and the Word of God. The basis of the disagreement has its parallel in the old argument about the *extra-Calvinisticum*, the Lutheran-Calvinist argument about the relation of divinity and humanity, of the transcendent and the immanent. Its significance for hermeneutical theory has, in my opinion, not sufficiently been discussed, and so it is necessary to give a short outline of the relevant issues.

The *extra-Calvinisticum* is a christological statement of the reformed tradition, saying that the eternal and divine *logos* remains separated from the flesh and the flesh separated from the *logos* when the *logos* enters the flesh: *Logos extra carnem, caro extra logon*. It was a polemical turn against the Lutheran tradition, which affirmed the *genus maiestaticum* of the *communicatio idiomatum*, i.e. that the divine attributes of Christ are also property of his human nature and thus that the *logos* is able to enter the flesh, yet without being exhausted in it. Calvin, however, teaches that 'even if the Word in his immeasurable essence united with the nature of man into one person, we do not imagine that he was confined therein.'[39] Yet Calvin keeps the divine and the human attributes of Christ as far apart as possible when, in the context of the Ascension, he states that 'we always have Christ according to the presence of majesty; but of his physical presence it was rightly said to his disciples, "You will not always have me with you" [Matt. 26:11]. For the church had him in his bodily presence for a few days; now it holds him by faith, but does not see him with the eyes.'[40] Luther, on the other hand, argues that 'Christ's body is at the right hand of the Father, as it is commonly known. The right hand of God, however, is everywhere [...] therefore it is as well in bread and wine on the table. Yet, where God's right hand is, Christ's body and blood must be.'[41] Luther is able to think the paradox that God can be within the flesh, and at the same time above all and outside all created things. This paradoxical statement that God is in the elements of the Lord's Supper and at the same time infinitely above them, which holds together the eternal and the temporal without collapsing them into each other, is an important feature of Lutheran theology.

---

38   Cf. Barth, Karl; *Rudolf Bultmann: Ein Versuch, ihn zu verstehen – Christus und Adam nach Röm. 5: Zwei theologische Studien*, Zürich (EVZ) 3/2(respectively)1964, 5f. Both essays were written 1952; ibid.

39   Cf. Calvin, John; *Institutes of the Christian Religion*, Book II, Ch. XIII:4.

40   Calvin; *Institutes*, Book II, Ch. XVI:14.

41   Luther; WA XXIII, 138ff.

The hermeneutical significance of this argument between Lutherans and Reformed becomes clearer in the other version of the *extra-Calvinisticum*: *finitum non est capax infiniti* (the temporal is not able to contain the eternal), which the Lutherans countered with their formula *finitum capax infiniti!* (the temporal can contain the eternal). Thus, in analogy with the christological question, in the reformed tradition the finite human word cannot contain the eternal Word of God. Lutherans, on the other hand, can see human word and Word of God in paradoxical identity.

If one sets the Barth-Bultmann discussion in the context of this debate, Karl Barth would take the side of the reformed tradition; his hermeneutics are based upon the Calvinist *finitum non est capax infiniti!* Bultmann, on the other hand, would counter with the Lutheran *finitum capax infiniti!* The discussion between Barth and Bultmann has, implicitly, this fundamental disagreement as its basis, which also accounts for Barth's and Bultmann's inability to understand one another.

There are only a few writings in which the two theologians refer directly to each other, among them their correspondence and Karl Barth's essay *Rudolf Bultmann: An attempt to understand him* (*Rudolf Bultmann: Ein Versuch, ihn zu verstehen*), to which Bultmann never replied in public but only in a personal letter,[42] and the latter's essay 'The Problem of Hermeneutic' ('Das Problem der Hermeneutik').[43] Yet for a full understanding of their respective positions it is certainly necessary to use their other publications as well.

Before beginning to discuss the controversy between Karl Barth and Rudolf Bultmann, we need to address one essential issue in Karl Barth's *œuvre*, which is the question of his alleged conversion from 'dialectics' to 'analogy', which is crucially important to any discussion of Karl Barth's thinking and any Barthian theology. Through the highly influential interpretation of Karl Barth by Hans-Urs von Balthasar, Barth's development is widely assumed to be discontinuous.[44] Balthasar assumes, that after the dialectical period of his work, Barth turned to a completely new approach, based on the principle of analogy rather than on that of *diastase* (separation) between God and humanity.[45] Neo-Barthian scholars usually follow Balthasar's interpretation. Watson, for example, indicates that he accepts

---

[42]   Barth, Karl – Bultmann, Rudolf; *Briefwechsel 1922-1966* (ed. by Bernd Jaspert), Karl Barth, Gesamtausgabe, V. Briefe, vol. 1, Zürich (TVZ) 1971, 169-195.

[43]   Bultmann, Rudolf; 'Das Problem der Hermeneutik' in: *Glauben und Verstehen* vol. 2, Tübingen (Mohr-Siebeck) [6]1993, 211-235.

[44]   Cf. McCormack, Bruce L.: *Karl Barth's Critically Realistic Dialectical Theology: Its Genesis and Development 1909-1936*, Oxford (Clarendon) 1995, 1-4.

[45]   Cf. Balthasar, Hans Urs von; *Karl Barth: Darstellung und Deutung seiner Theologie*, Köln (Jakob Hegner) 1951, 93f.

this reading of Barth's work by assuming a sharp differentiation between Barth's earlier and later work.[46] In Balthasar's opinion, after the turn to analogy, the human word can be identified with the divine word through the *analogia fidei* (analogy of faith),[47] so that God can be spoken of in human language. Yet this reading of Karl Barth has been challenged by Bruce McCormack, who, in his study *Karl Barth's Critically Realistic Dialectical Theology*, has pointed out that Barth has remained faithful to his insights of the dialectical period for his whole life, and that, therefore, his theology has never been changed fundamentally but developed continually.[48]

In the following discussion of the controversy between Karl Barth and Rudolf Bultmann, I am going to follow McCormack's view of a continuity in Karl Barth's epistemology. This will also be reflected in the choice of works discussed, which include Karl Barth's early work, as, for example, his *Epistle to the Romans* and others, as well as his later work from the *Church Dogmatics* to his last major work, the *Introduction to Evangelical Theology*.

Deus dixit: Word of God and Scripture

Fides quaerens intellectum

Before discussing the fundamental differences between Karl Barth and Rudolf Bultmann, it is necessary to highlight an important feature common to them both. Both agree on the presupposition that theology is essentially Christian and that the interpreter has to be part of the Church, i.e. the community of faith.

Karl Barth describes the relation between faith and theology through Anselm of Canterbury's phrase '*fides quaerens intellectum*' (faith seeking understanding). According to Barth, following Anselm, the presupposition of all theology is Christian faith,[49] having its source in the 'Word of Christ', which is indirectly identical with its reflection, particularly in the Bible.[50] Thus, the question of an external legitimisation of the revelation is entirely irrelevant; revelation as the source of all theology has to be acknowledged as the inner necessity of theology.[51] *Deus dixit*, 'God has spoken' is the

---

46   Ibid. 244.

47   Ibid. 117f.

48   McCormack; *Karl Barth's Critically Realistic Dialectical Theology*, 434-441.

49   Cf. Barth, Karl; *Fides quaerens intellectum*, 25f and Barth, Karl; *Einführung*, 112-115.

50   Cf. Barth; *Fides quaerens intellectum*, 20-22.

51   Cf. Bayer; *Theologie*, 324f. Cf. also Hunsinger, George; *How to read Karl Barth*, 49-64.

starting point of Barth's theology,[52] which has to be accepted by the theologian and the biblical interpreter in order to be admitted to the theological discourse. Thus, theology is a task exclusively of the Church, and it takes place only within the Church.

Since theology is, for Karl Barth, a task exclusively of the Christian Church, and presupposes Christian faith, there are important implications for his understanding of scripture. Barth thus asserts that the Bible is an authority which exists over against the Church.[53] This authority of the Bible does not need to be and cannot be justified by the Church since the Church is founded upon the biblical testimony to Jesus Christ. In fact, the Christian Church is the Christian Church only because she has accepted the Bible's witness to Jesus Christ, and therefore the Bible 'imposes itself' as normative upon the Church,[54] as Barth repeatedly insists. There is no means of going beyond this authority of the Bible, as it is self-evident for the Christian Church. Any attempt to question beyond the Bible's authority would inescapably lead to the Church's dialogue with herself. Barth sees this authority of the Bible also covering the biblical canon. For him, the Bible has 'imposed itself' as canon upon the Church; therefore scripture 'constitutes itself' the canon. The Church 'can only register this event as such, as the reality in which the Church is the Church.'[55]

For Bultmann, too, the Bible is the source of divine revelation and has to be accepted as that by the interpreter, although in a different manner than for Barth. Bultmann's presupposition is that to understand the Bible means to understand its message as questioning the interpreter.[56] For Bultmann, the Bible is the Word of God addressing the interpreter; it is a force that speaks into today's human existence and demands a decision either to accept or reject it.[57] The guiding question of the interpretation is that regarding God and his revelation.[58] As Word of God and Church belong intrinsically together,[59] theology is a task that takes place in the realm of the Church. Even the debate about his concept of demythologisation is, for

---

52 Bayer; *Theologie*, 322.
53 Cf. Barth; KD1/1, 108-110.
54 Ibid.
55 Cf. Barth; KD 1/1, 110.
56 Cf. Barth; *Rudolf Bultmann*, 11. Cf. Also Rudolf Bultmann's response in Barth, Karl — Bultmann, Rudolf; *Briefwechsel 1922-1966*, 173.
57 Bultmann, Rudolf; *Das Problem der Hermeneutik*, 233.
58 Ibid.
59 Cf. Bultmann, Rudolf; 'Zum Problem der Entmythologisierung' *K&M* II, 206. Cf. Also Schmithals, Walter; *An Introduction to the Theology of Rudolf Bultmann*, London (SCM) 1968, 225.

Bultmann, a discussion that takes place within the Church, although it is also intended to function as a catalyst for interdisciplinary discourse.[60]

Here, a main point of Barth and Bultmann's disagreement already becomes discernible. For Barth the presupposition of theology is that God *has spoken*, and has revealed himself once for all, which is reflected in the Bible, whereas for Bultmann God *speaks* through the Bible and addresses the reader or hearer. In order to pursue this point, we must discuss their respective understanding of the Word of God.

Logos extra carnem?

In short, Karl Barth sees the Word of God *behind* scripture, while Rudolf Bultmann finds it *in* scripture. For Karl Barth, on the one hand, the Word of God is absolutely transcendent, so that human language is incapable of referring to God or to the Word of God directly.[61] Thus, the Word of God is the 'Word within the words'[62] of the biblical text, which the interpreter must access through the text in order to understand. Karl Barth regards the Bible as one of three forms of the Word of God, i.e. revelation, scripture and the Church's proclamation. However, these three forms are only 'mirror images' (*Spiegelbilder*) of the one Word of God,[63] which cannot be expressed in human words. The relation between the human images of the word of God and the Word of God itself is that of simile (*Gleichnis*) rather than of equation (*Gleichung*).[64] Consequently, for Karl Barth there is an 'indirect identity'[65] between the Word of God and scripture.

For Rudolf Bultmann, on the other hand, the Word of God is present in the human language of the Bible. He sees the divine *logos* manifest in the external human word, in the proclamation of the Apostles, in the holy scriptures, and carried on in the Church's proclamation of Christ[66]: 'A human being like me speaks the Word of God to me; in him the *logos* is incarnate.'[67] The Word of God is present in the *verbum externum*, the actually

---

60   Bultmann, Rudolf; 'Zu J. Schniewinds Thesen' *K&M* I, 122-138, 138.

61   Cf. Hunsinger; *How to read Karl Barth*, 43.

62   Barth, Karl; *Der Römerbrief*, XIX.

63   Cf. Barth; KD1/1 136 and *Einführung*, 41. I believe that it is possible and legitimate to use parts from Barth's earlier and later work together in order to understand his hermeneutical approach – as we will see in the discussion below, there is much more continuity in Barth's work than some interpreters would allow.

64   Cf. Barth; *Einführung*, 152.

65   Cf. Barth; KD 1/2, 545.

66   Cf. Bultmann; 'Zum Problem der Entmythologisierung' *K&M* II, 206.

67   Op.cit., 206, fn.1.

spoken or written human word, in which a human being encounters God.[68] The Word of God, however, cannot be identified with the New Testament, and yet it is present within it: 'It is misleading if, in the discussion of methodological problems of New Testament hermeneutics, the New Testament and the Word of God are identified. The Word of God is present in the human word, and the New Testament is available as a literary document of history. [...] That it is the Word of God can only be seen in the event of believing understanding.'[69]

Already in this very short description of the two different positions it has become apparent that fundamental differences are at work here. Either the reader or hearer finds the Word of God behind the words of scripture or he or she finds himself or herself addressed by the Word of God through the human word of scripture.

Furthermore, for Karl Barth, the Word of God is God's revelation in his dealings with Israel and action through Jesus Christ as testified in the biblical scriptures. This testimony of scripture is not a monotony but a polyphony, which corresponds to the variety within God's word itself.[70] The Word of God is the one unfathomable truth, which is reflected in various ways in the Bible, and so through the manifold testimony of the scriptures the interpreter may come to a knowledge of the unfathomable mystery of God,[71] which is the one Word behind the multitude of words. Therefore, the aim of theology is 'knowledge of the "eternally rich" God, his one secret in the overflowing fullness of his counsels, his ways and judgements.'[72]

In order to achieve knowledge of God through the reading of the biblical scriptures, the interpreter has to read the texts in the spirit of obedience and with a willingness to understand.[73] Then the meaning of the text, i.e. the Word of God, will disclose itself to the reader. Through the text the interpreter will understand the subject matter as well as the author did, with the result that the reader almost forgets that he or she is not the author her- or himself. Eventually, the interpreter is wrestling with the subject matter itself, which in the case of the New Testament is the Word of God directly rather than only with its document.[74] Thus, true theology begins

---

68   Ibid. 204. Cf also Schmithals; *An Introduction to the Theology of Rudolf Bultmann*, 222f.

69   Bultmann in Barth – Bultmann; *Briefwechsel*, 188.

70   Cf. Barth; *Einführung*, 42.

71   Ibid. 42f.

72   Ibid. 43.

73   Barth; *Rudolf Bultmann*, 12f.

74   Barth; *Römerbrief*, XIX, and *Einführung*, 41. Cf. also the discussion of Barth's 'internal reconstruction' in Bayer; *Theologie*, 332-335.

where the letter of the text ends,[75] in the self-disclosure of God through the Holy Spirit.[76]

For Rudolf Bultmann, on the other hand, the Word of God is always address. Through the saving event, the cross and resurrection of Jesus Christ, which has happened once for all, God has addressed humanity and opened the possibility of living in faith. This saving event is present in the external word, in its proclamation.[77] Where Jesus Christ is proclaimed, the saving event is present, because through this proclamation the possibility of faith is opened. So we can say that in the proclamation of Jesus as the Christ humanity encounters God. 'We encounter God in his word',[78] and the word of God is *verbum externum*.[79] The Word of God is present in the *kerygma*, the proclamation of Jesus Christ. Since the New Testament is the proclamation of Jesus Christ as the risen Lord, the Word of God is present in the human words of scripture, though hidden.[80] Thus the Word of God, God himself, is addressing the reader or hearer through the words of the New Testament. The Word of God is, for Bultmann, the Word *in* the words, as opposed to Karl Barth, for whom the Word of God is to be found *behind* the words. Consequently, Bultmann's aim is to understand the New Testament in a way that the kerygmatic address is brought out, so that the text becomes meaningful to the hearer or reader. Interpreting the New Testament, his ultimate aim is to preach the text and thus to continue the proclamation of Christ, in order to call the hearer to faith.

For Bultmann the theologian should not be much interested in who God is *per se*, but how he acts and deals with humanity. He is not at all interested in the mystery of God, which Barth is keen to explore.[81] In this respect, Bultmann is in line with the traditional Lutheran position which was well expressed by Philipp Melanchthon in the introduction to the first edition of his *Loci Communes*: '*Mysteria divinitatis rectius adoraverimus quam vestigaverimus*' ('The mysteries of the divinity we should rather adore than explore').[82] As Bultmann is mainly interested in God addressing humankind through his Word, Bultmann's position can also be described with

---

75 Barth; *Fides quaerens intellectum*, 29f, 41f. Cf. Also *Römerbrief*, XXIXf.

76 Cf. Bayer; *Theologie*, 328-334.

77 Bultmann, Rudolf; *Theologie des Neuen Testamentes*, Tübingen (Mohr-Siebeck) ⁹1984, 309.

78 Bultmann; 'Zum Problem der Entmythologisierung' *K&M* II, 204.

79 Ibid.

80 Ibid. 200.

81 Cf. above, p.21.

82 Melanchthon, Philipp; *Loci Communes, 1521*, Latin and German, ed. Lutherisches Kirchenamt der Vereinigten Evangelisch-Lutherischen Kirche Deutschlands, transl. and annnotaded by H.G. Pöhlmann, Gütersloh (Mohn) 1993, 0.6, p.19.

Melanchthon's '*Hoc est Christum cognoscere beneficia eius cognoscere.*' ('To know Christ means to know his benefits.')[83] Martin Luther makes the same point when he states that the subject of theology is not God in himself, but the relation between human being and God: '*Subiectum Theologiae homo reus et perditus et deus iustificans vel salvator.*' ('The subject of theology is the human being, guilty and lost, and the justifying and saving God.')[84] Theology is, for Bultmann, about God's word to humankind, about his acting with humankind and not about God himself. Thus, his theology is about the proper understanding of God's address and therefore pertains primarily to making the kerygma within scripture speak and rendering its address audible. Theology is subservient to biblical interpretation; its function is only to help the reader understand the biblical texts properly and to bring about an encounter with God's word in scripture. Bultmann's theology is grammar of sacred scripture, whereas Karl Barth's theology is knowledge of the divine mystery.

A problem of Karl Barth's hermeneutical theory is in his insistence on the *diastase*, the absolute separation of transcendence and immanence, which traditionally is called *distinctio metaphysica*. This implies for Barth that the meaning of a text is transcendent, so that it cannot be *in* the text, but it must be *behind* the text, since for Barth the finite cannot contain the infinite.[85] The meaning of the text cannot be expressed in words, for it is behind the words, which only reflect the meaning like a mirror-image. If the text is read with the willingness to understand and in the spirit of obedience, the subject of the text will disclose itself to the reader. Thus, the Word of God, which is only reflected by (rather than contained in) the text, discloses itself to the faithful and obedient reader or hearer.

---

83 Melanchthon, Philipp; *Loci Communes*, 0.13., p.23. Barth has seen this parallel between Melanchthon and Bultmann, cf. *Rudof Bultmann*, 18.

84 Luther, Martin; WA 40 II, 328,1f.

85 Cf. Bruce McCormack's analysis of Karl Barth's epistemology: For Barth, revelation is an entirely 'unhistorical' event (cf. *Karl Barth's Critically Realistic Dialectical Theology*, 251), i.e. for him the new world opened up through revelation touches the old without extension in historical time, as a tangent touches a circle (ibid. 253, cf. Barth; *Römerbrief*, 6). The point of contact between the new world and the old is, for Barth, only the resurrection. Revelation of the new world, i.e. the resurrection, is not really part of history, but a 'suprahistorical' event. Bultmann, on the other hand, sees revelation happen in history, it is part of it. This understanding of the relation between the new world and the old is paralleled by that of the two natures of Christ in Antiochenian understanding (Karl Barth) and the Cyrillian-Alexandrian (Bultmann), which reflects the argument about the *extra-Calvinisticum*.

Thus Karl Barth's understanding of meaning and text, or, as in our case, Word of God and biblical text, is in danger of mysticism in relation to the Word of God. Understanding the New Testament is not at all an issue for Karl Barth, for he sees the biblical text only as a vehicle for the self-disclosure of the true meaning of the text, the Word of God through the Spirit. Karl Barth himself believed that his hermeneutical principles were drawn from scripture.[86] However, as Oswald Bayer has shown in a critical discussion of Barth's theology, the notion of the self-disclosure of the subject matter is more influenced by Hegelian philosophy than by the New Testament.[87] Barth, however, does not show any awareness of his own philosophical presuppositions but accuses Bultmann of being influenced by 'a certain philosophy'. Here, Karl Barth's thought shows an unfortunate lack of self-reflection and consistency.

On this basis, I believe that Rudolf Bultmann's view of the Word of God and the biblical text is to be preferred, as Bultmann does not separate the two elements, meaning and text, Word of God and human word, but he is able to hold them together. For Bultmann, the Word of God is in the text; it is in paradoxical identity with the text; i.e. the Word of God, which is essentially address, addresses the hearer through the human proclamation of the *kerygma*. In this respect the Word of God, the Gospel, is a living voice, for it is present in the proclamation. The immanent text may contain the transcendent Word of God, *finitum capax infinitum*. Thus for Bultmann the understanding of the text itself has priority over the understanding of what is behind the text. He does not distinguish between the immanent text and its transcendent meaning.

The notion of the subject matter being in paradoxical identity with the text is, in fact, a strong safeguard against postmodernist criticism of other views of reference and meaning, such as the Barthian model.[88] If the meaning of the text lies behind the words of the text, as Karl Barth assumes, then the hermeneutical approach is open to a postmodernist criticism, which finally cuts off the text from what it is supposed to refer to. In view of these considerations, one ought to follow Rudolf Bultmann's hermeneutical approach rather than Karl Barth's, as the former is able to avoid the difficulties arising from the latter's theory of language.

Because of his seeing the Word of God in the text, Rudolf Bultmann's aim is to make the text itself speak, and so he is able to see the particularity of each text. Bultmann wants to bring out what is in the text; his interpretation is *exegesis* in the literal meaning of the word. Karl Barth, on the other

---

[86]   Barth; *Rudolf Bultmann*, 57.
[87]   Cf. Bayer; *Theologie*, 328-335.
[88]   Cf. above, p.5.

hand, by giving priority to the Word of God behind the text, is in constant danger of practising *eisegesis*, for he can read theological meaning into an individual text which is not there.[89] When Barth reads the Bible, knowledge of God rules over against understanding the text.

In addition, for Karl Barth the Bible and the Church form a closed circle. The Church accepts the authority of the Bible without questioning; the Bible is, in turn, the only document of the Word of God on which the Church is founded. Thus, no adequate understanding of the biblical text is possible without the willingness to understand the Word of God behind the biblical text and without faith in the Trinitarian God. If this is so, any interdisciplinary dialogue about biblical interpretation is impossible. Yet for Bultmann the text can be understood without faith, for it is, being an address, a call to faith. The text has to be understood as a historical human writing, and thus the secular methods for interpreting historical texts have to be applied. Therefore, it is possible to enter a dialogue about biblical interpretation with other academic disciplines and other faiths.

Pre-understanding or Prejudice?

A major point of disagreement between Barth and Bultmann is the significance of pre-understanding for understanding the New Testament and for understanding in general. For Rudolf Bultmann a pre-understanding of the subject matter is essential for the process of understanding,[90] whereas Karl Barth treats any pre-understanding of the subject matter as an obstacle to understanding and as an expression of unwillingness to understand.[91] This important disagreement between the two scholars seems to be rooted in the fundamental difference in their concepts of Word of God.

As we have seen above, Karl Barth views the Word of God as absolutely transcendent and therefore beyond the words of scripture. As the Word of God is totally different from any worldly words, there cannot be any pre-understanding of the Word of God. We recall that for Barth the Bible is the mirror image of the Word of God, the human 'document' pointing at the subject matter. The Word of God itself is, consequently, totally different from all human words; God's revelation happens 'straight from above.'[92] Thus, it is impossible for humankind to know anything about God and his Word before having encountered it. The biblical texts are, obviously,

---

[89] Cf. Bultmann in Barth — Bultmann; *Briefwechsel*, 161-163.
[90] Cf. Bultmann; 'Das Problem der Hermeneutik' in: *Glauben und Verstehen* vol. 2, Tübingen (Mohr-Siebeck) ⁶1993, pp.211-235, 227-235.
[91] Cf. Barth; *Rudolf Bultmann*, 56-60.
[92] KD I/1, 348.

written in human words. These point at the divine revelation; through
them the interpreter comes to understand the Word of God. As the biblical
texts, however, deal with something of which no pre-understanding is
possible, it is not fruitful for exegesis to have a pre-understanding of the
subject matter of the text. If the texts are interpreted in the spirit of obedience, the subject matter, i.e. the Word of God, will disclose itself to the
interpreter through the text. In discussion with Bultmann, Barth stated:

> 'Would it not be better [...] to make great effort to be relaxed towards the text
> and to wait whether and how one will understand practically and factually (and
> thus will be able to understand) or, alternatively, will not understand (and thus
> will not be able to understand)? Rather than to take what one considers one's
> own ability to understand as catalyst for the New Testament text, to let the New
> Testament text be the catalyst of one's own understanding? Rather than to aim
> at an understanding of the text within the framework of one's own, supposedly
> authoritative self-understanding, to understand oneself the way in which one
> finds oneself understood by the text in order to understand the text better and
> better from the basis of this new self-understanding?'[93]

For Rudolf Bultmann, on the other hand, the subject matter of the text,
the Word of God, is not *behind* the text but *in* the text. The Word of God as
written or spoken word makes itself heard through the human words of
the text and calls the reader or hearer to faith in Christ. As the Word of God
is present in the human words, the human words have to be interpreted as
such, i.e. with all the methods necessary to understand human utterings.
Thus, it is the basis of interpretation that the human authors of the New
Testament had a certain understanding of the subject matter, i.e. human
existence and God, before they encountered the *kerygma*. Through their
faith their previous understanding of the subject matter was transformed,
yet they used their old language in a transformed way to express the
kerygma. Therefore, as Bultmann himself puts it very pointedly: 'The main
task of exegesis is to identify the ways of talking which are possible for the
author within the tradition in which he finds himself.'[94] The same is true
for today's interpreter. For Bultmann, everybody has an understanding of
human existence and divinity, although it may be different from that of
Christian faith. Through encountering the *kerygma*, a possibility of a completely new understanding of human existence and divinity is opened, so
the understanding of human existence and divinity is radically changed.
Without having a concept of human existence or divinity at all, there
would not be anything that could be transformed. Thus pre-understanding

---

93   Barth; *Rudolf Bultmann*, 57 (own translation).
94   Cf. Bultmann, Rudolf; *Das Evangelium des Johannes*, Kritisch-exegetischer Kom-
     mentar über das Neue Testament, Vol.2, Göttingen ²¹1986, 6 (own translation).

is necessary for understanding,[95] but it does not presuppose the outcome of the interpretation, for openness to have one's own pre-understanding transformed is a prerequisite of interpretation.[96]

This theory of understanding has the important advantage against Barth's perception, that it anticipates an important criticism postmodernism has brought forward against Barthian hermeneutics. Bultmann avoids this criticism by acknowledging that understanding without presuppositions is impossible. He recognises the part played by presuppositions and a pre-understanding of the subject matter in the process of understanding. Barth, on the other hand, believes that the interpreter should make himself or herself free of prejudices in order to understand the text in the spirit of obedience and faith. Exactly this attitude is criticised by postmodernist interpreters, who rightly assert that there is no such thing as an innocent reading,[97] but that it is always influenced by the reader's point of view. A hermeneutical theory following Bultmann will avoid the drastic conclusion to which postmodernist interpreters come, i.e. that the meaning of the text is actually created by the reader.[98] The reader approaches the text with a certain understanding of the subject matter and an expectation what the subject matter of the text will be, yet this is transformed by the encounter with the text, and thus understanding may take place between text and interpreter.[99] In this respect Bultmann's hermeneutical theory provides an important starting point for a discussion with post-modernist hermeneutical theories.

Another important factor in Karl Barth's disagreement with Rudolf Bultmann is Barth's identification of pre-understanding with prejudice.[100] Karl Barth does not appreciate that in Bultmann's thought the self-understanding and pre-understanding of the interpreter is not authoritative. It is impossible for him to understand a text without any presupposition of the subject matter. This pre-understanding is transformed in the course of the interpretation, and a new understanding of the subject matter is possible. In fact, this is the very aim of interpretation.[101] For Karl Barth, on the other hand, every pre-understanding of the subject matter of the text must be abandoned, and the text has to be listened to with openness, so that the text will disclose to the reader (or hearer) the

---

95   Cf. Bultmann; 'Das Problem der Hermeneutik' 227-235.
96   Ibid. 230.
97   Cf. *The Postmodern Bible*, 134f.
98   Ibid. 52-54.
99   Cf. Bultmann; 'Das Problem der Hermeneutik' 227-235.
100 Barth; *Rudolf Bultmann*, 58-60.
101 Cf. Bultmann in Barth — Bultmann; *Briefwechsel*, 188-190.

subject matter. Every supposition about the subject matter of the text is then, for Barth, a serious obstacle on the way to understanding.

In sum, for Karl Barth understanding consists of the self-disclosure of the subject matter of the text (*Die Sache des Textes*), whereas understanding for Rudolf Bultmann is to have one's own pre-understanding of the subject matter of the text transformed through the encounter with the possibility of understanding the subject matter which the text offers. Again, Bultmann's approach to human understanding seems to be more plausible to me than Barth's. Bultmann takes seriously the conditions of human understanding and the fact that the meaning of a text is *in* the text and not *behind* the text. Karl Barth, on the other hand, relies on the self-disclosure of a sovereign subject matter of the text, which is a concept that has rightly been questioned by post-modern literary theory.

Anthropology or Existentialist Interpretation?

Another major difference between Karl Barth and Rudolf Bultmann is the question of the legitimacy of Bultmann's existentialist interpretation. Karl Barth assumes that the existentialist interpretation is nothing more than anthropology. Barth claims that for Bultmann '[...] anthropology, or rather anthropology structured thus [i.e. by Heidegger's existentialist philosophy], is the subject matter of the New Testament!'[102] Hence, Bultmann reduces theological and biblical statements to statements about the inner life of the human being.[103] Against this criticism Bultmann insists that he does not talk just of human consciousness when he uses the term self-understanding, but of *existential* understanding,[104] which is an essential part of his epistemology. This means that a perception or knowledge of something can only be meaningful if it means something in the human being's life, if there is a life-relationship to the matter.[105] Just to assume that something is true does not constitute authentic understanding. Authentic understanding only takes place in action, by making something a part of the human self-understanding, by having a life-relationship to it.[106] Thus, in order to understand a text, it is necessary to understand what possibilities of human existence are opened by the text. For example, a biblical text offers a particular understanding of the world, seeing the world in relation to God and oneself addressed by God through Jesus Christ etc. It is not the

---

[102] Barth; *Rudolf Bultmann*, 45.
[103] KD III/2, 534f.
[104] Cf. Bultmann; 'Zum Problem der Entmythologisierung' *K&M* II, 201.
[105] Cf. Schmithals; *Introduction to the Theology of Rudolf Bultmann*, 235-237.
[106] Ibid.

aim of understanding just to know what the biblical text says and to assume that it is true or not, but to have understood the possibilities of
human life which derive from this knowledge and either to accept this
understanding of human existence and live accordingly or to reject it.

For Karl Barth, on the other hand, understanding takes place on a cog-
nitive level.[107] As already indicated, Barth's interpreter leaves the text behind and is able to deal with the subject matter of the text, in this case the
Word of God, directly rather than merely struggling to understand its human document. Eventually, Karl Barth deals with immediate knowledge of
the subject matter; the Word of God thinks itself in the mind of the theologian.[108] Based on this epistemology, Karl Barth cannot admit that theological statements have to be a part of human self-understanding. Rather, the
theologian is drawn into the self-understanding of divinity; he or she deals
with the absoluteness of divinity. For Karl Barth, knowledge of the divine
mysteries is the aim of theology, not the dialectics of the sinful and lost
human being and the saving God. The subject matter of the biblical text is,
for Barth, the divine mysteries, which are totally different from everything
humanity can know. Thus, a pre-understanding of the subject matter is
impossible, so that reflecting the pre-understanding of the subject matter
leads to the incapability to understand the qualitatively different Word of
God.

It is, in my opinion, unfortunate, when Barth accuses Bultmann of having made a certain philosophy ruler over his theology.[109] It is true that
Bultmann uses Heidegger's existentialist philosophy as a hermeneutical
key to the New Testament, yet, as discussed above, Karl Barth does not
show himself sufficiently aware of his own philosophical and epistemological presuppositions. Although Karl Barth believes that his hermeneutical
principles are drawn from scripture,[110] we have seen that his own hermeneutical principles are strongly influenced by Hegelian philosophy.[111]
Barth, however, does not reflect his own philosophical presuppositions but
accuses Bultmann of being influenced by a certain philosophy. Here, Karl
Barth's thought lacks adequate self-reflection and is therefore inconsistent.

This is not to say that philosophical presuppositions are generally
wrong in theology. On the contrary, there is no such thing as a theology
without influences of philosophy; e.g. all hermeneutical theories used in
theology are influenced by or drawn from philosophical discourse. It is,
however, necessary to reflect philosophical presuppositions, lay them open

---

107 Cf. Bayer; *Theologie*, 328-335.
108 Cf. Bayer; *Theologie*, 325f..
109 Cf. Barth; *Rudolf Bultmann*, 44f.
110 Cf. Barth; *Rudolf Bultmann*, 57.
111 Cf. above, p.24.

and expose them to discussion in order to enable theological discourse and understanding within the scholarly community.

However, having said that Bultmann's existentialist interpretation is not dissolving theology into anthropology, as Barth alleges, we should note that Barth's criticism is not completely unfounded. In fact, Bultmann is in danger of an anthropological diminution of theology, or, as Paul Ricœur puts it, theocentric personalism,[112] which is, however, distinctly different from dissolving theology into anthropology.

For Bultmann, God acts by addressing the human being 'here and now', in the present moment. Addressed by the *kerygma*, the listener has to decide whether he or she lives authentically in faith or rejects this possibility. Faith is, in this framework, basically authentic existence, i.e. life from the future.[113] It is 'the abandonment of man's own security and the readiness to find security only in the unseen beyond, in God'[114] and that 'which is lived from what cannot be seen, what is not at man's disposal. Such a life means the abandonment of all self-contrived security.'[115] The other possibility of human existence is inauthentic existence, i.e. seeking life in the disposable, to live from the worldly available rather than from God's future, and thus not accepting God as one's creator.[116] This decision between faith and unbelief, authentic or inauthentic existence is the centre of Bultmann's theology; every other aspect is derived from it. As Oswald Bayer has pointed out, this central principle of Bultmann's theology is a reception of Kant's *diastase* between what is and what should be.[117] For Bultmann,

> that which is can be experienced in space, time and in the combination of idea and concept (*Anschauung und Begriff*) and grasped in its objectivity. What should be belongs to another dimension. This dimension is not that of constant causally determined nature but the dimension of freedom, as it is known through the categorical law.[118]

As the dimension of that which is determined by the natural laws and causality, freedom is only possible at the moment, where the human being is free to take the decision. Thus Bultmann stands in a tradition of Kant and Kierkegaard when saying that authentic existence is only possible at the

---

[112] Ricœur, Paul; 'Preface to Bultmann' in: Ricœur, Paul; *Essays on biblical interpretation*, Philadelphia 1980, 49-72, 66.

[113] Cf. Schmithals; *Introduction to the Theology of Rudolf Bultmann*, 74-78.

[114] Bultmann, Rudolf; *Jesus Christ and Mythology*, London (SCM) 1960, 40f.

[115] Bultmann; *Neues Testament und Mythologie*, 35.

[116] Cf. Schmithals, Walter; *Introduction to the Theology of Rudolf Bultmann*, 74-78.

[117] Cf. Bayer; *Theologie*, 476-480.

[118] Ibid. 476.

present moment.[119] However, this means that Bultmann separates the natural and the historical (historical as the free decision here and now) and puts it into a dialectical relation: the human being is, on the one hand, living in the world and thus subject to causal determination and on the other hand an autonomous 'I', which has the freedom to take decisions.[120] The relationship between God and the human being is therefore reduced to the dimension of freedom, which, in turn, excludes the natural world. Theologically, the human being is only in view as isolated before God. Hence, Bultmann excludes the world as creation, as fallen and redeemed creation, from his theology. For him, the subject of theology is exclusively the lost and sinful human being and the saving God, whereas for Luther, from whom this definition of the subject of theology derives,[121] the human being is in view only as part of the world and together with his or her fellow-creatures. Whilst the subject of theology should be threefold, God, human being and world, it is only twofold for Bultmann, God and human being. Consequently, Bultmann arrives at a theocentric personalism, as Ricœur put it in his essay on Bultmann's hermeneutics.[122]

Similarly, Bultmann's approach to mythological language, his 'demythologisation programme', which is intrinsically linked with his existentialist interpretation, is in danger of narrowing language's function as the *bearer of meaning*. In the discussion of the question of demythologisation, Bultmann affirmed repeatedly that demythologisation does not mean abandoning mythological language from the New Testament but reinterpreting it, a point which played an important role in the initial debate about Bultmann's proposal to demythologise the New Testament.[123] Yet it can be argued that Bultmann reinterprets the mythological language in a way inappropriate to the *kerygma* by separating the *kerygma* as the inner meaning or the kernel of the New Testament from mythological language, which is but the wrapping of the *kerygma*.[124] Having interpreted and demythologised the language of the New Testament, Bultmann believes that it is possible to express the *kerygma* in neutral and 'innocent' language.[125] One can see a parallel between Bultmann's interpretation of mythological language and the so-called rhetorical understanding of metaphor, first suggested by Aristotle. In this tradition, metaphorical language is seen as

---

[119] Ibid. 476f

[120] Ibid. 477f, cf. also Bultmann; *Neues Testament und Mythologie*, 24.

[121] Luther, Martin; WA 40 II, 328,1f.

[122] Cf. Ricœur; 'Preface to Bultmann' 66.

[123] Cf. Körtner, Ulrich; 'Arbeit am Mythos?' 65f.

[124] Ibid. 169.

[125] Ibid. 169f.

merely a rhetorical figure and trope, which can be translated into non-tropical language without loss of meaning.[126]

Therefore, Bultmann reduces the meaning of mythological language in the Bible to the call to the existentialist decision before God, which can be expressed in neutral or 'innocent' language. He assumes that the meaning of the text can be separated from its actual language and that one can take the concepts contained in the text and interpret them existentially, understand and apply them directly.[127] Paul Ricœur highlights this issue in his essay 'Preface to Bultmann', saying that the meaning of the text is not available without the language of the text, which is the bearer of meaning.[128] Thus, 'there is no shorter path for joining a neutral existential anthropology, according to philosophy, with the existential decision before God, according to the Bible. But there is the long path of the question of being and of the belonging of saying to being.'[129]

At this point, Bultmann's understanding of the Word of God as *verbum externum* needs to be clarified. As I have pointed out in the discussion of the Barth-Bultmann debate, Bultmann sees the Word of God as present in the spoken or written human word, the external word.[130] The Word of God is, for Bultmann, the *kerygma*, the call to the existentialist decision between faith and unbelief. He understands it as present in the human word and not behind it, yet he narrows it down to the call to the decision; it is something that takes place only between the individual human being and God. Yet the further development of the theory of language has shown that it is not possible to assume that the Word of God (or anything else) can be expressed in a neutral language, that it can be distilled out of its linguistic form and treated as if isolated from it. Thus the following chapter will need to focus on the development of a wider understanding of the Word of God, which includes the whole of creation as part of the subject of theology, and a perception of the meaning of the New Testament as inseparably embedded in its linguistic form. In the course of this inquiry, we will follow the way suggested by Paul Ricœur, which is 'the long path of the question of being and of the belonging of saying to being.'[131]

---

[126] Ibid. 175f.
[127] Cf. Ricœur; 'Preface to Bultmann' 65f.
[128] Ibid. 68.
[129] Ibid. 72.
[130] Cf. above p.20.
[131] Ricœur; 'Preface to Bultmann' 72

Beyond Barth and Bultmann?

In the end, the question remains whether it is possible to find a synthesis between Barth and Bultmann and to overcome their controversy.[132] After the previous considerations, I assume that it is not possible to find a theology beyond the controversy between Barth and Bultmann. These two scholars approach theology as a whole and the New Testament in particular with irreconcilably different epistemologies and work with completely different conceptions of the subject of theology and the Word of God.

Karl Barth liked to use the picture of the whale and the elephant for Bultmann's and his own attempts to understand each other.[133] Being biggest animals of their realm, they happen to meet at the coast and try to communicate. Although they try every kind of gesture to make themselves understood, they are lacking the key to mutual understanding, and therefore communication between them is impossible. This analogy does, in my opinion, not apply exactly. It is true that Barth and Bultmann could not come to an agreement in hermeneutical issues, but they could have been able to understand the difference in their thought. This chance was missed for various reasons, one of which may well have been Karl Barth's lack of reflection on his own philosophical presuppositions.

After this discussion one must heed Karl Barth's advice not to try to develop a viewpoint beyond Barth and Bultmann, but to travel one of the two paths consistently to its end.[134] Therefore, I shall take Bultmann's path, but then go beyond Bultmann, and set out on 'the long path of the question of being and of the belonging of saying to being', as Paul Ricœur demanded.[135]

---

[132] Cf. Jeanrond; *Theological Hermeneutics*, 148f.

[133] Cf. Barth in Barth — Bultmann; *Briefwechsel*, 196.

[134] Cf. Barth, Karl; *Rudolf Bultmann: Ein Versuch, ihn zu verstehen — Christus und Adam nach Röm. 5: Zwei theologische Studien*, Zürich (EVZ) 3/2(respectively)1964, 5f. Both essays were written 1952; ibid.

[135] Ricœur; 'Preface to Bultmann' 72.

Chapter 4

The Long Path to Language

In this chapter, I will attempt to develop an approach to the New Testament, which takes seriously the three demands for a hermeneutical theory drawn from the previous investigations. Accordingly, first the proposed approach to the New Testament must see the Word of God as present in the human language of the New Testament as *verbum externum*. Secondly, the interpretation must be based on the existentialist interpretation. Thirdly, the hermeneutical theory needs to recognise language as the bearer of meaning and thus it must include a theological perception of the world into the hermeneutical process and into the horizon of the interpreter in order to avoid Bultmann's theocentric personalism. This will avoid Bultmann's assumption of an 'innocent' or 'neutral' language, into which the New Testament could be translated without loss of meaning. These three presuppositions will be contained in the approach to the New Testament which I am proposing.

In the first section of this chapter, I will establish the relationship between language and meaning, using, in an eclectic manner, insights gained through a discussion of the philosophies of Martin Heidegger and Hans-Georg Gadamer.

In the second section the historical conditions of understanding will be reflected in a discussion of Gadamer's hermeneutical theory. In this context, we will return to the question of the significance of pre-understanding for interpretation. The third section will focus on the question as to how language contains meaning. This will take place in discussion with Paul Ricœur's poetological theory of metaphor, which will allow us important insights into the function of language.

On the grounds of these considerations, a view of the genesis of the New Testament will be developed in the third and final section. Here the threads of the previous sections will be drawn together and a view of the New Testament will be presented, which can interpret it as a result of the early struggle for language in which to understand Christian faith and the new world opened through the cross and resurrection of Jesus Christ. This concept of the *Struggle for Language* will be the basis for the exegetical work in the subsequent chapters of my study.

Language and Meaning

As Ricœur claimed in the essay on Bultmann mentioned above, the interpreter must not aim directly at the concepts underlying the text, but has to
go through an analysis of language. A good starting point for the following
discussion is the key statement of Gerhard Ebeling's essay 'Word of God
and Hermeneutics': *'The primary phenomenon in the realm of understanding is
not understanding* OF *language, but understanding* THROUGH *language.'*[136] This
statement needs, certainly, some further explanation, which will lead us
directly to the heart of the problem. In order to understand what understanding *through* language means, we need to take a step back and enter a
discussion with the philosophies of the later Heidegger and of Hans-Georg
Gadamer.

After Heidegger in his early period analysed the human *Dasein* in his
work *'Sein und Zeit'* and subsequent works, he turned to language and its
relation to *Sein* (Being) itself. The starting point of Heidegger's approach to
language and being is his criticism of conceptualising thought. He argues
that the move towards objectifying thinking was a development in the
wrong direction. The right way of seeing the world is, according to Heidegger, to see it in relation to *Dasein*, i.e. not to objectify it. 'Through language, which does not only talk about single beings, or Essent (*Seiendes*),
but puts Being (*Sein*) and relation of Being (*Seinsbezüge*) into words, the
world is explicitly disclosed and communicable in its meaningful significance.'[137] In other words, language sets the subject matter in relation to the
world, i.e. the totality of Being and of the relations of Beings, and thus unveils Being.

Crucial within Heidegger's thought is his distinction between language
as *Geläut der Stille* (Chime of Stillness, or Sound of Silence) and as *Lauten des
Wortes* (Sounding of the Word).[138] First, language as *Geläut der Stille* is the
author of meaningful relationship between single Beings and World. In this
capacity, language is not the actually spoken language, but it is the disclo-
sure of meaningful relations between Essents and World.

Language, for Heidegger, originates in the *Unter-Schied* (Difference, but
Heidegger uses it differently). The *Unter-Schied* is the point of contact between the single thing and the world and also the painful difference between them. The *Unter-Schied* is, as it were, like a threshold, where the

---

[136] Ebeling, Gerhard; 'Wort Gottes und Hermeneutik' in: *Wort und Glaube*, Tübingen (Mohr-Siebeck) ³1967, 319-348, 333 (Ebeling's italics; English: 'Word of God
and Hermeneutics' in: Ebeling, Gerhard; *Word and Faith*, London (SCM) 1963,
305-332, 318).

[137] Jaeger, Hans; *Heidegger und die Sprache*, Bern (Franke) 1971, 15 (my translation).

[138] Cf. Jaeger; *Heidegger und die Sprache*, 89f, 106.

inside and the outside are ultimately close and yet definitely separated.[139] Because of this contact and separation, relations between beings are possible. The world, to which the single thing is so close and yet so painfully separated, is the totality of relations of beings and being. In the *Unter-Schied* the thing, the single being is set in its place in the world. Here, the thing is at rest, in Stillness, because it is in the place where it belongs in the world.[140] The *Unter-Schied* also gathers the world. It calls together the world as it is in contact with the single thing[141] and thus calls Being into presence (*Anwesen*). In this respect, language 'grants' us the things,[142] and so it makes them meaningful to us by showing us their place and meaning in the world. Without language the world and the single thing would be completely meaningless to us. This calling things into their being is, for Heidegger, the essence of language.[143] Heidegger names this calling of things into their being '*läuten*', the corresponding noun, in his idiosyncratic use of German, is '*Geläut*', which usually means 'chime'. Here it is 'sounding' or 'calling.'[144] Because of this gathering and dividing of things and world, setting them into their place, where they are at rest, at stillness, and calling them into their being, language is called the *Geläut der Stille*, which can be translated as 'Chime of Stillness' as well as 'Sound of Silence'. Heidegger sums up: 'Language speaks as *Geläut der Stille*.'[145]

Consequently, it is language that speaks, as it is the Sound of Silence (or the Chime of Stillness), which enables meaningful relations between single beings and the world. Therefore, language is grounded in Being itself, not in human thought, for things have their being not in themselves but in their closeness and difference to the world, in the *Unter-Schied*, which is the place where language 'dwells'.

Human language, language as *Lauten des Wortes*, can only answer what it has heard. It does not merely transmit concepts and information, but it passes on what language as *Geläut der Stille* has disclosed. The human being can only speak as listener,[146] answering the *Geläut der Stille*. Being is unveiled by language, and language is disclosed in the *Ereignis* (Event), which can be seen as the connection between language as *Geläut der Stille* and as *Lauten des Wortes*. Heidegger emphasises that the *Ereignis* is not the

---

139 Cf. Heidegger, Martin; *Unterwegs zur Sprache*, Stuttgart (Neske) [10]1993, 24-27.
140 Ibid. 29.
141 Ibid. 25.
142 Ibid. 25.
143 Ibid. 30.
144 Ibid. 29f.
145 Ibid. 30.
146 Ibid. 31f.

result of a cause; it is the giving of language.[147] In the *Ereignis* the human being encounters language, being is disclosed and the human being is enabled to speak. Language has given itself to the human being, and human language is the answer to language.[148] *Ereignis* is whenever a human being encounters Being, whenever the single thing in its relation and difference to the world is unveiled. The touchstone for authenticity of human language is, obviously, its closeness to the event. Authentic language answers the *Ereignis*.

It has been argued that Heidegger's theory of language is in danger of 'word-magic' and 'language-mysticism.'[149] And indeed, if the distinction between language as *Geläut der Stille* and the actually spoken language as *Lauten des Wortes* is missed, and thus language in the plain and everyday meaning of the word is understood as originating in the *Unter-Schied*, it looks suspiciously like language-mysticism and word-magic. However, one cannot take Heidegger's language literally here. Especially when Heidegger talks of language as *Geläut der Stille*, he does not speak about language in the common meaning of the word, but metaphorically. Heidegger does so to express the relation between Being and language and our perception of reality. It is, as it were, poetic language, that is able to express a thought that could not be expressed in another way. If Heidegger's theory of language and being is viewed in this way, the danger of word-magic is banished.

Heidegger's philosophy of language contributes to the present study a perception of the relation between language and meaning and being. For Heidegger, meaning and being is language, being can only be perceived through language, and language contains being: 'Words and language are not just wrappings, in which the things are packed for commerce in speaking and writing. Only in words, in language they become and are things.'[150]

Obviously, we need to develop this important insight into the nature of language, and make it practically adaptable. In this, Hans-Georg Gadamer's work proves instrumental, as he contributes significant insights to the question of meaning and language. This will be an important further step on our Way to Language. In addition, Gadamer's hermeneutical theory will be essential to an investigation into the historical conditions of human understanding, which will follow in the next section.

In his general approach to the problem of meaning and language, Gadamer follows the thought of his academic teacher Martin Heidegger.

---

[147] Ibid. 258.
[148] Ibid. 260.
[149] Cf. Thiselton; *The Two Horizons*, 337.
[150] Heidegger, Martin; *Einführung in die Metaphysik*, Tübingen (Niemeyer) ³1987, 11.

For him, as for Heidegger, language is the relation between the speaker, the single thing and the world in total.[151] Unlike Heidegger, Gadamer does not continue to think about language as *Geläut der Stille*, but about human language and how it evolves and is understood, and how it is the medium of human thought and understanding of the world. For Gadamer,

> Language is the universal medium in which understanding itself is realised. The mode of realisation of understanding is interpretation. [...] All understanding is interpretation, and all interpretation takes place in the medium of a language which would allow the object to come into words and yet is at the same time the interpreter's own language.[152]

Human thought is, according to Gadamer, intimately bound up with language.[153] Human beings can only think in language and, therefore, only understand through language, which, in turn, determines human thought. In addition, language is passed down in the linguistic tradition of one's culture. Thus, language and one's understanding of reality is actually inherited from the tradition in which one lives. In order to understand the reality that one encounters, one has to translate it into one's own language. Therefore, language provides the conceptual framework for the interpretation of the world. Although one's understanding of the world is determined by language, it has also the potential to develop, because language develops, too. As the understanding of the world changes, language changes as well.[154]

In this respect Gadamer can say that the world, as it is understandable, is language.[155] To have the world is, for Gadamer, to be above the rush of that which one encounters in the world.[156] The human being becomes free from the surrounding environment (*Umwelt*), from being bound by what one encounters in the world, by having language. Through language human beings gain a world-view, an understanding of their world. Through language the things one encounters are put into a meaningful relation to each other and to the horizon of the whole world.[157] Thus, world comes into language, so that Gadamer can say: 'Whoever has language "has" the

---

[151] Gadamer, Hans-Georg; *Wahrheit und Methode*, in: Gadamer, Hans-Georg; *Gesammelte Werke*, vol. 1: *Hermeneutik: Wahrheit und Methode: Grundzüge einer philosophischen Hermeneutik*, Tübingen (Mohr-Siebeck) ⁶1990, 473 (English: *Truth and Method*, London (Sheed and Ward) ²1979, 426)

[152] Gadamer; *Wahrheit und Methode*, 392 (Engl. 350).

[153] Cf. Thiselton; *Two Horizons*, 314.

[154] Ibid. 312.

[155] Cf. Gadamer; *Wahrheit und Methode*, 446f (Engl. 401f).

[156] Ibid. 447f (402f).

[157] Ibid. 462 (415f).

world.'[158] This implies that the world is language, and that everything that is understood is language. 'Being *(Sein)* that can be understood is language'[159] Thus, there is an inseparable unity between the subject matter and the language in which it is expressed.

By following the 'long path to language' we have arrived at an understanding of language which fulfils the demands made earlier. On the one hand, language is understood as being able to contain meaning (as opposed to only pointing at it, as Karl Barth assumes).[160] There is no difference between the immanent language and the transcendent meaning, or, in other words, the temporal is capable of containing the infinite, or *finitum capax infinitum!*[161] The *verbum interius* (internal word) is contained in the *verbum externum* (external word). Yet language is also understood in such a way that Bultmann's shortcut, excluding a perception of the world from theology, is avoided. It enables the interpreter to keep Bultmann's important insights regarding New Testament interpretation while avoiding his shortcomings, fulfilling Paul Ricœur's demand to take 'the long path of the question of being and of the belonging of saying to being'[162] to an appropriate understanding of biblical language.

Understanding and History

Following on from our discussion of the relation of language and being, we need to proceed to the issue of historical distance and understanding. What effect does it have on the understanding of a text if it is an ancient text as the New Testament? And what is the role of the tradition, which connects the ancient text and the modern interpreter?

It has become a commonplace statement that understanding a historical text works, according to Gadamer, through the fusion of the horizons of text and interpreter.[163] Text and interpreter have each their own horizon, which is formed respectively by the world in which the text was written and that in which the interpreter is living. These horizons form the background against which understanding takes place. Gadamer's definition of horizon[164] needs to be seen in the light of the 'ontological shift' in the third part of Gadamer's 'Truth and Method'. In Gadamer's hermeneutics,

---

[158] Ibid. 457 (411).
[159] Ibid. 473 (426).
[160] Cf. above 20.
[161] Cf. above, p. 20f.
[162] Ricœur; *Preface to Bultmann*, 72
[163] Cf. Gadamer; *Wahrheit und Methode*, 311 (Engl. 273).
[164] Ibid. 307f (269f).

someone's horizon is the world in which one lives. It is the world as a meaningful whole of relations which can be understood through language. In
this respect the ancient text and the reader are from different worlds, since
they are based each in a different meaningful whole of relations, thus having different horizons. Usually, there will be a relation between the horizon
of the interpreter and that of the text, since both take part in the same tradition of thought, which is continuously developing. Although the world
view may have changed significantly, there will still be a common basis, a
common origin. In order to understand a text, the interpreter places himself
within the tradition of which the text and the interpreter are a part. 'Understanding is [...] to be thought of [...] as the placing of oneself within a process of tradition, in which the present and the past are constantly fused.'[165]

The different horizons of interpreter and text lead to another feature of
Gadamer's theory of understanding, which is the role of the interpreter's
pre-understanding. The interpreter approaches a text already having an
understanding of the text's subject matter within the framework of one's
understanding of the world. Above we have seen that understanding the
world is determined by the language in which one lives, which, in turn, is
passed down through the tradition. The presuppositions of interpreters,
formed by their understanding of the world, are a product of the language-
tradition in which they find themselves. Consequently, since text and interpreter have different horizons, the text is alien to anyone approaching it.
But there is also a certain familiarity between the text and its interpreters,
for they are part of the same tradition. Therefore, the text influences the
way its interpreters approach it through the tradition that connects them.
In addition, there is the whole tradition of interpreting the text placed between the text and the interpreter. A text has been interpreted from the first
time it was read and thus a tradition of interpreting and understanding the
text started; contemporary interpreters find themselves at the (for the moment) final point of this tradition. Thus, interpreters are in a certain familiarity with the text, since they are part of the same tradition. On the other
hand, through the meeting of past and present in the act of interpretation,
the text has also the power of saying something new, to speak anew in the
situation of its interpreters and thus to say something unexpected, which
has not been recognised before. Therefore, the text is also a stranger to its
interpreters. 'The place between strangeness and familiarity that a trans-
mitted text has for us is that intermediate place between being a historically
intended separate object and being part of a tradition. The true home of
hermeneutics is in this intermediate area.'[166]

---

[165] Ibid. 295 (258).
[166] Ibid. 300 (262f).

In this intermediate area between being a historically intended separate object and being part of a tradition, new truth can emerge. 'In as much as the tradition is newly expressed in language, something comes into being that had not existed before and that exists from now on.'[167] Through the fusion of the horizons a new horizon emerges which is larger than just the two horizons that existed before. The meaningful relations that constitute the respective worlds of text and interpreter add to each other in such a way that completely new relations become visible and thus new truth is unveiled. The subject matter is revealed in a new way by the encounter of presence and tradition.

Interpreters encounter a text, as Gadamer suggests, by approaching the text with certain questions in mind, which the text is expected to answer. Every text is, according to Gadamer, an answer to a question or a whole set of questions, and thus the text speaks only in relation to the questions that it is asked.[168] The questions with which a text is approached are themselves a part of the tradition in which its interpreters find themselves, either because they are given to the interpreters by the tradition or they evolve from the continuous development of the tradition of thought. These questions can be new questions which the text has never been asked before and which have not been in the mind of the author, but the text may have the potential to answer these questions. If a new question is found to which the text offers a meaningful answer, understanding takes place. Thus interpretation takes place as a dialogue between the text on one end of the tradition and the interpreter on its other end. Between them is the gulf of the tradition in which text and interpreter are placed, which is not something to be bridged but the bridge between them. This tradition enables the interpreter to formulate questions to the text and then to check whether they are valid by seeing them within the now common horizon of text and interpreter. Within this process of interpretation the questions of the interpreter may also be changed and more appropriate questions, that have been a part of neither the text's nor the interpreter's world, may be recognised. The result of this debate will be that the text speaks in the world of the interpreter and establishes new meaningful relations and new meaning.

However, the important question remains as to whether the encounter between text and interpreter always work. For Gadamer and the related New Hermeneutics the task of interpretation is to ensure that understanding happens. In this context, Ebeling says:

---

[167] Ibid. 466 (419).
[168] Cf. Grondin, Jean; *Einführung in die philosophische Hermeneutik*, Darmstadt (Wissenschaftliche Buchgesellschaft) 1991, 150f.

[...] interpretation, and therefore also *hermeneutics*, is *requisite* only in the case *where the word-event is hindered* for some reason or other. But for that reason also the hermeneutic aid can only consist in removing hindrances in order to let the word perform its own hermeneutic function.[169]

The main hindrance of understanding is, certainly, that the text simply does not make sense to the interpreter. This may be the case especially when a text from an unknown background is interpreted. In this case the horizon of the text has to be investigated so that the text can be understood against this background. Thus, historical research is necessary for the understanding of the text. In addition, to investigate the world of the text historically brings about the text's otherness so that wrong familiarity will be destroyed. This move is important to alienate the text as a step towards a fresh understanding of it, through which new truth can happen.

There are certainly different possible understandings of a text. For example, the historical background of the text may be reconstructed differently, which could lead to different interpretations of the text. Thus, there will be a certain range of possible and valid interpretations, and if a particular interpretation leaves this range, it has to be falsified in the scholarly dispute and will probably be ruled out.

As there are ever new interpretations, and a conflict of competing interpretations, temporal distance has an important positive and valuable effect; 'not only are fresh sources of error constantly excluded, so that the true meaning has filtered out of it all kind of things that obscure it, but there emerge continually new sources of understanding, which reveal unsuspected elements of meaning.'[170]

An important issue in contemporary hermeneutics is the identification and critique of ideological and hidden agendas as well as power structures underlying the text. This concern can be taken seriously using a hermeneutical approach like Gadamer's. The ideological presuppositions which can be found in the text are intrinsically part of its horizon, so they need to be explored and how far they influence understanding of the text must be investigated. This is still part of the exploration and explanation of the horizon of the text, and if this task is fulfilled carefully and with awareness of ideological agendas, it can be discerned how far they influence the meaning of the text and whether they need to be rejected or not. Being made explicit, it is not likely that they will influence the interpreter unconsciously. For example, John's Gospel has often been said to contain a strong anti-Semitism. If the interpreter is aware of this notion, then he or she can

---

[169] Ebeling; 'Wort Gottes und Hermeneutik' 334 (English: 'Word of God and Hermeneutics' 318f).

[170] Gadamer; *Wahrheit und Methode*, 303 (Engl. 265f).

take the agenda underlying the text into account, and explain its origin and the way in which it works. Then understanding the text can take place without the danger of any unconscious ideological indoctrination, thus bringing out the particular Johannine contribution to Christian thought and its meaning for today. Yet in this framework the text needs to be accepted as an authority which has to say something new to the interpreter, though as an authority the text is open to critique. Therefore, ideological criticism fulfils an important role in the process of understanding without silencing the text. In fact, through this critical component of interpretation a better and deeper understanding of the text will be facilitated, for the text and the interpreter are challenged, and a deeper interaction can take place. Although these considerations are, to my knowledge, not included in Gadamer's work, I believe that his hermeneutical theory is open to the inclusion of a critical perspective within the process of interpretation.

What implications do these considerations have for the interpretation of the New Testament? It is a key issue of this study, which will be discussed in depth below,[171] that the scriptures of the New Testament are a result of a struggle for a language to express the new truth that had been encountered in Jesus' cross and resurrection. The authors of New Testament literature found idioms to understand this new truth within the framework of their world. Today's humanity certainly understands the world in a very different way than people in antiquity did. Therefore, interpreters today encounter the biblical texts as strangers. Yet interpreters are connected with the New Testament through the Christian tradition; they will probably know Christianity and thus there is already an understanding of what these texts say. They are somehow familiar to modern readers. This intermediate area between strangeness and familiarity is the true home of hermeneutics.[172] In order to bring about this intermediate area, the interpreter must rid himself or herself of wrong familiarity with the text; the text's otherness and strangeness must be rediscovered. This is the alienating function of historical research. In addition, it is necessary to explain the horizon of the historical text in order to understand the world of the text in a way that it can be fused with the horizon of the interpreter.

An essential part of the interpreters' horizon is their ecclesial background. The interpreters' view of Christianity, even their whole world view is strongly influenced by the Christian tradition. The tradition will, certainly, have an impact on the result of the act of understanding, and thus influence the meaning the biblical text has for today's community of faith. This does not, however, mean that theologians from different

---

[171] Cf. below p.47.
[172] Cf. Gadamer; *Wahrheit und Methode*, 300 (Engl. 262f).

traditions cannot discuss their interpretations of a text. Whatever the theological persuasion, the implications of philological and historical evidence can be discussed by scholars from different backgrounds. Furthermore, the dialogue between the Christian denominations and traditions is something most important for the development of Christian theology.

Finally, theological tradition is important for the understanding of the New Testament. This is because being aware of the history of their own theological tradition makes interpreters conscious of their own background and thus helps to clarify their presuppositions, so that they can be reflected and become a conscious part of interpretation rather than influencing it as a subconscious hidden agenda. Secondly, the theological tradition provides countless examples of how the biblical texts have been applied to the different situations and world views interpreters have found themselves in. Dealing with these previous interpretations shows the variety of possible interpretations and applications of the texts. New relations between the texts and the world can be seen in these interpretations and enrich the horizon of the interpreter. Apart from that it may be helpful to see that certain ways of interpreting the texts have been tried before and were not successful, so that these attempts do not have to be repeated by every generation of interpreters.

Poetic Language: Metaphor and Symbol

In the former sections of this chapter I have discussed the relation between language and meaning and the historical conditions of understanding. As a last step in my investigations into the nature of language I shall explore how language contains and expresses meaning. Mythological language as we encounter it in the Bible, is, in my opinion, poetic language, functioning analogically to Paul Ricœur's poetological theory of language.[173] I use the term *poetic* in the sense of the Greek term, where ποίησις has an interesting double meaning. On the one hand, it means 'making', 'fabrication', 'creation' and 'production', on the other hand it means 'composition', or the 'writing of a poem'. These two meanings together constitute what may be termed *poetic*. Poetic language in this sense is not necessarily metric language, but language that creates new meaning through composition.[174] In the context of this investigation, I will limit myself to a discussion of non-narrative poetic language, for including a theory of narrative language

---

173 Körtner, Ulrich; 'Arbeit am Mythos?' 175f.
174 Another term for the theory of language I propose here is that of the 'absolute metaphor', as it is suggested by Körtner; 'Arbeit am Mythos?' 175f. For the terminology cf. Aristotle; *Poetics* I, 1447a, 1-1447b, 29

would not add any significant gain to the understanding of our question. A theory of narrative language would follow, however, from a discussion of Paul Ricœur's work in his book '*Time and Narrative*'[175] in the light of the insights of this study.

Paul Ricœur has described his understanding of the functioning of poetic language concisely and clearly in his book '*Interpretation Theory*'.[176] In this section, I am going to follow his argument laid out in this work, and to make use of his insights in the light of my earlier hermeneutical investigations. For Ricœur, metaphor is not just a trope or a figure of speech, but a semantic device which bears meaning that could not be expressed in any other way. Ricœur does not view the individual word as the bearer of metaphorical meaning, but the metaphorical utterance on the level of the sentence as a whole.[177] In a metaphorical utterance, two elements are combined that, on the literal level, do not make sense together. 'The metaphor is the result of the tension between two terms in a metaphorical utterance.'[178] Yet it is not merely a semantic deviance,[179] but through this tension between the two terms new meaning is disclosed, because they are seen in the light of each other and thus give new meaning to each other.

> What is at stake in a metaphorical utterance [...] is the appearance of kinship where ordinary vision does not perceive any relationship. [...] It is, in effect, a calculated error, which brings together things that do not go together and by means of this apparent misunderstanding it causes a new, hitherto unnoticed, relation of meaning to spring up between the terms that previous systems of classification had ignored or not allowed.[180]

Through metaphor, a new view of the subject matter is offered. A new range of references or relations of being (*Seinsbezüge*) is opened and the reader is invited to see the subject matter in the light of these new relations. Thus the meaning of the subject matter is changed. In this process the world of the reader is altered by the implementation of new relations of being into the reader's previous system of relations. 'A metaphor, in short, tells us something new about reality.'[181] Metaphor only works in the realm

---

[175] Ricœur, Paul; *Time and Narrative* (3 vols.), Chicago and London (Chicago University Press) 1984-88.

[176] Ricœur, Paul; *Interpretation Theory: Discourse and the Surplus of Meaning*, Fort Worth (Texas University Press) 1976.

[177] Ricœur, Paul; *The Metaphorical Process as Cognition, Imagination, and Feeling*, Critical Inquiry 5, 1978, 143-160, 145.

[178] Ricœur; *Interpretation Theory*, 50.

[179] Ricœur; *The Metaphorical Process*,145. Cf. also Ricœur; *Interpretation Theory*, 49.

[180] Ricœur; *Interpretation Theory*, 51.

[181] Ibid. 53.

of language and meaning, i.e. of discourse (*logos*), because it creates new relations between beings, thus not having a direct relation to the physical life (*bios*). Or, as Ricœur puts it, 'Metaphor occurs in the already purified universe of the *logos*.'[182]

The connection between the realm of life (*bios*) and discourse (*logos*) is made by the symbol, which Ricœur discusses after his treatment of metaphor. Ricœur sees symbol as hesitating 'on the dividing line between *bios* and *logos*.'[183] Through symbol, something in the world, which can be seen, touched or experienced, is linked with an additional meaning. The single thing as a symbol signifies more than is visible, and in symbolic language, the symbol stands, on the one hand, for the literal meaning, on the other hand for that to which the symbol also points.

Finally, another important means of expressing new meaning is, as Ricœur calls it, the root metaphor.[184] Root metaphors are metaphors which are rooted in other metaphors and symbols; they are part of a whole system of symbols and metaphors. In this system, all metaphors and symbols are related to each other so that, if one of them is used, all of them contribute their meaning to the one which is used. In the same way, metaphors and symbols can be combined so that one or both elements of the metaphors are symbols. In this case, the whole meaning of the symbol is contributed into the metaphor.

In this respect, Gadamer's insight into the nature of language becomes important again. According to Gadamer, 'every word causes the whole language to which it belongs to resonate, and the whole of the perception of the world, that it is based upon, to appear.'[185] This statement must be seen in the context of Gadamer's general theory of language, which I have discussed in the previous section. If one word or idiom is used, it contains all the meaning it has in the world, in the world of the text as well as in that of the interpreter. Every term therefore carries with it the whole weight of its meaning. Unlike symbols, 'ordinary' terms do not point at something transcendent, although they too contain a surplus of meaning like metaphors and symbols. They always have to be seen against their own horizon, i.e. as a part of the world from which they come.

In religious language, metaphor and symbol become extremely important, since the subject matter in this kind of language is the divine, the transcendent. One way of speaking about the divine is the language of metaphysics, which is highly abstract and cannot really talk about the experience of the divine and its meaning in the life world of humankind.

---

182 Ibid. 59.
183 Ibid. 59.
184 Ibid. 64.
185 Gadamer; *Wahrheit und Methode*, 434 (Engl. 415f).

Poetic language, on the other hand, is able to communicate the experience and the meaning of the divine in a way that conceptualising language cannot do. This kind of religious language is earthly language speaking about the divine and its mystery, yet without collapsing the distinction. Heaven and earth, the divine and the human, are put into meaningful relation and the divine becomes speakable without losing its mystery. Immanent human language thus can contain transcendent meaning, *finitum capax infiniti!*

In order to interpret the mythological language of the Bible in the light of this theory of language, we need to analyse first how the terms, concepts and figures of speech, metaphors in particular, relate to each other and understand the network and development of meaning within the text. Secondly, the range of meanings of the terms and concepts within the text must be established; light needs to be shed on the world they make resonate, and the meaning which they carry with them has to be made explicit. The first task is a literary one, whereas the second one is a historical one. These two investigations are, as it were, two sides of a coin, they cannot be separated from each other and proper understanding of the text can only be gained through both.

The New Testament as a Reflection of the Early Christian Struggle for Language

The results of the above investigations have, certainly, important implications for our understanding of the New Testament. In analogy to Ebeling's above statement that the task of interpretation is not the understanding *of* language but *through* language, we can say that the task of New Testament interpretation is not the understanding *of* the New Testament but the understanding of Christian faith *through* the New Testament.

The same way today's interpreter understands Christianity through the New Testament, the New Testament authors, followed by the whole of Christianity, understood their faith through the language they created. Obviously, Christianity was founded through the ministry, the cross and resurrection of Jesus Christ. For those who encountered it, it gave a new meaning to the world. Their faith in Jesus Christ as the risen Lord transformed everything for them. God was understood differently, but also the world, humanity and, last but not least, the human self. To use the Heideggerian terminology, new *Seinsbezüge*[186] (relations of being) were unveiled. Through this event, a new world, a new creation was opened. It is, indeed, a new world that had been opened, not only a new relation between God and the human self, or the possibility of authentic existence. This new

---

[186] Cf. above, p.35.

world in which the first Christians found themselves, was understood through language. Since there was no ready language at hand to understand the new world, they had to create language, a new language for a new creation. The Christian struggle for language had begun.

The natural framework of language, in which the new faith could be understood, was the language of Judaism, since the first Christians were originally Jews, and the ministry of the earthly Jesus, at least partly, that of a Jewish teacher. Traditional religious language of Judaism was used, but it was given a new meaning, by combining known terms and concepts in a creative, a poetic way so that new meaning was disclosed and thus the new creation could be understood through language. For example, the well known term 'Kingdom of God' played an important part in the proclamation of early Christianity, being originally a term that had its place in Jewish terminology. It was, however, used to describe something different from what is described in traditional Jewish religious language. The 'Kingdom of God'[187] was, in Christian language, connected with Jesus' person. The Kingdom of God, with all its connotations, had arrived in Christ. So all the contents of the traditional language of the Kingdom of God were connected with Jesus, and so both Jesus and the 'Kingdom of God' gained new meaning, a meaning that was needed to understand faith in Jesus Christ as the crucified and risen Lord. In the same way early Christianity took many elements of traditional Jewish religious language and gave them a new meaning by connecting the known concepts creatively among each other and with the person of Jesus.[188]

Early Christianity used the languages not only of different Jewish traditions, but also that of other Hellenistic religious thought. As the horizon of Christianity grew, its language grew, making use of elements from religious languages of different backgrounds for a better understanding of the new faith. These borrowed elements of religious language were transformed in order to express the Christian faith, the Christian world by using them in a new context and combining them poetically. This is certainly only an oversimplifying account of the development of Christian thought. However, the History of Religion school is right when it says that Christianity is a synthesis of Jewish and Hellenistic thought. But it is not the religions that have been fused, but the language-worlds of the different world-views in order to express the unique message of Christianity. Struggling for a language to express Christian faith, elements of the different world-views, which we find as background of the New Testament writ-

---

[187] For a thorough discussion of the development of the concept of the 'Kingdom of God' cf. below, p.99.

[188] Cf. Luz, Ulrich; 'βασιλεία τοῦ θεοῦ' in: *EWNT* 481-91.

ings, were combined in a poetic way, and through this combination new meaning, the new message of Christianity, was brought out. Through language, Christianity found ever new ways to understand itself.

It may be worth remarking that what was to be brought out was, in fact, the Christian *kerygma* of cross and resurrection of Jesus Christ and its power to transform the (language-) world. Therefore it does not seem plausible to assume, for example, that parts of the New Testament, such as the Johannine writings, were docetic and did not know of the cross of Jesus, but only of his returning to the father, as Käsemann and others have suggested, and were made acceptable for the Church only at a later stage through an 'orthodox' redaction.[189] Here, in my opinion, the order of the development has been turned around. Early Christianity struggled for a language to express the experience of the cross and resurrection and, subsequently, brought about the scriptures of the New Testament. Later, some currents left the mainstream that was only later seen as orthodoxy. They interpreted Christianity in a Gnostic way and docetism became their way of understanding.[190] But this was, in my opinion, a later development away from the struggle for a language to express the identity of the crucified one with the resurrected one.

Certainly, this struggle for language led to different results, as we can see in the different approaches the New Testament provides, not to mention all the non-canonical early Christian writings. Early Christianity, owing to the different situations in the various corners of the ancient world where the Church was growing, created a different language to express and understand what Christianity was about. Thus a wide range of theology developed, depending on the background from which the authors came and for what type of audience they were writing. Any attempts to harmonise the differences in the New Testament writings would, in my opinion, neglect this plurality. However, already in early Christianity there were attempts to unify the different languages that were used to express the new world of Christianity. Approaches which were found inadequate were ruled out and seen as heresy. Through the development of the theology of the early church up to the creeds of the ecumenical councils, a language evolved to unify the different interpretations of Christianity. The New Testament as it is, however, represents an early stage of this development towards a unifying Christian language, and it is still full of the variety of interpretations gained by earliest Christianity. Nevertheless, the movement towards unification can be seen already in later layers of the

---

[189] Cf. Käsemann, Ernst; *Jesu letzter Wille nach Johannes 17*, Tübingen (Mohr-Siebeck) [4]1980, 26-35.

[190] Cf. below, pp.65f.

New Testament, e.g. the ecclesiastical redaction of John's Gospel, through which the language of John was brought in line with the developing mainstream Christianity,[191] or in the later epistles like the Pastorals or 2 Peter or Jude. For this very plurality, I thoroughly agree with Käsemann's famous statement that the canon of the New Testament does not found the unity of the Church but the plurality of denominations.[192] Different currents within early Christianity emphasised different aspects of the Christian proclamation, and Käsemann gives a concise account of the most important and obvious theological and historical differences within the canon.[193] The same way we find these differences in the New Testament, Churches and Christian groups through all history have emphasised some traditions within the New Testament more than others.[194] In fact, even those groups that claim to weigh all writings of the New Testament equally usually emphasise certain aspects of the New Testament more than others.

This view of the genesis of the New Testament involves, certainly, consequences for its interpretation. First, the theory of language and the view of the genesis of the New Testament presented here involve seeing the Word of God within the biblical text. There is no way of finding the Word of God behind the text in some pre-verbal form, as Karl Barth and the neo-Barthians do.[195] The New Testament contains the Word of God in its lingual form. The Word of God is, to refer again to Melanchthon's famous statement,[196] the proclamation of the *beneficia Christi* (benefits of Christ), which takes place in the *verbum externum* (external word), in the human language of the Bible. The *beneficia Christi* are seen in the transformation of the world. The language of the Bible and all Christian proclamation displays a transformed world, a new creation. It invites the recipient to enter this new world and have his or her own language-world transformed and thus to live in the world of Christianity. This implies that all Christian and biblical language is an open language-system, not esoteric. It is accessible from the outside, it is comprehensible without approaching it with particular presuppositions or from within a certain community. It is language which can be understood (to be accepted or to be rejected) by everyone willing to take it seriously. The language-world of Christianity is fundamentally open and comprehensible.

---

191 Cf. below, p.68.
192 Käsemann, Ernst; 'Begründet der neutestamentliche Kanon die Einheit der Kirche?' in: *Exegetische Versuche und Besinnungen*, vol 1, Göttingen (Vandenhoek und Ruprecht) 1960, 214-223, 221.
193 Ibid. 214-221.
194 Ibid. 221.
195 Cf. above, p.20.
196 Cf. above, p.23.

Secondly, the historical nature of the New Testament must be taken seriously. The interpreter has to be aware that the New Testament deals with a historical person, who lived in history, at a particular time and place, from the time when Cyrenius was governor of Syria until the crucifixion under Pontius Pilate, and who was understood in the framework of history, of the particular time and place in which the authors of the New Testament lived. The task of interpretation is, therefore, to understand the world of the New Testament in its historical and geographical context, in its closeness and familiarity as well as in its otherness and strangeness. Through this understanding of the New Testament the interpreter will be enabled to enter the language-world of the Bible and to become part of the new reality which the New Testament opens. Thus the interpreter's world will be transformed, and he or she becomes part of the new creation within today's world. Then the interpreter can translate the language of the Bible into the language of today's communities in order to open the world of Christianity to others. In short, today's theologian is still involved in the struggle for language; he or she is struggling to understand the world of Christianity through the Bible, entering its language-world and attempting to find a language to make this world accessible for others, to transform our world through the faith which is opened through the New Testament. As early Christianity struggled for a language for its faith and created it, today's Church is in need of an adequate understanding of the ancient language of faith, as well as creating a language for faith nowadays, which can only be based on the faith that found its expression in the language of the New Testament. In order to translate the texts of the New Testament and to let them speak in our time, we have to take part in the *Struggle for Language*, which is Christianity.

Chapter 5

Interpreting John:
Introductory Questions

If we understand the New Testament as part of the Christian *Struggle for Language*, this will have implications for its interpretation. The following chapters will present some case studies, in which I will demonstrate the methodological framework which follows from the previous hermeneutical insights. Therefore, after a brief discussion of introductory questions in this section I interpret three texts from John's Gospel.

In this present chapter, I am going to outline some thoughts on introductory questions only very briefly. A broader discussion of relevant issues will follow in the course of the exegesis in the next three chapters. First we will consider the relevance and use of parallel texts for New Testament interpretation. Second, we will reflect on the relevance of research into the social setting of the text, and of the reconstruction of the community from which a text evolved. Third, we will discuss some questions of literary criticism. This will be followed by a fourth section on the history of tradition behind John's Gospel aimed at reconstructing its genesis. In the light of these insights I highlight the issue as to how, during the development of John's Gospel, a language of faith was found and developed to understand Christianity, or, in other words, how the *Struggle for Language* took place within John's Gospel.

The following three chapters are dedicated to the interpretation of selected texts from John's Gospel. I chose these particular texts, the Hymn which is contained in the prologue (John 1:1-18), the Nicodemus Discourse (John 3:1-21) and the final Prayer (John 17), because they represent, as I am going to show, different stages in the development of the fourth gospel . The Hymn represents a text which had been written before the composition of the gospel by the evangelist and goes back to the earliest period of the Johannine community; the Nicodemus Discourse depicts a text which is a composition of the evangelist, and the final Prayer is a text which has been inserted into John's Gospel by a later redaction, but still before the so-called ecclesiastical redaction took place.[197] All three texts are non-narrative texts, they are poetry, dialogue and speech. I chose non-narrative texts for this study because interpreting narrative texts would have involved a discussion of the theory of narrative[198] in addition to that of poetic language, metaphor and symbol above.[199] This additional discussion would not contribute essentially new insights to this study, since the functioning of language as bearer of meaning is sufficiently explored in the discussion of poetic language.

It may be worth pointing out that the different historical findings and insights which I am presupposing and arguing in this study are not essential to the relevance of the main thesis. The texts are interpreted as carefully and thoroughly as possible in order to demonstrate my hermeneutical approach to the New Testament and the methodology which follows from it. The guiding question in the interpretation is how the authors involved in the composition of John's Gospel have combined elements from other religious languages in order to understand and communicate the Christian *kerygma*. What I try to understand is how the early Christian authors understood their faith. Yet the approach I am using is, in my opinion, generally valid for the interpretation of the New Testament. The concept of the *Struggle for Language* is not restricted to highlighting how the evangelists, authors, bearers of traditions and redactors struggled for language themselves but it is relevant for every historical interpretation with theological concern. Since there is no such thing as a presuppositionless and objective exegesis, every interpretation of the New Testament is governed by a theological agenda and is, therefore, never purely descriptive. Therefore, to insert a section after the allegedly descriptive interpretation of the text, which is meant to provide the fusion of horizons for the reader, as Ben Witherington III's commentary on John's Gospel[200] attempts to do, only bears witness to hermeneutical ignorance and does not take seriously the complexity of understanding. This kind of exegesis assumes that there is a purely descriptive exegesis which needs to be appropriated. Yet already the interpretation is governed by the theological agenda of the interpreter. Already in the 'descriptive' part a fusion of horizons has taken place.

As the aim of the second part of the study is, however, to demonstrate the functioning of the concept of the *Struggle for Language* and its methodological implications, I have concentrated on the way the writers involved in the composition of John's Gospel approached (probably

---

197 For a description of the terminology cf. below, p.63.
198 Cf. Ricœur, Paul; *Time and Narrative.*
199 Cf. above p. 44.
200 Witherington, III, Ben; *John's Wisdom: A Commentary on the fourth Gospel*, Louisville, Kentucky (Westminster John Knox Press) 1995.

unconsciously) the hermeneutical task and created a language in which to understand and communicate their faith. This investigation displays how the earliest church approached the hermeneutical problem posed by the very nature of Christianity, and its implications for our dealing with the same task, which has not changed significantly during the last two thousand years.

It is almost certain that the historical insights and assumptions of my argument will be challenged. However, apart from the fact that the results of this study are based on serious exegetical effort and that I am prepared to defend them, their falsification should not affect the general thesis, which is the suggestion of a hermeneutic of the New Testament and a resulting methodology. The aim of the exegetical part of this study is to demonstrate that my concept of the *Struggle for Language* enables an understanding of the New Testament as sacred scripture of Christianity, taking seriously the historical conditions and circumstances under which it developed. Yet the basis on which the discussion of the results of my exegesis must take place is the hermeneutical approach developed in the first part of this study and the resulting methodology based on which I interpreted the individual texts. Therefore, the results of this study are, though secondary, not arbitrary, for they represent my insights into the theology of Johannine Christianity, gained through the exegetical means available to me.

The Relevance of Parallels for Interpretation

Earlier in this study, I have suggested the way in which the horizons of the interpreter and the text are fused when understanding takes place.[201] In order to make this fusion of horizons possible, the interpreter has to establish the horizon of the text, as far as it is possible. This is where parallel texts are crucial to biblical interpretation.[202]

It is essential for biblical interpretation, as for all interpretation of ancient texts, to compare the text in question with available parallels. Yet a parallel text does not explain the text in question, but it sheds light on its environment. It is essential for interpretation to understand what the words of the text mean. All terms and concepts can mean something different in different times, different places and circumstances. Thus it is necessary to establish how a term would have been used at the time when and in the context in which the text was written. As Gadamer said, 'every word causes the whole language to which it belongs to resonate, and the whole

---

[201] Cf. above, p.39f.
[202] For the argument in this section cf. Sandmel, Samuel; *Parallelomania*, JBL 81, 1962, 1-13.

of the perception of the world, that it is based upon, appears.'[203] Thus, in order to understand a text, the world of the text, the whole network of its linguistic connections to other texts need to be established. The interpreter must hear, as it were, how the world of the text resonates with each word. To establish the meaning of a particular term, parallels have to be found and compared with the text. Parallels do not determine the meaning of the word or of the text, yet they illustrate how a term or a concept was used and which range of meaning it had at the time in which the text was written. Against this background the meaning of the language of the biblical text can be established.

Many biblical texts, whole books or epistles as well as single passages, are an attempt to answer a particular question or to deal with a particular problem which was a matter of concern and discussion at the time of the text. Certain questions were dominating the religious and philosophical discourse at particular times, they are thus reflected in the writings of that period. Therefore, these terms, which are part of the discussion, will be found in all writings dealing with this particular problem. For example, the Greek term *logos* (word) occurs in a huge range of writing during the first two or three centuries AD. *Logos* was the key term in the discussion about how the transcendent God could interact with the immanent world. This question was reflected, amongst others, by Philo, John's Gospel, Hermetic writings and Stoicism.[204] Thus it is not surprising that the term *logos* is found in the writings of all these authors and traditions and is used similarly. Yet this does not mean that there is mutual dependency amongst these writings, but that the authors of the different texts were all working on their own solutions to the problem given. A careful investigation shows that all of them are using the concept of *logos* in a different way to solve the problem of the relation of transcendent God and world. It is necessary to investigate these different concepts of *logos* in the light of the problem they try to solve in order to understand each of them appropriately. For example, to understand the concept of *logos* in the prologue to John's Gospel it is necessary to know the question which the author tries to answer in order to understand his thought. So the context in which he is writing has to be established; thus different approaches to the same problem have to be compared with that of the prologue to John's Gospel. If the term *logos* occurs somewhere in first or second century literature, the whole of the period thought on that matter resonates.

In this respect later parallels to the text in question are significant, too, because they contribute to the interpreter's understanding of the discussion

---

[203] Gadamer; *Wahrheit und Methode*, 434 (Engl. 415f).
[204] Cf. below, pp.80-84.

of which the text is a part. They can show the interpreter how the use of a term or concept developed, and how it was used in later antiquity, thus giving valuable insight into the meaning of a term. In addition, literary parallels which are dependent on the text interpreted may highlight how the text or concepts of the text have been understood by contemporary readers and thus how the author might have understood it himself. To use a contemporary example, if an interpreter of Kant two thousand years from now endeavoured to understand what the term *Vernunft* means, it would not be absurd to use texts of the nineteenth and twentieth century as parallel, for example the idealist philosophy or the neo-Kantians of the beginning of this century or the positions which argue against Kant's perception of the issue. Certainly, the interpreter then has to be aware that the parallels are later, yet they highlight the variety of meaning and the potential of the given term. Hence, for example, Hermetic parallels are relevant for the interpretation of John's Gospel, although they are chronologically later than the fourth gospel. They too are a part of the great discussion of religious questions which took part in the later ancient world and thus shed light on the meaning of the fourth gospel.

In addition, there is always the possibility that an author used another writing as a model for his own. In this case, it is essential to the understanding of the text to compare it with the source. However, the aim of interpretation is not merely to establish the source, but to find the author's creative work and learn what he made of the source to fit it into his own agenda. Only then we can find out how the thought of the author was shaped by contemporary thought and what was his individual contribution, so that we may understand the meaning of the text in its context.

Finally, not only a knowledge of related texts and traditions is essential to biblical interpretation, but also a thorough knowledge of ancient literature, philosophy and history in general, for only then can the texts be seen in their context in the world from which they originate.

The Social Background of the Text

In the current debate, an important issue is the relevance of the sociological background of a biblical text. In this context, we need to discuss two important questions. First, some scholars have argued that John's Gospel is the arcane scripture of a sect which lived in complete separation from its environment and thus that John's Gospel is written in a language which is only accessible to the initiated and completely incomprehensible to outsiders.[205] We will discuss this claim in the light of the insights gained in the previous chapters of this study. Secondly, we will discuss the position on the other extreme, i.e. Richard Bauckham's thesis that the community from which a text originates is irrelevant for its interpretation.[206]

In Johannine interpretation, it has often been argued that through the Gospel text the history of the Johannine community can be reconstructed. This type of research into John's Gospel has been introduced by Louis J. Martyn in his influential work *History and Theology in the Fourth Gospel*.[207] For him as well as for his main followers, most eminently Wayne A. Meeks and Raymond E. Brown, John's Gospel evolved from an isolated group of Christians, the history of which is found in the narrative of the gospel in a coded form and can be deciphered. It is more or less agreed amongst these scholars that the Johannine group was a sect in opposition to the sect of John the Baptist, the Jewish community and even the 'Apostolic Christians', the group which became later the catholic church.[208] John's Gospel is then seen as a text that is, on one level, written 'to make sense of all these aspects of the group's history',[209] and is seen as written more or less exclusively for this distinct community. R.E. Brown even tries to reconstruct the whole history of this isolated community from the evidence found in the gospel.[210] Wayne A. Meeks even goes as far as saying that John's Gospel is the arcane scripture of an isolated community or sect, that 'not only describes, in etiological fashion, the birth of that community; it also provides reinforcement of the community's isolation.'[211] The gospel is written in a way, that

> only a reader who is thoroughly familiar with the whole Fourth Gospel or else acquainted by some non-literary means with its symbolism and developing themes [...] can possibly understand its double entendre and its abrupt

---

205 Cf. Meeks, Wayne A.; 'The Man from Heaven in Johannine Sectarianism' in: Ashton, John (ed.); *The Interpretation of John*, Issues of Religion and and Theology 9, Philadelphia (Fortress) and London (SPCK) 1986, 141-173.

206 Bauckham, Richard; *For whom where the Gospels written?* in: Bauckham, Richard (ed.); *The Gospels for All Christians: Rethinking the Gospel Audiences*, Edinburgh (T&T Clark) 1998, 9-48.

207 Martyn, J. Louis; *History and Theology in the Fourth Gospel*, Nashville, Tennessee (Abington) ²1979.

208 Brown, Raymond E.; *The Community of the Beloved Disciple: The Life, Loves, and Hates of an Individual Church in New Testament Times*, New York, Mahwah (Paulist Press) 1979, 59-91.

209 Meeks; 'Man from Heaven' 145.

210 Brown; *Community*.

211 Meeks; 'Man from Heaven' 163.

transitions. For the outsider — even for an interested inquirer (like Nicodemus) — the dialogue is opaque.[212]

Brown does not go as far as Meeks, and does not see the community in this complete isolation from the rest of Christianity. However, he suggests that, although separated from the mainstream church, and tending towards sectarianism, the Johannine community did not break communion with the 'Apostolic Christians'.[213] Yet can we really assume such a separated group of Christians, something like the Johannine community, in and for which John's Gospel has been written? And if so, can we reconstruct its history through the sociological deciphering of the gospel narrative?

For a comprehensive critical evaluation of these theories of a closed community behind the fourth gospel, it would be necessary to discuss the structuralist presuppositions at work behind these proposals, as they seem to be governed by structuralist anthropology.[214] But this discussion would be far too extensive within the framework of this study, and so I shall confine myself to some historical and linguistic arguments.

First, it is difficult to imagine that such an isolated, sectarian church, supposedly having daughter churches, could flourish in centres of early Christianity, like Ephesus or Syria,[215] independent of other Christian groups and not seeing itself as part of the larger church.

The fourth gospel was written well before the formation of the early catholic church in the second half of the second century, which in itself was a reaction to the crisis of the church caused by the Gnostic movement. It was only in this context, that the rule of faith, the canon of the New Testament and the monarchic episcopal office developed. Before that, at the time in question, a much wider variety of theologies and spiritualities was possible and, as far as we know, no fixed structure of organisation existed in the church. Before the Gnostic crisis, there would have been space in the church for a group like the Johannine without it being sectarian. In addition, it is hard to imagine how such a group could have developed. In Syria or Asia Minor we know of Christian churches from the Pauline missions. The area in which the Johannine churches are usually located is, so to speak, the heartland of early Christianity. Thus, the 'main stream church' is

---

[212] Meeks; 'Man from Heaven' 152.

[213] Brown; *Community*, 89-91.

[214] Cf. Barton, Stephen C.; 'Early Christianity and the Sociology of the Sect' in: Watson, Francis (ed.); *The Open Text: New Directions for Biblical Studies?*, London (SCM) 1993, 140-162, 147.

[215] Cf. Brown; *Community*, 98. For the location of the Johannine group in Syria cf. Köster, Helmut; *Einführung in das Neue Testament: im Rahmen der Religionsgeschichte und Kulturgeschichte der hellenistischen und römischen Zeit*, Berlin-New York (de Gruyter) 1980, 616.

strongly present here and develops ecclesiastically and theologically. It is, in my opinion, implausible to assume that in such an environment a separate church could grow entirely independently from the rest of the church and even develop daughter churches in other towns.

Furthermore, and this is a main point of my argument, Johannine language is not an arcane language incomprehensible to the uninitiated. On the contrary, it is an open system of language, drawing concepts and symbols from the Christian and non-Christian environment and combining them in a poetic way.[216] Therefore, the language of John's Gospel would have been, and still is comprehensible for anybody familiar with its contemporary thought, especially for members of Christian communities. The fourth gospel needs to be seen as a means to communicate theological insights and a particular interpretation to the community from which the gospel originated as well as to the church and beyond.

However, on historical and linguistic grounds it is possible to recognise distinct traditions at work behind or within John's Gospel. These allow us to identify a particular type of Christianity which is different from that of the synoptic gospels. Thus it is legitimate to say that the Gospel of John is a text which evolved from a particular group within the early church, and which was written within a context of a distinct theology and spirituality. There is not, however, enough evidence to suppose an isolated church or sect. In fact, the main feature of this group is, as far as we can reconstruct it, that it developed a particular theology. The development of a distinct theology does not, however, necessarily presuppose that the group deviated from orthodoxy, especially since orthodoxy and the rule of faith became important only later, after the Gnostic crisis of the early church. Therefore, we can see John's Gospel as a development within the variety of early Christian theology and language, a development which brought about an impressive system of language as well as of theology. Its theological language is not arcane, but it could be understood by Christians as well as everyone familiar with its contemporary religious thought.[217] It invited the reader or listener to enter the world which is brought about through its language. John's Gospel is not a document of a group which separated itself from the church, but it is an offer to the church, and which the wider church finally accepted.

The other extreme position is held by Richard Bauckham, who suggests that early Christianity was, because of the travelling activity of Bishops, missionaries and messengers, in such a close contact, that the 'global village'

---

[216] Cf. above, 48f. Cf. also Barton; 'Early Christianity and the Sociology of the Sect' 148.

[217] Cf. below, p.116.

was realised by the early Church. For Bauckham 'the early Christian movement was a network of communities in constant communication with each other, by messengers, letters and movements of leaders and teachers — moreover, a network around which Christian literature circulated easily, quickly and widely.'[218] In Bauckham's view of early Christianity there is not much space for the development of distinct groups having their own traditions, because every leading Christian figure is well travelled and has much experience of other local churches,[219] and literature from each Christian group circulated quickly, so that no author could expect to address only a particular community, but his work would very soon be distributed throughout the Christian world.[220]

There are three points of criticism which need to be discussed here. First, Bauckham gives an impressive account of the travelling activity in early Christianity. Yet he does not recognise that these journeys do not stand for an infinite amount of travelling messengers and clergy. The long distance journeys which Bauckham uses as examples have been documented because they were something unusual and not everyday business. In addition, journeys through the Roman empire in that period took a very long time. For example, when Ovid travelled from Rome to his exile in Tomi at the Black Sea, it took him from Autumn 8 AD until mid- 9 AD.[221] As travelling was such a time-consuming business, it did not facilitate 'constant communication' and 'quick circulation of literature.' Thus, it is likely that, despite the travelling-activity of the early Church, strong local traditions and local groups of Churches with distinct theological and spiritual features could develop. It is also possible that leaders stayed in a Church which they had founded and which thus shared their theological thought, with the result that their writings, e.g. Gospel writings, were primarily written for their particular community and recognising their particular needs. In this case, investigation into the community from which a particular writing evolved may be relevant for biblical interpretation.

Secondly, it is striking that none of the earlier versions of John's Gospel were circulated and thus known to us. If literature was distributed as

---

[218] Bauckham; *For whom where the Gospels written?*, 44.

[219] Ibid. 33-38.

[220] Ibid. 11f.

[221] Ovid's journey into exile is a particularly interesting example for he had been under pressure to travel as fast as possible. So his instance shows us how fast it was possible to travel through the Roman Empire of that period without using the fast imperial postal system. For Ovid's journey cf. Duff, J.Wight; *A Literary History of Rome: From the Origins to the Close of the Golden Age*, London (T. Fisher Uwin) [5]1923, 584f and Ovidius Naso, Publius; *Tristia Epistulas Ex Ponto*, Latine et Germanice, ed. by Georg Luck, Zürich (Artemis) 1963, X-XI.

quickly and easily as Bauckham assumes, earlier versions of John's Gospel, which are very likely to have existed,[222] would have been circulated and preserved. Thus, the fact that none of the earlier versions of John's Gospel have been received strongly suggests that it is possible that a Christian community did not live in 'constant communication' with the rest of Christianity and did not take part in the 'quick circulation of literature.' In the same way it is striking that, on the ground of the internal evidence, John's Gospel obviously ignores synoptic traditions and it is very likely that they were not known to the evangelist and redactors. If such a constant communication, as Bauckham assumes, really took place and led to such an interchange of thoughts and traditions, there would be noticeable traces of synoptic traditions in the fourth gospel, which are, however, strikingly absent.

Thirdly, Bauckham does not envisage that early Christian literature is rarely the work of a single author, but is rooted in communities which carry particular traditions which are shaped by their particular circumstances and environment.[223] The author of the gospels is not the far travelled and cosmopolitan individual, who is modelled after the modern scholar who travels from conference to conference to meet his fellow scholars and who is able to accept positions in nearly every part of the world. On the contrary, the gospels were written by communities within the early Church, which have their distinct traditions and customs. In addition, since a huge diversity of opinions and positions was acceptable to the early church, even the exchange between different Christian communities did not lead to uniformity of thought and customs. This is, contrary to Bauckham's thesis, the background of early Christian literature, which was directed at a particular audience.

In sum, it is possible and even likely that the fourth gospel originates from a community with its own traditions and theology and that it is written for this particular community in the first place. Nevertheless, it is not the arcane scripture of a sect, but that of a distinct group, which is part of the wider church. As we will see in the course of the interpretation of Johannine texts, the fourth gospel was comprehensible and meaningful to the rest of Christianity. Thus it is appropriate and necessary for New Testament interpretation to investigate the particular background of John's Gospel, and to identify particular traditions and theological approaches which may have been part of that community. If available, even sociological

---

[222] Cf. below, p.62, 'The Development of John's Gospel'.
[223] Cf. Becker, Jürgen; *Das Evangelium nach Johannes*, Vol 1: ÖTK 4/1, Gütersloh (Mohn) [3]1991, 36-38.

factors will play a part in exegesis. In sum, we must see John's Gospel somewhere in-between sectarianism and universal communication.

The Development of John's Gospel

A major issue in Johannine studies has always been the reconstruction of the original order of the fourth gospel and the underlying traditions and sources.[224] Starting point for most of the investigations into these questions is the chronological and local inconsistency of the text. This has led to theories like Bultmann's hypothesis of 'external disorder', i.e. that the pages of the original manuscript were mixed up by accident.[225] The other strand of research is to concentrate on the underlying sources which the evangelist may have used. Authoritative in this field has been Bultmann's analysis again, which suggested three sources behind the gospel, the Signs Source, the Revelation Discourse Source and the Passion Narrative.[226] Bultmann's theory and the following discussion have been discussed broadly and controversially in the years subsequent to their publication.[227] For the purpose of the present study, however, it may be sufficient to summarise that there is no widely shared consensus about the sources of John's Gospel.[228]

In my opinion, it is very likely that the evangelist drew on traditions and made use of them for his composition of his gospel. Yet I do not believe that it is possible to reconstruct the underlying sources sufficiently for conclusions to be drawn, since the evangelist used the sources as material, which he transformed in order to express his theology. For example, even if the so-called Signs Source was used in the composition of John's Gospel,[229] the evangelist did not use it simply by quoting it or copying it, but he changed the miracle-accounts of the source significantly so that they con-

---

[224] Cf. Kümmel, Werner Georg; *Einleitung in das Neue Testament*; Heidelberg (Quelle & Meyer) ²¹1983, 162-183; Lohse, Eduard; *Die Entstehung des Neuen Testaments*, Theologische Wissenschaft Vol. IV, Stuttgart, Berlin, Köln (Kohlhammer) ⁵1991, 103-114. Cf also Thyen, Hartwig; 'Aus der Literatur zum Johannesevangelium' *TRu* 39, 1979, 1-69, 222-252, 289-330; *TRu* 42, 1977, 211-270; *TRu* 43, 1978, 328-590; *TRu* 44, 1979, 97-134; Becker, Jürgen; 'Aus der Literatur zum Johannesevangelium (1978-1980)' *TRu* 47, 1982, 279-301, 305-347 and Becker, Jürgen; 'Das Johannesevangelium im Streit der Methoden (1980-1984)' *TRu* 51, 1986, 1-78.

[225] Cf. Bultmann; *Johannesevangelium*, 178, fn 3.

[226] Ibid. 489-491.

[227] For a concise picture of the discussion cf. Kümmel; *Einleitung*, 162-183.

[228] For the disagreement even about a presumed consensus within the discussion cf. Becker; *Johannesevangelium*, 39f and Kümmel; *Einleitung*, 165-183.

[229] Cf. Becker; *Johannesevangelium*, 134-143.

vey his own theology. Only the plot of the miracle-account of the source would have remained, yet the form of the narrative and the theological content would be the work of the evangelist. Hence it is unlikely that it is possible to reconstruct the sources which underlie John's Gospel and so to identify their theological agenda. The part of the Gospel which is the work of the evangelist is, in my opinion, an original work which is based upon earlier traditions.

Therefore, I propose an approach to the fourth gospel which starts at the level of the evangelist and takes seriously his theological work. From that level it is possible to identify traditions which the evangelist used for his compositions. We will need to identify the way in which the evangelist transformed his material. It is also possible to detect the work of later redactors, who inserted larger passages like the extensions of the farewell-discourse[230] or ch.21. There is also a further, later redaction, commonly called the ecclesiastical redaction, which inserted short glosses and possibly changed passages carefully in order to bring them in line with the predominant theology of their time.[231] We will have to discern and evaluate older traditions and later redaction in each individual case.

On these grounds I suggest a simple theory of the genesis of the fourth gospel. First, the evangelist, drawing on different oral and written traditions and maybe also on sources, composed the first version of John's Gospel. Secondly, the redactor, either during the lifetime of the evangelist or after his death, inserted additional pieces and speeches. These are the extensions of the Farewell Discourses, the second ending in ch.21 and possibly the appendices after the conclusion of a passage (3:31-36, 10:1-18, 12:44-50).[232] Later, the ecclesiastical redaction inserted smaller additions, like 5:28f or 6:51c-58.[233] Redaction of the fourth gospel, however, did not take place at once, but in different stages. For example, the Farewell Discourses were added in three identifiable stages.[234] This process of John's Gospel came to an end with its 'canonisation' and coming into liturgical use. From

---

230 John 15:1-17:26. Cf. Becker; *Johannesevangelium*, 39-41.
231 Becker also names the former stage of redaction the ecclesiastical redaction (*Kirchliche Redaktion*, cf. Becker; *Johannesevangelium*, 39-41). I do not find that title appropriate for this particular redaction, for it did not bring John's Gospel in line with the thought of the main-stream Church. Thus I use 'ecclesiastical redaction' only for the redaction for which I have used it here. The other redaction I only call 'redaction' without further specification.
232 Cf. Becker; *Johannesevangelium*, 39-41.
233 Ibid.
234 Cf. Becker, Jürgen; 'Die Abschiedsreden Jesu im Johannesevangelium' *ZNW* 61, 1970, 215-246.

that time on copies had to be made and circulated, so that John's Gospel became the property of the wider church.

The literary development of the fourth gospel also reflects an evolution of theological thought. On the one hand, ongoing theological reflection led to new insights and ideas, which are echoed in the different stages of John's Gospel. On the other hand, external factors like sociological developments or the relation to other groups brought new problems that had to be solved and ideas that could be built into the theology of the Johannine Churches. For example, the growing tension between the Johannine community and its environment is likely to have lead to an elaboration of the dualist world-picture. The closer contact with the growing Church led the Johannine community to adapt its theology, especially its perception of Eschatology and Sacraments. It is an important part of this study to bring out this development, to highlight its main threads and draw conclusions for Johannine interpretation.

The Development of the Johannine Churches

After the previous discussion of the literary history of John's Gospel it is necessary to engage in an investigation into the history of Johannine Christianity[235] and its traditions. In the course of this inquiry I am going to base my assumptions on reasons drawn from the history of tradition behind John's Gospel. It is not possible, in my opinion, to reconstruct the sociological conditions of the Johannine group, as for example Brown attempts in his book *The Community of the Beloved Disciple*.[236] In this respect I agree with Jürgen Becker, who argues that nobody who is able to distinguish between the literary world and lived history can read John 1-4 as an immediate reflection of the early history of the Johannine community.[237]

Theologically and literarily the oldest layer in John's Gospel is the hymn underlying the prologue. As I will demonstrate below in the following chapter 'The Prologue: John 1:1-18',[238] the theology of the hymn is strongly influenced by Jewish wisdom-speculation close to that of Philo of Alexandria.[239] This influence points at the origin of the Johannine community; it is

---

[235] By 'Johannine Christianity' (or synonym terms like 'Johannine churches', 'Johannine group' etc.) I mean the branch of Christianity from which the fourth gospel originated. Although it may be an anachronism to call it Johannine before the writing of the gospel, this terminology helps to identify this particular branch of Christianity.

[236] Cf. above, p.57, fn.208.

[237] Cf. Becker; *Johannesevangelium*, 54.

[238] Cf. below, p.69.

[239] Cf. below, pp.80, 85.

very likely that Johannine Christianity developed within a Jewish context which was part of the wisdom-circles, probably before the final separation of the Christian church from the Synagogue. During the first century AD tensions grew between early Jewish Christianity and other heterodox groups within the Synagogue on the one side and orthodox Judaism on the other, until it came to the final expulsion from the Synagogue after the inclusion of the *Birkath ha-Minim*, the cursing of heretics, into the prayers of the Synagogue.[240] The complete break with Judaism caused the development of a particular Johannine literature, which created the basis of a distinct Christian identity of the Johannine group.

Some scholars have suggested that the Johannine circle developed from a group which dissented from a group worshipping John the Baptist as the Messiah.[241] Though this interpretation of the evidence (especially the passages about John the Baptist, John 1:19ff, 3:23-30, 10:40-42) is not impossible, it is more likely that the Johannine community grew within the framework of the Synagogue. Yet after the expulsion from the Synagogue it is possible that the Johannine church came into close contact with other heterodox Jewish groups which had been excluded from the Synagogue as well, like the followers of John the Baptist or early Gnostics.[242] The Johannine church, beginning to develop its own identity, started a dialogue with those groups, which led to the rejection of the claims of the followers of John the Baptist, which is reflected in the John the Baptist-passages. The dialogue with Gnostic groups, however, led to a much closer interaction.

The nature of this interaction between Gnostic and Christian thought has been widely discussed, and no consensus has been achieved in the debate. On the one hand, scholars like Hengel or Yamauchi argue that there is no evidence for a non-Christian or pre-Christian Gnosis, which might have influenced the early church and its writings.[243] On the other hand, there is a number of scholars arguing for a non-Christian origin of

---

[240] Cf. Becker; *Johannesevangelium*, 56 and Schmithals, Walter; *Neues Testament und Gnosis*, in: 'Erträge der Forschung' 208, Darmstadt (Wissenschaftliche Buchgesellschaft) 1984, 113-115.

[241] Cf. Becker; *Johannesevangelium*; 55; Bultmann; *Johannesevangelium*, 4f, Brown; *Community*, 27-31.

[242] Cf. Perkins, Pheme; *Gnosticism and the New Testament*, Minneapolis (Fortress) 1993, 40-42.

[243] Cf. Yamauchi, Edwin; *Pre-Christian Gnosticism: A Survey of the Proposed Evidences*, London (Tyndale Press) 1973 and Hengel, Martin; *Der Sohn Gottes*, Tübingen (Mohr-Siebeck) 1975.

Gnosis.[244] These scholars agree that Gnostic thought developed alongside the New Testament and shares the same origin, which is heterodox Judaism.[245] These scholars say that Gnosticism is far from being a closed speculative system or an established religion, but that

> there were certainly Gnostic religions and Gnosticizing interpretations of religious traditions and mythical materials, pre-Christian and Christian, Jewish and pagan. [...] And all these Gnostic religions, in spite of the vast difference of the materials they interpret, exhibit a high degree of affinity and congeniality. It is, therefore, quite legitimate to speak of a phenomenon 'Gnosis' in general [...]
>
> As Christian religion, in the early Christian period as well as today, cannot be grasped in the abstraction of a theological and cultural system, Gnostic religion in its origin and development cannot be understood through the reconstruction of a general system in mythological and philosophical terms, but only in the analysis of Gnostic interpretations of the traditions of myth and cult in the specific religious communities.[246]

This theory is much more able to account for the parallels between Gnostic and Christian thought than the assumption that there is no pre-Christian Gnosis. It sees both groups as referring to the same authorities, to the Jewish tradition, from which both of them originate. In addition, it is likely that two groups on the fringe of Judaism and expelled from the Synagogue at roughly the same time were in contact with each other.[247]

It is important at this point to observe that early Christianity before the so-called Gnostic crisis in the second century was not a homogenous movement but it allowed a huge variety of approaches to the Christian faith, so that Gnosticising thought would have been tolerated in earliest Christianity.[248] Early Christianity and Gnosis were both movements with-

---

[244] Cf. Schmithals; *Neues Testament und Gnosis*; Perkins; *Gnosticism and the New Testament*; Köster, Helmut; 'The History-of-Religion School, Gnosis and Gospel of John' *ST* 40 (1986), 115-136.

[245] Cf. Perkins; *Gnosticism and the New Testament*, 40-42.

[246] Köster, 'The History-of-Religion School, Gnosis and Gospel of John' 131f.

[247] The main problem in defining the relation between earliest Christianity and Gnostic thought is that there is no evidence outside the New Testament. When the first distinct Gnostic writings occur in the second century, the previous existence of Gnostic thought has to be assumed. Thus every argument in favour or against non-Christian Gnostic thought, which might have influenced Christianity, must be circular, as it can only build on the evidence in the New Testament (Cf. Schmithals, *Neues Testament und Gnosis*, pp.16-21). In my opinion the assumption of a non-Christian Gnosis which may have influenced Christianity explains the internal evidence of the New Testament much better then the opposite position. Cf. (amongst others) below, pp.101, 129, 134.

[248] Cf. Wisse, Frederik; 'Prolegomena to the Study of the Testament and Gnosis' in: Logan, A.H.B. and Wedderburn, A.J.M. (eds.); *The New Testament and Gnosis: Es-*

out a fixed organisation or a defined orthodoxy. Christianity developed these features only in its struggle against Gnosticism and the resulting evolution of early catholicism in the second century. Thus a far-reaching interaction between Christian and Gnostic thought was possible and took place in the first and early second century, for Christianity had not yet recognised the danger Gnosticism would constitute for the Christian church. Consequently, the development of Gnosticism and Christianity overlapped widely and influenced each other during the first and the early second century until the two movements finally separated.

Within this historical framework it is likely that a group like the Johannine was in close contact with Gnostic groups and that mutual influence took place. Even within the Johannine community Gnosticising tendencies grew. This position is confirmed by the internal evidence we find in John's Gospel, i.e. the strong parallels to Gnostic thought in the Nicodemus Discourse[249] and the increasing influence of these ideas in John 17.[250] This parallel development of Johannine Christianity and (Johannine) Gnosticism continued until the Johannine group had to take a clear stance towards Gnosticism, especially towards docetic ideas, and turned towards the developing and increasingly anti-Gnostic early Catholic church.

Within this historical framework, it is likely that the Johannine church was, at least at some stage of its development, open to Gnostic ideas, which are reflected in the parallels to Gnostic thought pointed out in the case-studies below.[251] Yet tensions between 'main-stream Johannine Christianity' (i.e. as it is known from the Gospel as it is received and the epistles) and Johannine Gnostics grew to a point when it came to a split in the community, which is reflected in 1 John. Certainly, the final dissent of the opponents of 1 John may have been motivated by many reasons; for example sociological factors may have played an important role in the split of the Church. These non-theological elements in the history of the Johannine church, however, are not relevant to the study of the history of tradition of Johannine theology. The theological thought which is found in the Johannine writings is, in fact, sufficient to understand the development of Johannine theology as far as it is needed for the interpretation of Johannine writings. There are certainly other questions for which the non-theological factors may be relevant, but this is beyond the scope of this study.

---

says in honour of Robert McL. Wilson, Edinburgh (T&T Clark) 1983, 138-145, 141. Cf. also Bauer, Walter; *Orthodoxy and Heresy in Earliest Christianity*, in: The New Testament Library, London (SCM) 1972, 229-231.

[249] Cf. below, pp.101f.
[250] Cf. below, pp.129f, 134f.
[251] Cf. (amongst others) below, pp.101, 129, 134.

After the final split of the Johannine church, the dissenters moved towards Gnosticism and contributed to its development, especially bringing with them the high estimation of John's Gospel, which is found in later Gnosticism. The remaining group, however, took an anti-Gnostic stance and embraced the developing early catholic church. In this time the ecclesiastical redaction took place, which aligned John's Gospel with the theology of the main-stream church.

This is certainly far from a comprehensive discussion of Johannine history and of the other introductory questions. Yet it is not meant to be a comprehensive study into the matter, but only to provide the historical framework in which the interpretation of the fourth gospel may take place. In the study of the individual passages those questions relevant to the interpretation will be discussed in more detail.[252]

---

[252] It must be remarked here that the development of Johannine theology is a continuous movement. Because of the outline of this study, discussing three texts which represent particular levels of the development of Johannine thought in relative isolation, it may appear as if these stages are only loosely connected. This is, however, not the case. Rather, they represent important stages in the history of Johannine theology, which are connected not only by the continuous thought-process, but also by texts which mirror the transition from one stage to the next. To identify and discuss these texts, however, would be a another book.

Chapter 6

The Prologue: John 1:1-18

Introduction

Hardly any other passage of the New Testament has attracted so much scholarly attention as the Prologue to John's Gospel. It is, in fact, one of the most fascinating texts of the New Testament, so familiar and yet totally strange. It has played a crucial part in the formation of the church doctrine and was also popular amongst heretics. And it is no surprise that Goethe's Faust turns to this very text when he starts to translate the Bible — only to meet the devil.

There is a confusing multitude of literature on the prologue,[253] much of which has been engaged in reconstructing the underlying hymn or arguing against its existence. In contemporary exegesis, however, it is more or less a consensus that the prologue to John's Gospel consists of an older, traditional hymn and annotations by the evangelist.[254] Since there is broad disagreement among scholars as to which parts of the prologue belong to the hymn and which to the evangelist, I shall try to establish criteria for evaluating the different theories and make a decision for a particular reconstruction of the hymn. This exercise will involve a detour into the wider context of Johannine theology and history of Johannine Christianity.

This will be followed by an interpretation of the underlying hymn, in order to demonstrate how the hermeneutical ideas outlined earlier can be applied to the prologue. We will focus on the development of those concepts which are the basis of the language of the hymn, in order to see how they are combined in new and creative ways in order to express the new interpretation of the Christian proclamation and the world. In addition, I am going to highlight how the language of the hymn is a further

---

[253] Cf. the bibliographies in Thyen, Hartwig; 'Aus der Literatur zum Johannesevangelium' *TRu* 39, 1979, 1-69, 222-252, 289-330; 42, 1977, 211-270; 43, 1978, 328-590; 44, 1979, 97-134; Becker, Jürgen; 'Aus der Literatur zum Johannesevangelium (1978-1980)' *TRu* 47, 1982, 279-301, 305-347; Becker, Jürgen; 'Das Johannesevangelium im Streit der Methoden (1980-1984)' *TRu* 51, 1986, 1-78.

[254] Cf. Hofius, Otfried; 'Struktur und Gedankengang des Logos-Hymnus in Joh 11-18' *ZNW* 78, 1987, 1-25, 1; Thyen, Hartwig; 'Aus der Literatur zum Johannesevangelium' *TRu* 39, 1979, 1-69, 53-69.

development of earlier languages and how it relates to the later language of the main body of the gospel.

The Hymn

The Problem of the Reconstruction

As pointed out earlier, there is a broad consensus in modern scholarship that the prologue to John's Gospel is based upon an older hymn.[255] But as much as the scholars agree on the existence of the hymn, so strongly they disagree about its extent. I cannot give an outline of the recent discussion of this matter here, but excellent reviews are available.[256] There are, as far as I can discern, two basic methods of reconstructing the hymn. On the one hand, some scholars attribute to the evangelist only those parts which are undoubtedly prose and do not fit into the context of the hymn. On the other hand, some scholars have achieved remarkable results and impressive reconstructions of the hymn by larger and sometimes rather speculative operations. In the following, I am going to discuss two reconstructions, that of Otfried Hofius[257] as an example of the former approach and that of Jürgen Becker[258] as a model for the latter. I chose these two approaches, because they are sufficiently recent to represent the latest state of the debate. In fact, Hofius' essay is the most recent work on that matter that has come to my notice. In addition, Hofius is able to attribute to the evangelist only the minimal number of verses possible and to reconstruct a plausible (and beautiful) hymn. Becker's reconstructed hymn measures only two thirds of Hofius', because Becker attributes much more material to the evangelist, and his investigations result in a plausible hymn as well. Becker, however, not only ascribes much less material to the hymn, which makes him a representative of the second group of scholars, but also sees a complex history of redaction at work in the genesis of the prologue. This makes him a profitable partner for discussion in order to gain a deeper understanding of the prologue. In dialogue with these two interpretations of the prologue, which represent a good sample of recent scholarship, my own view on the prologue will be developed and discussed.

---

[255] Cf. Hofius; 'Struktur und Gedankengang des Logos-Hymnus in Joh 1:1-18' 1.

[256] Cf. Thyen, Hartwig; 'Aus der Literatur zum Johannesevangelium' *TRu* 39, 1979, 1-69, 222-252, and Becker, Jürgen; 'Aus der Literatur zum Johannesevangelium (1978-1980)' *TRu* 47, 1982, 279-301, 305-347, esp. 317-321.

[257] Cf. Hoius, Otfried; 'Struktur und Gedankengang des Logos-Hymnus in Joh 1:1-18' ZNW 78, 1987, 1-25.

[258] Cf. Becker; *Johannesevangelium*, 79-104.

There are, nevertheless, important scholars who do not treat John 1:1-18 as a hymn with annotations. C.K. Barrett, for example, rightly observes in his commentary on John's Gospel that the prologue is not Greek poetry.[259] Not being classical Greek poetry, however, does not disprove that it is a hymn which follows different, more Semitic poetic rules, that of the christological hymns we find in different places in the New Testament. In this case, Barrett is wrong saying that it is 'impossible to strike out certain passages as prose insertions into an original "logos-ode".'[260] In addition, as a multitude of scholars have demonstrated, the passage does not show a 'marked internal unity', or 'a distinct unity of theme and subject matter with the remainder of the gospel' as Barrett assumes,[261] but evidence of different layers of tradition and redaction . I am going to elaborate that in more detail in my further discussion of the prologue.

Both, Hofius[262] and Becker[263] agree with Bultmann[264] that vv.6-8,12c (v.12c=τοῖς πιστεύουσιν εἰς τὸ ὄνομα αὐτοῦ)+13,15,17+18 are additions to the hymn. Apart from a few scholars who disagree about single verses,[265] it seems to be a minimal consensus among scholars that these verses are not part of the underlying hymn. Hofius stops here and attributes the rest of the prologue to the hymn, whereas Becker goes further and also excludes vv.2,9+10,14d from the hymn. Hofius' reconstruction results in a hymn of four stanzas, which are each divided into two half-stanzas, Becker assumes a hymn of three stanzas. The exact shape of the two reconstructions can be seen below, where the assumed original forms of the hymn are given.

---

[259] Barrett, Charles K.; *The Gospel according to St. John*, London (SPCK) ²1978, 150.

[260] Barrett; *John*, 150.

[261] Barrett; *John*, 150.

[262] Cf. Hofius; 'Struktur und Gedankengang des Logos-Hymnus in Joh 1:1-18' 2.

[263] Cf. Becker; *Johannesevangelium*, 82f.

[264] Bultmann; *Johannesevangelium*, 29, 37f, 50, 53f.

[265] Cf. for example Schmithals (Schmithals, Walter; 'Der Prolog des Johannesevangeliums' *ZNW* 70, 1979, 16-43), who attrinutes v.17 to the hymn.

Becker's and Hofius' Reconstructions
of the Hymn in John 1:1-18 in Synopsis

<table>
<tr><td>

Becker

First Stanza

(1) Ἐν ἀρχῇ ἦν ὁ λόγος,
καὶ ὁ λόγος ἦν ἐν ἀρχῇ πρὸς θεόν,
καὶ θεός ἦν ὁ λόγος.
(2)
(3) πάντα δι' αὐτοῦ ἐγένετο,
καὶ χωρίς αὐτοῦ ἐγένετο οὐδὲ ἕν.

(4) ὃ γέγονεν ἐν αὐτῷ ζωή ἦν,
καὶ ἡ ζωὴ ἦν τὸ φῶς τῶν ἀνθρώπων

Second Stanza

(5) καὶ τὸ φῶς ἐν τῇ σκοτίᾳ φαίνει,
καὶ ἡ σκοτία αὐτὸ οὐ κατέλαβεν.
(6-10)

(11) εἰς τὰ ἴδια ἦλθεν,
καὶ οἱ ἴδιοι αὐτὸν οὐ παρέλαβον.
(12) ὅσοι δὲ ἔλαβον αὐτόν,
ἔδωκεν αὐτοῖς ἐξουσίαν
τέκνα θεοῦ γενέσθαι, (12I)

</td><td>

Hofius

First Stanza

A.(1) Ἐν ἀρχῇ ἦν ὁ λόγος,
καὶ ὁ λόγος ἦν ἐν ἀρχῇ πρὸς θεόν,
καὶ θεός ἦν ὁ λόγος.
(2) οὗτος ἦν ἐν ἀρχῇ πρὸς τὸν θεόν.
B.(3) πάντα δι' αὐτοῦ ἐγένετο,
καὶ χωρίς αὐτοῦ ἐγένετο
οὐδὲ ἕν ὃ γέγονεν.

Second Stanza

A.(4) ἐν αὐτῷ ζωή ἦν,
καὶ ἡ ζωὴ ἦν τὸ φῶς τῶν ἀνθρώπων
(5) καὶ τὸ φῶς ἐν τῇ σκοτίᾳ φαίνει,
καὶ ἡ σκοτία αὐτὸ οὐ κατέλαβεν.(6-8)
B.(9) Ἦν τὸ φῶς τὸ ἀληθινόν,
ὃ φωτίζει πάντα ἄνθρωπον,
ἐρχόμενον εἰς τὸν κόσμον.

Third Stanza

A.(10) ἐν τῷ κόσμῳ ἦν,
καὶ ὁ κόσμος δι' αὐτοῦ ἐγένετο,
καὶ ὁ κόσμος αὐτόν οὐκ ἔγνω.
(11) εἰς τὰ ἴδια ἦλθεν,
καὶ οἱ ἴδιοι αὐτὸν οὐ παρέλαβον.
B.(12) ὅσοι δὲ ἔλαβον αὐτόν,
ἔδωκεν αὐτοῖς ἐξουσίαν
τέκνα θεοῦ γενέσθαι, (12a, 13)

</td></tr>
<tr><td>

Third Stanza

(14) Καὶ ὁ λόγος σὰρξ ἐγένετο
καὶ ἐσκήνωσεν ἐν ἡμῖν,
καὶ ἐθεασάμεθα τὴν δόξαν αὐτοῦ
(14a)
πλήρης χάριτος καὶ ἀληθείας. (15)
(16) ὅτι ἐκ τοῦ πληρώματος αὐτοῦ
ἡμεῖς πάντες ἠλάβομεν
καὶ χάριν ἀντὶ χάριτος· (17,18)

</td><td>

Fourth Stanza

A.(14) Καὶ ὁ λόγος σὰρξ ἐγένετο
καὶ ἐσκήνωσεν ἐν ἡμῖν,
καὶ ἐθεασάμεθα τὴν δόξαν αὐτοῦ
δόξαν ὡς μονογενοῦς παρὰ πατρός,
πλήρης χάριτος καὶ ἀληθείας. (15)
B.(16) ὅτι ἐκ τοῦ πληρώματος αὐτοῦ
ἡμεῖς πάντες ἠλάβομεν
καὶ χάριν ἀντὶ χάριτος· (17, 18)

</td></tr>
</table>

Becker's and Hofius' Reconstructions
of the Hymn in John 1:1-18 in Synopsis

Becker

First Stanza

(1) In the beginning was the Logos,
and the Logos was with God,
and the Logos was God.
(2)
(3) All things came into being through him,
and nothing came into being without him

(4) What was made, he was life in it.
And the life was the light of all people.

Second Stanza

(5) And the light shines in the darkness,
and the darkness did not take possession of it.
(6-10)

(11) He [i.e. the Logos] came into his own
but his own did not accept him.

(12) All who accepted him,
to them he gave power
to become children of God. (12c)

Third Stanza

(14) And the Logos became flesh
and dwelled among us.
And we saw his glory (14d)
full of grace and truth. (15)

(16) Because from his fullness
we have received,
even grace upon grace. (17,18)

Hofius

First Stanza

A.(1) In the beginning was the Word,
and the Word was with God,
and the Word was God.
(2) And he was in the beginning with God.
B.(3) Everything came into being through him,
and nothing came into being without him,
of that which came into being.

Second Stanza

A.(4) In him was life,
and the life was the light of all people.
(5) And the light shines in the darkness
and the darkness did not overcome it. (6-8)

B. (9) He was the true light,
which gives light to all people,
coming into the world

Third Stanza

A.(10) He was in the world,
and the world came into being through him,
yet the world did not know him.
(11) He came into his own,
and but his own did not accept him.

B.(12) All who accepted him,
to them he gave power
to become children of God. (12d, 13)

Fourth Stanza

A.(14) And the Logos became flesh
and dwelled among us
and have seen his glory
the glory of the only Son of the Father,
full of grace and truth. (15)

B.(16) Because from his fullness
we all have received
grace upon grace. (17, 18)

In terms of the extent of the hymn Hofius' reconstruction is to be preferred over Becker's. Hofius rules out only those parts of the prologue which cannot be a part of the hymn, whereas even Becker says that his own operations beyond this are more controversial, though necessary, because he thinks that the result of the previous operations is not yet satisfying.[266] Therefore he starts literary operations, which are possible, though not necessary. His investigations result in a plausible hymn, but his findings in those places where he goes beyond Bultmann and Hofius[267] are, in my opinion, too speculative, especially as Hofius has shown that it is possible to reconstruct a plausible hymn from the given material. Therefore I shall follow Hofius' reconstruction, which includes another disagreement between Becker and Hofius, which is the extent of the sentence in v.3. Two readings are possible, depending on where the interpreter sets the full stop. The full stop is situated either after the οὐδὲ ἕν or after the ὃ γέγογεν; both readings have sufficient manuscript evidence. In my opinion, Hofius' arguments for the full stop after ὃ γέγογεν are plausible. He resolves the assumed rhythmical problems by dividing v.3 into three parts rather than into two. Thus the inclusion of the ὃ γέγογεν in v.3 does not spoil the rhythm of the hymn, but fits into the overall structure of the hymn.[268]

An advantage of Becker's approach, however, is that he recognises that it is possible not only that two hands have been at work in the prologue, as Hofius assumes, but that the received form of the prologue is the result of a number of redactions. He assumes that the hymn consisted originally of stanzas one and two and that the third stanza had been added before the composition of the gospel.[269] The evangelist used this hymn and annotated it for the prologue to the gospel, and in a fourth step, after the completion of the gospel, the ecclesiastical redactor added v.13. That vv.14ff are not part of the original hymn has already been argued by Käsemann.[270] Käsemann sees a hymn with annotations in vv.1-13, but assumes that vv.14-18 are all written by the evangelist. The question of whether vv.14-18 contain a part of the original hymn and how they relate to the rest of the prologue will have to be discussed later.[271] Yet even if one assumes with Käsemann that vv.14-18 do not contain a part of the original hymn, one cannot assume that vv.14-18 are a literary unity, because v.15 interrupts the flow of the

---

[266] Cf. Becker; *Johannesevangelium*, 83.

[267] Cf. Becker; *Johannesevangelium*, 85.

[268] Cf. Hofius; 'Struktur und Gedankengang des Logos-Hymnus in Joh 1:1-18' 4-8.

[269] Cf. Becker; *Johannesevangelium*, 86f.

[270] Cf. Käsemann, Ernst; 'Aufbau und Anliegen des johanneischen Prologs' in: *Exegetische Versuche und Besinnungen*, vol.2, Göttingen (Vandenhoek und Ruprecht) 1964, 155-181.

[271] Cf. below, pp.75-78.

text, as Christian Demke has convincingly shown.[272] Therefore, Demke assumes that vv.14+16 are a hymn of another provenance. These two hymns, the first one a *Gesang der 'Himmlischen'* (chant of the heavenly beings) and a *auf diesen Gesang antwortendes Bekenntnis der 'Irdischen'* (responding confession of the earthly ones to the chant), have been adopted for the prologue to the gospel by the evangelist.[273] Becker follows Demke's argument and builds his reconstruction of the prologue upon Demke's and Käsemann's assumptions. He combines their insights with the more recent discussion of the subject and the greater knowledge about different redactions in John's Gospel for his reconstruction of the genesis of John 1:1-18.

The main problem for the interpretation of the prologue now is to establish whether John 1:14-18 are originally part of the hymn or a new creation of the evangelist according to his theological agenda. In this respect it is also important to establish the relation between the prologue and the rest of the gospel. Käsemann assumes that the underlying hymn was of Christian origin and had been adopted by the (Christian-) Gnostic evangelist.[274] Bultmann, on the other hand, found the hymn to be originally Gnostic and adopted by the evangelist, who had converted from Gnosticism to Christianity.[275] This shows how closely the reconstruction of the prologue is connected with the interpretation of the history of religion background of the gospel and the relation between the prologue on the one hand and the rest of the gospel on the other. Therefore, before I can come to a decision on the reconstruction of the hymn, I have to establish the relation between hymn and gospel and the underlying theological agendas.

The Hymn and the Gospel

An important step forward in the investigation into the background and genesis of John's Gospel was, certainly, the discovery of the connection between the history and social setting of Johannine Christianity and the evolution of the gospel, connected with a careful analysis of the history of tradition of the gospel. One of the most significant works in this area is, in my opinion, J. Louis Martyn's *History and Theology in the Fourth Gospel*[276] where Martyn shows convincingly the Jewish background of John's Gospel and demonstrates that the Johannine community was, originally, a heterodox Jewish group which had been expelled from the Synagogue and

---

272 Cf. Demke, Christian; 'Der sogenannte Logos-Hymnus im johanneischen Prolog' *ZNW* 58, 1967, 45-68.
273 Cf. Demke; 'Der sogenannte Logos-Hymnus' 64.
274 Cf. Käsemann, 'Aufbau und Anliegen'.
275 Bultmann; *Johannesevangelium*, 4f.
276 Martyn, J. Louis; *History and Theology in the Fourth Gospel*.

formed its own community. These findings have been broadly agreed,[277] and I am going to base my analysis of the prologue on these insights. Which particular strand of ancient Judaism is to be identified as the background of John's Gospel and the Prologue in particular, I leave open here, since this will become clear through the analysis of the Prologue, in which I shall engage later in this chapter.

This view of the background of Johannine Christianity has certain implications for our reconstruction of the prologue. First, it is likely that the history of religion background of the hymn contained in the prologue is of Hellenistic Jewish-Christian origin. Secondly, it is likely that it stems from an earlier stage of the development of Johannine Christianity. We can identify important elements of Hellenistic Jewish-Christian thought, such as the concept of the *logos* of 1:1+2,14, as well as a basically dualistic world view (1:4+5,10-12). The later gospel emphasises the cosmological dualism and radicalises it, but it does not use the *logos*-Christology anymore, as the evangelist thinks in terms of his messenger-Christology (*Gesandtenchristologie*),[278] which is, in turn, unknown to the prologue. Therefore, the hymn, in the form in which the evangelist found it and used it, has its place between the expulsion from the synagogue and the development of the messenger-Christology.

But why does the evangelist include a tradition which competes with his theology? There are indeed important differences between the theology of the prologue and that of the gospel. Apart from the differences in Christology, which I have already mentioned, the prologue talks about the creation of the world by God through the *logos*. It is striking that the evangelist does not take up this important thought again in his gospel. In fact, he never even mentions again that the world is divine creation.[279] In the same way, the evangelist never comes back to the important concept of incarnation, but uses a different concept to describe Jesus Christ's coming into the world, i.e. the sending of the son rather than the incarnation of the *logos*.[280] Here, as well as in the Christology, a certain tension between prologue and gospel is obvious; thus we can say that different theologies are at work here. But there are also important parallels between prologue and gospel, e.g. the cosmological dualism and the emphasis on the rejection of the *logos* in the prologue and that of Jesus in the main body of the gospel. I

---

277 Cf. Brown; *Community*; Becker; *Johannesevangelium*, 47-62 and Dunn, James D.G.; 'Let John be John' in: Stuhlmacher, Peter (ed.); *Das Evangelium und die Evangelien*, WUNT 28, Tübingen (Mohr-Siebeck) 1983, 309-339, 318-321.
278 Cf. Becker; *Johannesevangelium*, 484-494. For Messenger-Christology and the hymn cf. 94-98.
279 Cf. Becker; *Johannesevangelium*, 93, 96.
280 Ibid.

suppose that the evangelist used the traditional hymn in order to embed his work in the tradition of his branch of Christianity. It is obvious that, while Johannine Christianity developed, its theology did not remain static but developed as well. From the early Jewish-Christian origin to the developed theology of John's Gospel, especially to its highest developed form in John 17, it is a long way, and the hymn marks one stage of the development of Johannine thought. Since Johannine Christianity drew its legitimisation from the presence of the Paraclete, who ensures the authenticity of Johannine teaching,[281] a radical break from the tradition is hardly possible, because the previous insights of the school must have been inspired by the Paraclete as well. Thus, a strong sense of continuity in teaching is necessary. This finds its expression in the fact that development in thought has not led to abandoning the earlier writings, but to editing them and to adopting them for the new context; thus the fourth gospel went through a number of editions marking further developments of Johannine thought. In the same way, the author of the gospel used older material in order to keep continuity with the tradition, which he could not dismiss, for it too was inspired by the Paraclete. In such a context it seems to be plausible to place a prominent piece of the older tradition in front of a later writing in order to maintain this important notion of continuity.

If this view of the relation between prologue and gospel is right, then it is not necessary to harmonise them. The conceptuality of the prologue, and of the hymn in particular, is perceived as one possible and true interpretation of the Christian proclamation. What the main body of the gospel offers is another, a later view of Christianity. Both are seen as true; they are not the same but they complement each other. Because of the changing historical context in which Johannine Christianity found itself, it was seen as necessary to annotate the hymn in order to avoid misunderstandings and misinterpretations, which also helped to make a connection between the well-known hymn and the main body of the gospel. Therefore, the tension between prologue and gospel is intended, and through this combination of two different interpretations of the Christian teaching, the truth about Jesus Christ can emerge fuller and richer than only through one of the two elements. They complement each other by being different. I will have to come back to the relation between prologue and gospel in greater detail after the reconstruction and interpretation of the hymn.

---

[281] Cf. Becker; *Johannesevangelium*, 50, 566f and Dietzfelbinger, Christian; 'Paraklet und theologischer Anspruch im Johannesevangelium' *ZTK* 82 (1985), 389-408, 402-408.

The Hymn and the Prologue

After we have established the relationship between the hymn and the gospel and seen that differences in theology and conceptuality are actually intended, we can return to our attempt to find a plausible reconstruction of the hymn which had been the basis for the prologue. Since there is no need to harmonise the hymn with the rest of the gospel or to find traces of the evangelist bringing the prologue in line with his theology, the main criterion for the reconstruction of the hymn should be linguistic observations. In this case, only the parts excluded from the hymn by Hofius seem to be plausibly excluded; anything else would be too hypothetical. This point of view is confirmed by the fact that Hofius is able to arrange the material into a plausible (and beautiful[282]) hymn. Therefore, I am going to use Hofius' reconstruction of the hymn as a basis for my interpretation.

On linguistic grounds alone, it is impossible to assume that the hymn is of a pre-Christian origin. Käsemann has plausibly shown that the part of the hymn which is embedded in vv.1-12 is of Christian origin,[283] especially since the prologue seems to talk about the *logos ensarkos* (the word that became flesh) from an earlier point than v.14. Käsemann suggests v.5 as the introduction of the *logos ensarkos*,[284] Hofius sees the *logos ensarkos* as the subject of the hymn from the second stanza (v.10) onwards.[285] Each of them seems to be right in the context of his own reconstruction of the hymn, but both agree over against Becker,[286] who assumes that the first two stanzas of the hymn (up to v.12) are pre-Christian and therefore cannot refer to the *logos ensarkos*. If the whole hymn is of Christian origin, then it is no longer a question whether vv.14,16 are a Christian redaction of the hymn. The differences between vv.1-12 and 14,16 do not necessarily point to a different origin, but it is likely that the fourth stanza in the original composition of the hymn was the responding confession of the earthly ones to the heavenly and cosmological events sung of in the first three stanzas. This conception can well be explained by the original liturgical setting of the hymn, for it is very likely that this text, as a hymn, was used within worship. It is not necessary to assume with Demke[287] that this responding confession is a later addition.

---

282 Hengel (Hengel, Martin; *Die johanneische Frage*, WUNT 67, Tübingen (Mohr-Siebeck) 1993, p.252, fn.156; only in the German edition) remarks that Hofius' reconstruction of the Hymn is 'nearly too beautiful to be entirely convincing.'
283 Cf. Käsemann; 'Aufbau und Anliegen' 164.
284 Cf. Käsemann; 'Aufbau und Anliegen' 162.
285 Cf. Hofius; 'Struktur und Gedankengang des Logos-Hymnus in Joh 1:1-18' 21.
286 Cf. Becker; *Johannesevangelium*, 89-92.
287 Cf. Demke; 'Der sogenannte Logos-Hymnus' 64.

The Language of the Hymn

After we have established the extent of the hymn, we can start the investigation into the meaning of the hymn, especially within the framework of
the concept of the *Struggle for Language*. The difficulties of interpretation
start at the very beginning of v.1. The hymn uses the concept of *logos* to
describe its subject. The term *logos*, however, is used in a huge multitude of
ways and by nearly every Hellenistic school of thought. As understanding
the concept of *logos* is crucial to understanding the hymn, I must expand on
its origin and meaning. In addition, the term *logos* in the prologue is a good
example for the concept of the *Struggle for Language*, since in this term we
find the creation of a new terminology, which re-interprets the Jewish and
Hellenistic heritage and sheds new light on the significance of Christ. In the
usage of the term '*logos*' in the hymn, we see how, in early Christianity,
concepts of different traditions are taken and transformed so that Christianity can gain a better understanding of itself. As the hymn is, as we have
seen above, older than the gospel,[288] the interpreter is able to see it as a step
in the development towards the language of John's Gospel. Therefore, it is
valuable for our understanding of John's Gospel in the context of the *Struggle for Language* to investigate the usage of the term *logos* in the hymn.

At first sight, the ἐν ἀρχῇ alludes clearly to the 'In the beginning...' of
Gen. 1:1. In fact, it is a literal quotation from the Septuagint version of Gen.
1:1. The *logos* exists already at the beginning of creation, he is pre-existent
before creation, not part of it. Verse 3 says that πάντα δι' αὐτοῦ ἐγένετο
(everything came into being through him), which makes a connection to
the 'God spake' of Gen. 1. The *logos* is God's creating and maintaining
power, which is 'hypostatised'[289] here; that is, it is seen as a distinct person
who is with God. There are many possible origins for this type of language.

An important background for the concept of the *logos* is the Jewish
sophia (wisdom)-speculation.[290] In the later writings of the Old Testament,
especially in the Apocrypha, the concepts of *logos* and *sophia* are fused and
logos takes over the meaning of *sophia*. As Ashton argues in his essay '*The
Transformation of Wisdom*',[291] through the fusion of these two terms, *logos*
was given the general meaning of 'plan of God.'[292] Thus Ashton sees the

---

[288] Cf. above, pp.75-78.
[289] Cf. Kleinknecht, H.; 'λέγω B: Der Logos in Griechentum und Hellenismus'
    ThWNT IV, 76-89, 86-88.
[290] Cf. Ashton, John; 'The Transformation of Wisdom' in: Ashton, John; *Studying
    John: Approaches to the Fourth Gospel*, Oxford (Clarendon) 1994, 5-35.
[291] Ashton, John; *Studying John: Approaches to the Fourth Gospel*, Oxford (Clarendon)
    1994, 5-35.
[292] Cf. Ashton; 'The Transformation of Wisdom' 22.

hymn as a 'meditation on wisdom offering a variation on a traditional theme; it is also a hymn to the Incarnate Word.'[293] It is about the 'divine plan seen at work throughout the history of Israel' which 'has actually taken flesh in him [sc. Jesus].'[294] Ashton has his finger on a most important point, but, in my opinion, it is questionable whether wisdom-speculation alone is sufficient as a background for the *logos*-hymn. Although the identification of *logos* and *sophia* is highly significant for the understanding of the hymn, we must assume that the background of the *logos*-concept of the hymn is much more complex. Since the background of John's Gospel and the hymn is likely to be Hellenistic Judaism, it is probable that some Hellenistic concepts also had an influence on its composition. Doubtlessly, there were concepts of *logos* known at the time when John's Gospel was composed, and we have to investigate whether they can be helpful for our understanding of the hymn.

First, Philo of Alexandria uses the concept of *logos* in a way similar to the hymn underlying the prologue to John's Gospel. Philo, amalgamating Jewish religious thought with Greek philosophical speculation,[295] sees *logos* as a god, but of the second rank ('But the primal existence is God; and next to Him the word of God, but all other things subsist in the word only').[296] He usually indicates this by using θεός without the article for the *logos* and with the article for God.[297] The *logos* is, for Philo, 'a mediating figure which comes forth from God and establishes a link between the remotely transcendent God and the world or man, and yet which represents man to God as a high-priest [...] and advocate [...], i.e. as a personal mediator and not just in terms of the genuinely Gk. ἀνα-λογία.'[298] In addition, Philo follows the movement, which we have discussed above, of letting the concept of the *logos* take the place that *sophia* had been occupying in earlier Hellenistic Judaism[299] and identifies *logos* and *sophia* ('This [River] issues forth out of Eden, the wisdom of God, and this is the Word of God').[300] The important

---

293 Cf. Ashton; 'The Transformation of Wisdom' 31.
294 Cf. Ashton; 'The Transformation of Wisdom' 31.
295 Cf. Kleinknecht; 'λέγω Β' 86-88.
296 τὸ δὲ γενικώτατόν ἐστιν ὁ θεός, καὶ δεύτερος ὁ θεοῦ λόγος, τὰ δ' ἄλλα λόγῳ μόνον ὑπάρχει (Philo; *Allegorical interpretation of Genesis II., III.*, II:86 (in: Philo I, ed. and trans. by F.H. Colson and G.H. Whitaker, in: Loeb Classical Library 226, Cambridge, Massachusetts, London (Harvard University Press) 1929, 278)) Cf. also Kleinknecht; 'λέγω Β' 76-89, 87.
297 Cf. Becker; *Johannesevangelium*, 88.
298 Kleinknecht; 'λέγω Β' 87 (Translation from ThDNt IV, 89)
299 Barrett, Charles K.; *The Gospel according to St. John*, London (SPCK) ²1978, 154.
300 αὕτη ἐκπορεύεται ἐκ τῆς Ἐδεμ, τῆς τοῦ θεοῦ σοφίας· ἡ δέ ἐστιν ὁ θεοῦ λόγος (Philo; *Allegorical interpretation of Genesis II., III.*, I:65 (Philo I, 188 — translation modified)) Cf. also Kleinknecht; 'λέγω Β' 87, FN 88.

difference between Philonic thought and wisdom-speculation is that Philo, much more than Jewish wisdom-speculation, consistently sees the *logos* as a hypostasis and thus as a divine person.[301] In addition, Philo sees the *logos* essentially within a dualistic context. God is, for Philo, completely different from the world, he is inaccessible and absolutely transcendent[302]; furthermore, God is absolutely good while matter is evil, thus God cannot be in direct contact with matter. Thus Philo needs a device by which God can be viewed as connected with the world, which is the *logos*.[303] The cosmological dualism in Philo finds its parallel in the hymn, where, on the one hand, God does not deal with the world himself, but only through the *logos*. On the other hand, there is also a dualism between the *skotia* and the *phōs*, the divine and its opponent. Although the dualism of the hymn is different from Philo's, as it does not speak of the opposition of the divine or the rational and the material; the idea of a radical cosmological dualism is common to both, but is not present in wisdom-speculation. Ashton, assuming that the hymn exclusively draws upon wisdom-speculation, actually does not acknowledge the radical dualistic element of v.5. Therefore, I assume that Philonic thought is a useful background for the interpretation of the hymn in the Prologue to John's Gospel, which can help us to clarify the meaning of the hymn.[304]

---

[301] Cf. Kleinknecht; 'λέγω Β' 86-88 and Sandmel, Samuel; *Philo of Alexandria: An Introduction,* New York and Oxford (Oxford University Press) 1979, 94f, 148f. L. Hurtado, on the other hand, argues that the *Logos* is not an own hypostasis but a metaphorical concept (cf. Hurtado, Larry W.; *One God, One Lord: Early Christian Devotion and Ancient Monotheism,* London (SCM) 1988, 44-48). In fact, this particular detail may be very important for the interpretation of Philo, yet it does not matter for the exegesis of the hymn underlying the prologue to John's Gospel. The particular usage of the term *logos* as God's creating and maintaining power has been introduced by Philo, and it could be and was understood as an own hypostasis by contemporary readers. At some point in the reception of Philo the interpretation of the *logos* as a hypostasis had been introduced and in the context of this study it does not make any significant difference whether Philo himself, the author of the hymn or somebody between them first saw the *logos* hypostatised.

[302] Cf. Sandmel; *Philo,* 94f.

[303] Cf. Sandmel; *Philo,* 94f.

[304] In order to clarify the meaning of the hymn, we do not have to assume that the author of the hymn drew upon Philo directly. It is also possible and does not devaluate Philo for our understanding the hymn that both the hymn and Philo came from a similar background, which was based in Hellenistic Judaism and Hellenistic eclecticism, fusing Jewish and Hellenistic thought, cf. Wilson, Robert McLachlen; 'Philo and the Fourth Gospel' *ExpTim* LXV, 1953, 47-49 and Sandmel; *Philo,* 158f. For the similarities in the understanding of the *logos* between

Secondly, apart from the Philonic influence, there are also interesting parallels with the mystico-religious speculations of Hermeticism.[305] In Hermetic writings, Hermes Trismegistos is the hypostatised revealing and cosmogonic principle of the *logos*, which is essentially a cosmic and creative potency, the guide and agent of knowledge, increasingly represented as a religious doctrine of salvation, the revealer of what is hidden.[306] He is also the mediator and revealer of the will of the Gods. The *logos* can even be described as God's son and the λόγος θεοῦ. The similarities between the concepts of *logos* in Hermeticism and the prologue to John's Gospel are unlikely to be accidental; they will have their origin in the common intellectual and spiritual environment, in which John's Gospel, Philo and Hermetic thought may have evolved.

Thirdly, there are parallels between the Stoic concept of a divine *logos* and the hymn. I assume, however, that there is no direct Stoic or other Greek philosophical influence on the hymn; rather I assume that Stoic concepts are mediated through eclectic thinking in Hellenistic Judaism, as we see it, e.g. in Philo. Through Philo or similar thought the parallels between Stoa and the hymn can easily have been brought about.

In sum, there was a metaphysical question in late antiquity, which theological and philosophical thinkers attempted to solve: If God was wholly transcendent, how could the gap between transcendent divinity and immanent humanity be bridged? The concept introduced was the *logos*, which was used differently by the various schools of thought. In this context, the author of the hymn underlying the prologue to John's Gospel finds a distinctly Christian solution to the problem, while building upon earlier ideas. As we will see, his particular view of the *logos* is unfolded in the further course of the hymn.

In the first two stanzas of the hymn, the *logos* is further qualified. The first stanza describes in the first semi-stanza (vv.1+2)[307] the relation between *logos* and God, in the second semi-stanza (v.3) the role the *logos*

Philo and the fourth gospel cf. also Dodd, C.H.; *The Interpretation of the fourth Gospel*, Cambridge (University Press) 1953, 66-73 and Argyle, A.W.; 'Philo and the Fourth Gospel' *ExpTim* LXIII, 1951, 385-386. It must not be forgotten, however, that all these authors compare Philo with the whole of John's Gospel. The similarities between Philo and the hymn, which is older than the main body of the gospel, are, in fact, much more striking than those between Philo and the whole of the gospel. Therefore, the Philonic parallels to the hymn have to be taken seriously, even if the exact nature of the relation between the two cannot be established here.

[305] For the relevance of Hermetic parallels cf. pp.65f.

[306] Kleinknecht; 'λέγω B' 85f.

[307] Cf. above p.72.

played in creation. The whole first semi-stanza is playing only with the terms ἐν ἀρχῇ, λόγος and θεός and combines them in different ways in order to describe the relation between God and the *logos*. It is, in my opinion, too easy directly to identify the *logos* with Jesus, and to interpret the whole first semi-stanza as a definition of Jesus and his relation to the Father, and say with Karl Barth that the prologue states the

> Identification of the essence of two distinguished persons. For to the person which has been named ὁ θεός has come the *logos* even in person, and takes part in the same θεότης [divinity].[308]

In fact, I assume that the text is not really interested in objectifying the relation between Father and Son, but is saying something important and new about the *logos*. Contrary to Karl Barth's assumptions I assume that the recognition of a pre-understanding of the terms used is necessary. When the term *logos* is used here, it already has a meaning, which is transformed when it is combined with ἐν ἀρχῇ and θεός.

The first important statement is that the *logos* pre-existed creation. The Philonic *logos*, for example, is part of creation, although he is the first and oldest of creation, belonging to the noëtic realm, not to matter. This notion is explicitly contradicted in v.1. The *logos* was there already in the beginning, he precedes creation and is therefore entirely divine and not created. The hymn is not interested in what happened before the beginning; there is no cosmogony or any explanation how the *logos* came into being; he is just there, not created but with God in the beginning, which is another important predication of the *logos*. The *logos* is together with God, and even more, he is divine himself. The use of θεός without the article can result from θεός being the predicate-noun to ὁ λόγος, as Hofius assumes,[309] or it can be an influence from Philonic thought, since in Philo's terminology the *logos* is differentiated from God by using ὁ θεός for God and θεός for the *logos*, which means that the *logos* is divine, but not of the same rank as God.[310] Both interpretations are possible; however, it is going too far if one uses the former interpretation to read an almost Nicean theology into the hymn, as Hofius does, when he says that the 'the linguistic findings in v.1c can only mean that the Logos is *God* — true and real God.'[311] The hymn does not say anything in detail about the relation of the Father to the Son, because this question arose only c.200 years later in the struggle that led to the formulation

---

[308] Barth, Karl; *Erklärung des Johannes-Evangeliums (Kapitel 1-8)* (ed. by Walther Fürst), Karl Barth, Gesamtausgabe, II. Akademische Werke, 1925/26, Zürich (TVZ) 1976, 35.

[309] Cf. Hofius; 'Struktur und Gedankengang des Logos-Hymnus in Joh 1:1-18' 16f.

[310] Cf. Becker; *Johannesevangelium*, 88.

[311] Cf. Hofius; 'Struktur und Gedankengang des Logos-Hymnus in Joh 1:1-18' 17.

of the creeds of Nicea and Constantinople. Thus it seems far-fetched to read a Nicean interpretation into the hymn. However, the hymn does say that the *logos* is divine and with God from the beginning, already there in the creation, and not part of it.

The second semi-stanza (v.3) is about the part the *logos* played in creation. Here, a more traditional view of the *logos* is taken up again. The *logos/sophia* as mediator of creation is found in Philo[312] as well as in Jewish wisdom-speculation.[313] Another traditional Jewish idea used here is that of creation out of nothing. Remarkably, this motif of the world as divine creation does not occur again in the body of the Gospel,[314] and so the dualism expressed in the hymn is different from that in the main body of the gospel. We will return to that in the discussion of the second stanza. Here, in v.3, any idea of an anti-divine cosmological power, which has been there before creation, is strictly rejected. The whole world is created by God through the *logos*, and any notion that the world could be evil in itself or opposed to the divine is contradicted.

The second stanza (vv.4+5+9) introduces, in its first semi-stanza (vv.4+5), the notion of cosmological dualism by contrasting the *logos*, which is the *phōs* (light), the life-giving and maintaining principle of the universe and of humanity, with the *skotia*, the darkness, its opponent. As the first stanza does not say anything about how the *logos* came into being, this stanza does not speculate about the origin of the darkness, but only establishes that the darkness is there. Again, any kind of supralapsarian speculation as well as mythological language is rejected. As v.1 gives evidence that the hymn knows of Gen. 1, it is almost certain that the author of the hymn knew the Old Testament-tradition of creation and fall. The result of the Old Testament myth is presupposed in the hymn, but the language seems, if one may use this term here, to be demythologised, to be kept free of any supralapsarian speculation, and to be rationalised. This indicates that the origin of this hymn is likely to be within Hellenised Diaspora-Judaism. There seem to be parallels between the rationalising approaches of the Stoa and Philo and the hymn, which amalgamates rationalising thought and biblical conceptuality. In this framework, the dualism of the light and the darkness is a radical expression of what is the fallen nature of the world in the language of Genesis.

The cosmological dualism of the hymn seems to be quite different from that of the main body of the gospel. In the hymn, the whole world is divine creation, which seems to stem from the Jewish legacy to Johannine theology,

---

[312] Cf. Kleinknecht; 'λέγω Β' 87.
[313] Cf. Ashton; 'The Transformation of Wisdom' 18-23.
[314] Cf. Becker; *Johannesevangelium*, 93, 95f.

whereas the main body of the Gospel moves into the direction of a more radical dualism by avoiding saying that the whole world is created by God. I do not assume that the evangelist abandoned the concept of the world as divine creation completely or deliberately. Rather, I suppose that this matter was not a theological issue when the main body of the gospel was written. This theory is supported by the fact that he integrated the traditional hymn, which contains this concept, into his gospel. Thus it was possible to read the Gospel in the light of the tradition behind the Gospel, i.e. Judeo-Christian thought. Then the world is certainly seen as divine creation. Nevertheless, this tradition could be ignored and then used by a theological current within Johannine Christianity that will dissolve into Gnosticism later. The implications of these different interpretations can be seen in the argument underlying 1 John, where an 'orthodox' interpretation of John's Gospel is asserted over against a Gnosticising tendency.[315]

The origin of the terms φῶς, σκοτία and ζωή seems to be the same as that of the λόγος, i.e. Hellenistic Diaspora-Judaism, influenced by Philo or other similar thinkers. Again, the similarities between the hymn and Philonic thought are striking. First, as we have seen above when discussing the term λόγος, there is an influence of wisdom-speculation, which is adopted in a Philonic way. Light is connected with wisdom, the wise, i.e. righteous, good and happy man is enlightened, and the divine law is compared with the light.[316] For both the author of the hymn and Philo, φῶς is opposed by σκοτία, which is folly and wickedness.[317] In wisdom-speculation, however, light and darkness are only seen as moral categories and lack the cosmological dimension they have in the hymn, which is paralleled by Philonic thought. For Philo, light is wisdom and knowledge of God's claim and of his will.[318] The divine world and God himself are light, too, and they can be reached by means of mystical ascent.[319] Thus, both Philo and the author of the hymn see λόγος, φῶς and σκοτία as part not only of a moral, but also of a cosmological dualism. Another important parallel between Philo and the hymn is the identification of the *logos* with the light. The *logos*, being the middle being between God and humanity and the light, is the enlightening power in the world; only through him the light can be perceived.[320] There is, however, an important difference between Philonic thought and the hymn in John 1 which must not be overlooked: Philo contrasts the light

---

315 Cf. above, p.67.
316 Cf. Conzelmann, H.; 'φῶς κτλ.' ThWNT IX, 302-349, 314f.
317 Cf. Conzelmann, H.; 'φῶς' 314f, and Conzelmann, H.; 'σκότος κτλ.' ThWNT VII, 424-446, 431f.
318 Cf. Conzelmann, H.; 'φῶς' 322-324.
319 Ibid.
320 Ibid.

with the darkness in a rather different way from the hymn; the cosmological dualism of light and darkness is not part of his world view.[321] A much better parallel to the dualism of light and darkness in the hymn is offered by the Hermetic writings. Here, light and darkness are cosmological powers, which are opposed to each other,[322] and coming to the light is identified with salvation.[323] But there are significant differences between Hermeticism and the hymn. Hermeticism sees human beings as originally heavenly beings, which are alienated from themselves; enlightenment leads them back to their true identity. The means to this is asceticism.[324] This has no parallel in the canonical Johannine writings. However, I suppose that this aspect of Hermetic thought is a further development of the type of dualism found in the hymn, which, in turn, is a step on the way which can lead to Johannine Gnosis as well as Johannine 'orthodoxy'.

The particular dualism of the hymn seems to be an original creation of Johannine theology. It is likely, that an earlier theology, originally a Christian adaptation of Philonic (or similar) thought, was transformed under the pressure of the events in which the community was involved. Above I have located the time of the composition of the hymn between the separation from Judaism, i.e. the expulsion from the Synagogue and the later development of Johannine theology.[325] Under the impression of the rejection of the Christian proclamation by the former fellow-Jews, a Philonic system of thought could well have been modified, and its dualism radicalised. True faith had to be separated more sharply from unbelief, and this happened through the introduction of the darkness as the opponent of the light as an expression of the radical fallenness of the world, and thus cosmological dualism developed. An existing language of faith was transformed in order to interpret the world of the community in the light of the Christian proclamation.

Another important transformation of language takes place in the use of the term ζωή. In the traditional usage, ζωή means physical life and as well as 'the leading of life', the moral quality of life.[326] True life 'is attained when life corresponds to a transcendent norm',[327] which is living according to God's demand. This can be living according to the law, as in Hellenistic

---

[321] Ibid.

[322] Cf. Conzelmann, H.; 'σκότος' 435f.

[323] Cf. Conzelmann, H.; 'φῶς' 325-327.

[324] Cf. Conzelmann, H.; 'φῶς' 327.

[325] Cf. above p. 76.

[326] Cf. Bultmann, R.; 'ζάω κτλ. D.: Der Lebensbegriff des Judentums' *ThWNT* II 856-862, 861f.

[327] Cf. Bultmann, R.; 'ζάω' 559f.

Judaism, or living apart from the body, as Philo teaches.[328] In v.4, the ζωή is now identified with the λόγος. This is a further expression of the *logos* as the mediator of creation, a continuation of the thought of the first stanza. Physical life is created, and the *logos*, being the creative power, is also the giver of life; he has life and gives it to creation. Yet life in v.4 cannot mean merely physical life, since life is identified with light. Light is, as we have seen above, wisdom and knowledge of God's will. Therefore, life must have a moral quality in this context, i.e. living according to a transcendent norm. This life of humanity, the physical as well as the moral, is in the *logos*. This implies that life, true or authentic life, is not something human beings can achieve, but it exists only in the *logos*. The *logos* gives this life to those belonging to him, to those that see the light — and know that life is not a human possibility but only a gift from God through the *logos*. Neither mystical ascent, as Philo teaches, nor moral attitudes lead to life, but only the recognition of the *logos* as the life-giving principle. Other views are rejected, although the community from which the hymn evolved must have known them; when all religious thought was reinterpreted after the community accepted the Christian proclamation, they were led to an entirely new view of what life really is: faith in Christ.

Where the light is not seen, there is darkness, of which v.5 speaks, and those that do not see the true light are excluded from life. That the light shines in the darkness means that it could be known that the revelation of the light is available, but it is rejected. Here, I suppose, the experience of the congregation, that the Christian proclamation had been rejected, helped to shape this dualism. Verse 5b explains this matter further: the light has not been grasped or understood by the darkness, which is the reason for the darkness being darkness. I agree with Schnackenburg against Barth and Hofius, that καταλαμβάνειν means comprehend rather than overcome.[329] The concept of a cosmological fight between light and darkness would clash with the imagery of the hymn, which speaks of a dualism of belief or unbelief and not of darkness as a cosmological power, which might be able to wage war against the light. In addition, a cosmological fight between powers would contradict the rationalising and demythologising tendencies of the hymn. Moreover, the meaning 'to grasp', 'to comprehend' for καταλαμβάνειν would be in line with the notion that the world did not know the *logos* (ὁ κόσμος αὐτόν οὐκ ἔγνω) of v.10 and his own did not accept him (οἱ ἴδιοι αὐτὸν οὐ παρέλαβον) of v.11. The darkness, which is where the

---

[328] Cf. Bultmann, R.; 'ζάω' 561f.
[329] Cf. Schnackenburg, Rudolf; *Das Johannesevangelium*,Vol.1, HTKNT 4/1, Freiburg (Herder) 1965, 222f; Barth; *Johannes-Evangelium*, 57f; Hofius; 'Struktur und Gedankengang des Logos-Hymnus in Joh 1:1-18' 19.

light is not accepted and understood (cf. v.5), is not a power of its own, but only the rejection of the only power, the light.

The second semi-stanza (v.9) deals with the phenomenon of the rejection of the light again. The light shines for every human being which has come into the world.[330] Thus the perversity of the darkness becomes obvious; although the light shines for everybody and can be seen and grasped by everybody, it is rejected by a part of humanity. Being in the darkness is, therefore, perversion of true humanity, even ridiculous. The predication of the light as τὸ φῶς τὸ ἀληθινόν seems to point to the Philonic distinction between the heavenly, true light and the earthly light, which is inferior to the divine light. To prevent any misunderstanding it is made clear that the *logos* is the true and heavenly light,[331] to which everybody should be able to come, as opposed to the earthly light.

As a whole, the second stanza says something new about the *logos* again by combining known terms and concepts in a creative way. The terms φῶς, σκοτία and ζωή are already available in the environment and tradition of the community, but they are combined so that their meaning is transformed and the Christian teaching of the community finds an expression. The dualism of the hymn seems to stand between the Philonic type of Hellenistic-Jewish thought, and the more developed dualism of the main body of the gospel, in which darkness is seen as a power opposed to the light; here, darkness is the realm where the light is not accepted. The step towards a cosmological dualism has been taken, but there is still a long way to go to such pointed statements like John 17:14-16, where the believers do not belong to the world at all anymore.[332] The main body of the gospel, however, keeps the conceptuality of the hymn, but in a form which is further developed and radicalised.

To sum up our findings so far, the first two stanzas of the hymn explain what the *logos* is, they define it by setting it in relation with God, creation, life and humanity by combining known terms and concepts in a new way. These terms still carry their meaning, but it is transformed by their new use and thus new meaning is brought about. The cosmological background is thus set up for the event which will be described in the next two stanzas.

---

[330] I agree with Hofius ('Struktur und Gedankengang des Logos-Hymnus in Joh 1:1-18' 8-10) that the ἐρχόμενον εἰς τὸν κόσμον relates to πάντα ἄνθρωπον. Schnackenburg's argument against this interpretation (*Johannesevangelium*, 230f) does not take into consideration that the text is a hymn and that, therefore, poetic language is employed. In poetic language it is possible to use the term itself and another description for the same.

[331] Cf. Conzelmann, H.; 'φῶς' 322.

[332] Cf. below, pp.130-132.

The subject of the last two stanzas of the hymn (III: 10-12c; IV: 14+16) are the events which take place within the cosmological setting. The third stanza deals with the *logos* coming into the world and being rejected. The concept of the *logos* coming into the world is nothing entirely new. In Hellenistic thought, the *logos* is known as mediator between the divine and the world[333] and the coming of the *logos* into the world or his being in the world is a well known thought. Yet this can only be thought as the divine presence in the world, which is still distinct and separate from the world. The incarnation of the *logos* is a concept completely alien to ancient thought, where the immutability of God is one of the most important presuppositions of metaphysics. The incarnate *logos*, Jesus Christ is already implicitly subject of this stanza, but he is not made explicit yet. The third stanza can be seen as a climax and summary of the first two stanzas, leading towards the fourth. Already in v.3 it is made explicit that the *logos* came into the world, but it is possible to understand the *logos* only as divine principle. Then this idea would be, implicitly, part of the light-darkness symbolism of the second stanza. Yet if read in the context of the fourth stanza, the coming of the *logos* into the world has to be made explicit in the third stanza, in v.10 in particular, in preparation for the shift in the perspective. Thus the angle of the hymn changes already at this point: From a comprehensive cosmological view it shifts to a focus on the world, the *kosmos*, where the incarnation, the real subject of the hymn, is going to take place. The paradox of the rejection of the *logos*/light is expressed very pointedly in this stanza: The *logos* is the creator of the world, and the world does not accept the one who brought it into being. Verse 11 repeats the same subject matter, but in another way, now talking about the *logos*, as creator, coming into his own and not being accepted.

The main term of v.10 is κόσμος, which occurs three times, in each of the three first verses of the third stanza. In New Testament usage, *kosmos*[334] can mean either 'adornment' a meaning that clearly does not apply here, or the world 'as the universe, the Sum of all Created Being', or the world 'as the Abode of Men, the Theatre of History, the inhabited World, the Earth' or the world 'as Humanity, Fallen Creation, the Theatre of Salvation History.' Bultmann assumes, that, in v.10, *kosmos* is the fallen world, unable to accept God.[335] It is, in my opinion, questionable whether the evaluation of the world is already part of v.10. Rather, the world seems to be the place where revelation, rejection and acceptance of the *logos* takes place. This place is the world of humanity and human affairs, which is capable of

---

[333] Cf. above pp.80f
[334] Cf. Sasse, H.; 'κόσμος κτλ.' *ThWNT* III, 867-898.
[335] Cf. Bultmann; *Johannesevangelium*, 33f.

knowing or not knowing its maker.[336] The rest of creation, not having the same relation to the divine as humanity, is not within the range of the hymn. It is the world of humanity, which is involved in the dualism of light and darkness, of accepting and rejecting the *logos*. In this respect, the hymn stands somewhere between the optimistic openness towards the world of Hellenistic Judaism, a view that is also shared by Philo, and the profound pessimism of apocalyptic thought.[337] While the former is also, as we have established above, the original background of the Johannine community, Johannine thought shifts more and more towards the latter. In the hymn we still find a moderately positive or neutral view of the world as the place where the decision for or against the *logos* takes place, but in the main body of the Gospel, a more negative view of the world begins to develop, which finds its climax in the Farewell Discourses and the so-called highpriestly prayer of ch.17.[338]

The next verse (v.11) takes up the same point, now focusing on the world as God's, and therefore also the *logos'* own. It has been argued that τὰ ἴδια/οἱ ἴδιοι refer to Israel as God's own people.[339] I agree, however, with the majority of scholars[340] who prefer to relate v.11 to v.5, so that τὰ ἴδια/οἱ ἴδιοι refers to the created realm. The phenomenon of the rejection of the *logos* in the world is mentioned a second time in order to underline the perversity of the unbelieving world and to emphasise the cosmological dualism, before in v.14 the main point of the hymn is made.

The second semi-stanza of stanza 3 contrasts the rejection of the *logos* with its acceptance by the believing community, which is, certainly, the community in which the hymn was used. As the first semi-stanza stated that the *kosmos* is rejecting the *logos*, the (Johannine-) Christian community sees itself as an exception from the world. The reward for the accepting of the *logos* is that the community members become God's children. The idea of becoming τέκνα θεοῦ through the *logos* is, as Becker points out,[341] of

---

[336] Cf. Barrett; *John* 161. Cf. also Barth; *Johannes-Evangelium*, 78f.

[337] For the two views of the world in ancient Judaism cf. Sasse, 'κόσμος' 891. For Philo cf. ibid., 876-878.

[338] For the worldview of the main body of the Gospel cf. Sasse, 'κόσμος' 894-896. Sasse does not take into account that there may be different conceptions of the world at work in different layers of John's Gospel, but the negative perception of the world in the main body of the gospel comes out clearly in his article. Cf. also Bultmann; *Theologie des Neuen Testamentes*, 378-385.

[339] Cf. Barrett; *John* 163; Brown, Raymond E.; *The Gospel according to John*, Vol. 1, The Anchor Bible 29, New York (Doubleday) 1970, 10; Dodd; *Interpretation*, 402.

[340] Cf. Barth; *Johannes-Evangelium*, 82-84; Becker;*Johannesevangelium*, 90f.; Bultmann; *Johannesevangelium*, 34f; Hofius; 'Struktur und Gedankengang des Logos-Hymnus in Joh 1:1-18' 21f; Schnackenburg; *Johannesevangelium*, 236.

[341] Cf. Becker; *Johannesevangelium* 90f.

Philonic origin again. Philo sees the *logos* also as the mediator of sonship, which is the aim of salvation and the fulfilment of creation. As a whole, the third stanza does not contribute an entirely new meaning to the hymn; rather it shifts from general cosmology to a perception of the world as humanity encounters it. Viewed without the previous and following stanzas, it could be read in a 'conventional' Philonic way. In the context of the hymn, it condenses the meaning unfolded in the previous stanzas and prepares for the turn the hymn takes in v.14.

That the community sees itself as an exception from the world is a concept, which can be developed further into the more radical dualism and rejection of the world which we find in the main body of the gospel, and in ch.17 in particular. While, in the hymn, the world is seen as the place where the *logos* is rejected (rule) or accepted (exception), the *kosmos* is, in the later development of Johannine theology, only the fallen world, which is opposed to the revelation and to God, and the Christian community is not part of the world anymore, but taken out of it.[342]

The *logos*, which is not too unusual a concept in ancient thought, is now identified with the *logos ensarkos*, the incarnate Son of God, Jesus Christ. This happens, on the one hand, through the fourth stanza, where the incarnation of the *logos* is explicitly subject (although without mentioning Jesus Christ as an individual person) and on the other hand through the liturgical setting, since this hymn would have been sung in a liturgical context in which Jesus Christ must have had a prominent place. An incarnation of the *logos* is unthinkable in Hellenistic thought. In fact, the divine and the human are separated in a way which does not allow the divine to become human. The heavenly revealer, like Hermes Trismegistos, may appear in a human figure and teach or reveal cosmological truths, but he cannot possibly be human. Therefore, the καὶ ὁ λόγος σάρξ ἐγένετο is indeed a *skandalon*, since the divine *logos* is a man, a thought which is impossible in any non-Christian Greek or Hellenistic thought. For the interpretation of v.14 I can only point at Bultmann's impressive explanations in his *Theology of the New Testament* and in his commentary on John's Gospel:[343] 'In pure humanity he is [i.e. the *logos*] the revealer. Certainly, his own see his δόξα (v.14b); and if it had not been visible, it would not be possible to speak of revelation. Yet this is the paradox, which is found in the whole gospel, that the δόξα is visible not besides the σάρξ or through it, as if it was transparent, yet nowhere else but in the σάρξ. The eye has to bear having the σάρξ

---

[342] Cf. John 17:14-16, and below, pp.130-132; cf. also Sasse, 'κόσμος' 894-896.

[343] Cf. Bultmann; *Johannesevangelium*, 40f and *Theologie des Neuen Testamentes* 392-402.

in view without being distracted if it wants to see the δόξα. Revelation is present only in peculiar disguise.'[344]

Through this identification of the eternal *logos* with a historical man, who, in the end, even died on a cross (which must have been said in the liturgical context of this hymn), both concepts are understood anew in a different way. On the one hand, the concept of the eternal and divine *logos*, which is known from Hellenistic and Hellenistic-Jewish thought, is radically transformed, while on the other hand, the person of Jesus is understood in a new way as well. Jesus, the man who had been crucified, is now understood as the eternal and divine *logos*; this concept is used in order to understand what cross and resurrection of Jesus the Christ, which was without doubt at the heart of the proclamation of early Christianity, meant. The cross and resurrection of Jesus Christ do not need to be mentioned in this hymn explicitly, as it is embedded in a liturgy which must have carried all the other elements of Christian proclamation. Therefore, one cannot conclude from the silence about the suffering of the incarnate *logos* that the hymn represents a docetic theology. This would see the hymn separated from its liturgical setting. Within this setting the hymn is about who Jesus Christ, the crucified and resurrected one, really is; and it understands him as the divine *logos*, though in a way which changes the understanding of *logos* and Jesus.

Through the combination of hymn and gospel, the horizon against which Jesus Christ can be understood is broadened even more. As we have seen above, the fourth gospel understands Jesus Christ in terms of the messenger-Christology.[345] This means that the ancient 'messenger-law'[346] is used to describe the sending of the son by the father and the relation between God and Jesus. This concept, however, is paired with the Christology of the hymn. The Gospel is understood through the hymn, the cosmological setting presented in the prologue is connected with the rest of the gospel in a creative way: the one who is sent by the Father is the eternal *logos*, the one who fulfils the will of the father is the one who has been with the Father from the very beginning before creation. In this respect the competing concepts of understanding Jesus Christ, one in the main body of the gospel and the other one in the prologue, work like the two parts of a metaphor. They produce a fruitful tension, through which a broader understanding of the subject matter becomes possible.

When the hymn had been connected with the gospel, it was necessary to make links between the hymn and the beginning of the gospel-narrative,

---

344 Bultmann; *Johannesevangelium*, 40f (my translation).
345 Cf. above, p.76 and below, p.113.
346 Cf. Becker; *Johannesevangelium*, 484-494.

i.e. the testimony of John the Baptist, so that the hymn would not stand out of the gospel but be harmonically embedded. This connection is made through the insertion of vv.6-8,15, which makes an explicit link to the beginning of the narrative in vv.19ff, and, at the same time, rejects a possible interpretation of the hymn which takes John the Baptist as the light.

Verses 12c+13,17+18 were inserted as theological explanation to the hymn. They function to ensure that the hymn is interpreted along the lines of the development of 'orthodox' Johannine theology as it can be seen in the main body of the gospel and the epistles, and so to reject any other interpretation, e.g. an interpretation along the lines of the position of the opponents of 1 John, who deny the identity of the eternal *logos* (or the *Christ*) with the man Jesus.

As we have seen in this chapter, the prologue to the fourth gospel is a fine example of how the language of Christianity develops in order to gain a deeper understanding of Jesus Christ. Johannine Christianity used concepts of different origin in order to realise the truth about Christ, and concepts developed later, such as that of the messenger, are combined with earlier ones, like the *logos*-Christology. These concepts are in a certain tension, but this tension initiates a metaphorical process, in which the sum of meaning is more than the two elements. In addition, the keeping of older concepts and connecting them with newer ones shows an awareness of tradition within Johannine Christianity. The old is valid as well, since it is accorded the same legitimacy as the newer findings. The old is one understanding of the message of Christianity, as are the more recent insights, and only together they bring about a larger part of the unfathomable truth of the Christian Gospel.

Chapter 7

Jesus and Nicodemus: John 3:1-21

In the previous chapter of this study I have discussed the implications of the hermeneutical concept of the *Struggle for Language* for the interpretation of the hymn underlying the prologue to John's Gospel. In the course of the discussion we have seen that the evangelist inserted an annotated hymn into the prologue of his gospel in order to embed his own work in the framework of the Johannine tradition. The following case-study is going to focus on the original work of the evangelist by analysing the creation of language in the Nicodemus-dialogue, John 3:1-21. This passage shows how the evangelist, i.e. the author of the main body of the gospel,[347] uses different traditions and motifs of religious language in order to find a way to express the *kerygma*. The previous case-study has dealt with the hymn underlying the prologue to John's Gospel, which represents a stage of the development of John's Gospel previous to the work of the evangelist and thus an earlier step in the evolution of Johannine theology. So this study considers the work of the evangelist and the way he transformed his material in order to express his theology and how Johannine theology was further developed, built upon the earlier Johannine tradition and influenced by thought of the contemporary environment.

In order to create new language for his interpretation of the Christian Gospel by forming new, unexpected relations between known terms and concepts, the evangelist combines motifs from different religious languages in a poetic way; through his invention of new language he unveils a new world, the world of Christianity as his community interprets it. The evangelist weaves, as it were, a new web of meaning, using material which has been passed down to him through the tradition of which he is a part.

The passage John 3:1-21 is a text particularly suitable for an investigation into how the evangelist creates meaning by connecting known terms and concepts poetically, because in this text a comprehensive world-picture is painted this way. Starting with the question as to who is Jesus and the statement that 'no one can see the Kingdom of God without being born from above' (v.3) a whole theology *in nuce* is developed and

---

347 Cf. above, pp.62f.

communicated. Following this development will help us to understand creation of language, even of a whole language-world. Hence we will see how the evangelist takes part in the *Struggle for Language* to understand faith in Jesus Christ.

As in the previous chapter, we will identify relevant parallels to the language used by the evangelist in order to investigate the meaning they carried at that time. Then the creative way in which these terms and concepts are combined will be investigated, so that we can discern the processes through which the evangelist understood and communicated his interpretation of Christian faith. Since the evangelist used known terms and concepts in order to create a language of faith, his language-world is, as I shall show, an open system which the reader or listener is invited to enter, just as in the discourse Nicodemus is invited to do so by Jesus.

Introductory Questions

Before discussing the Nicodemus Discourse, we need to establish the extent of the passage, which has been subject to debate among New Testament scholars. In particular, the relation of the passage 3:31-36 to the discourse 3:1-21 on the one hand and that of the second half of the discourse (vv.13-21) to the first (vv.1-12) on the other hand has been questioned.

It has been suggested, that the Nicodemus passage originally extended only from 3:1-12, followed by the testimony of John the Baptist (22-30) and continuing with Jesus' decision to leave Judea and go back to Galilee (ch.4).[348] In this case, 3:13-21+31-36 together would form a speech or a sermon by the evangelist which has been later inserted or which is a composition by the evangelist that had not been intended to be a part of the Nicodemus-passage itself. This assumption presupposes that the kerygmatic speech 3:13-21+31-36 has been divided by the insertion of the testimony of John the Baptist. The passages 3:12-21 and 3:31-36 are, as Schnackenburg points out, an independent document, whose original order was 3:31-36, 3:12-21. This document was added to the gospel by disciples of the evangelist, who inserted the two loose pages, on which the speech was found, after v.12 and v.30. Thus the passages 3:12-21 and 3:31-36 are not part of the literary composition of the gospel. I do not agree that the internal evidence in the text is sufficient to support so radical an approach. Schnackenburg's theory presupposes Bultmann's theory of 'external disorder.' [349] It is, in my opinion, not plausible to assume that the disciples of the evangelist first divided a speech which they wanted to include, and then inserted it in

---

[348] Cf. Schnackenburg; *Johannesevangelium* I, 374-377.
[349] Cf. above, p. 62.

the wrong order. Furthermore, I regard the passage 3:1-21 as sufficiently consistent to be interpreted as a single literary composition. Finally, the passage 3:31-36 does not connect smoothly enough with 3:13-21 to argue that these two sections originally belonged together as a literary unity.

Bultmann argues that John 3:31-36 is a part of this discourse, separated from its main body by the insertion of the testimony of John the Baptist (vv.22-30) in the course of the redaction[350] and originally directly following v.21. Yet, as Dodd points out, the connection between 3:1-21 and 31-36 remains awkward: 'If, by way of experiment, we disregard verses 22-30, we find that the verses 31-6 are indeed germane to the preceding discourse, but they cannot be said to be an appropriate continuation of it.'[351] Therefore, a direct connection between the Nicodemus Discourse and the speech 3:31-36 is not likely. In addition, the discourse as a whole contains a movement of speech (*Sprachbewegung*) in which each element builds upon the former and enlarges the understanding of the subject matter by introducing new terms or new relations between terms that are already used. This passage represents, as we will see below, the construction of a whole language-world, and each successive section of the discourse adds something new to it. The passage vv.31-36 does not introduce any essentially new meaning to the world of vv.1-21, yet it repeats elements of it. It is about the 'Mystery of the Testimony',[352] but the theme of Jesus' testimony has already been explored in vv.11-13. In fact, vv.31f take up vv.11-13 and v.6, not creating any new relation between the elements. Verse 36 repeats vv.14f, combining it with the element of God's wrath or judgement, something that already happened in the main body of the discourse. Verses 33f have no direct parallel in vv.1-21, but they do not contribute any new meaning that would not be implicit in the main body of the discourse. Therefore, the speech 31-36 does not fit into the composition of the Nicodemus Discourse as an immediate part of it, and therefore I am not going to interpret it in this particular context. It is a separate speech which is, nevertheless, closely connected with the Nicodemus Discourse. As Dodd and Becker have pointed out, it can be seen as an explanatory appendix to the discourse,[353] but not as a part of it.

Yet how can the break between v.12 and v.13 be explained? Obviously, there is a change in the mode of speech between vv.1-12 and vv.13-21. Bultmann assumes that the evangelist drew on different sources for the two

---

[350] Cf. Bultmann; *Johannesevangelium*, 92f.
[351] Dodd; *Interpretation*, 309.
[352] Bultmann; *Johannesevangelium*, 116.
[353] Dodd; *Interpretation*, 311 and Becker; *Johannesevangelium*, 154.

parts of the passage.[354] Bultmann sees the first part of the dialogue as a composition of the evangelist based upon a traditional saying by Jesus,[355] and the second as taken from the source of the revelation-discourses and used by the evangelist for his composition in an edited form. Although it is not impossible that the evangelist used different sources for the composition of this passage, this does not in any event prohibit an analysis of the original work of the evangelist. Even if the evangelist used different sources, he did not merely quote them, but transformed them so that they represented his own theological agenda. Thus it is not satisfying to assume that a break in the text is to be explained by the use of different sources. This would be to underestimate the creative activity of the evangelist. In addition, this text is, in my opinion, a composition in which the evangelist worked with different literary forms, not attempting to write a realistic scene, but to create a language-world to communicate the *kerygma*. As the following analysis shows, everything in the passage builds upon what was said previously, and the text presents a consistent train of thought and as a unity discloses reality by combining the different elements in a poetic way. Therefore, it is neither the historical Jesus speaking in the passage nor a Gnostic source, but the evangelist himself, who freely and creatively composed material available to him. He drew, I assume, mainly on earlier Christian thought, religious and philosophical ideas and concepts from the Hellenistic world and Jewish religious teaching as well as on the Old Testament.[356] The evangelist took up concepts from these sources and combined them creatively, thereby unveiling new meaning and bringing out the world opened by the *kerygma*.

The passage John 3:1-21 can be divided into three main parts. The change in the mode of speech between vv.12+13 indicates a break in the text; the form of a dialogue is given up and a speech or monologue about Jesus as the heavenly Son of Man begins. This indicates that a new part of the passage begins here. The first half of the passage, a dialogue between Jesus and Nicodemus, contains two parts. First, from vv.1-8, Nicodemus' initial question and Jesus' reply with a statement about supernatural regeneration are the subject of the dialogue. The second part of the dialogue is about the source of knowledge of divine revelation, which is the testimony of Jesus; it can be described as being about the 'epistemology of

---

[354] Bultmann assumes, as we have seen above, that the second part of the discourse contains vv.13-21+31-36. Although I have shown above that vv.31-36 are not likely to be part of the original composition, Bultmann's observation is correct that the break between vv.1-12 and vv.13-21 needs to be explained.

[355] Cf. Bultmann; *Johannesevangelium*, 93, 95f.

[356] Cf. Barrett; *John*, 27.

faith.' Thus, the following structure will be the basis of the interpretation of John 3:1-21:

1-8:   Supernatural Regeneration
9-12: An Epistemology of Faith
13-21: Jesus as the heavenly Son of Man

Creation of Language: 'Sprachbewegung' in John 3:1-21

Verses 1-8: Supernatural Regeneration

The dialogue between Jesus and Nicodemus is, on one level, a discourse about salvation and Jesus' person. Yet, on another level, we can use it to demonstrate how language of Christian faith is developed in order to communicate the *kerygma* as the evangelist interprets it. The dialogue is opened (v.2) by Nicodemus presenting a statement about Jesus' person, and sets the agenda of the dialogue: who is Jesus and how can he be understood? He attempts to understand Jesus in his terms and concepts as a teacher, yet as a teacher with a special divine legitimisation through the miracles, or even as a prophet. Nicodemus is the archetype of those who understand Jesus only in terms of the miracles he is performing or of his teaching, rather than as what he really is: the proclaimed rather than the proclaimer, the heavenly Son of Man. This insufficient understanding of Jesus' person can be found outside Christianity, e.g. in Judaism, or even among Christian groups which understand Jesus in those terms.[357] Jesus rejects this approach to his person by his response in v.3: if one is not born from above/again, one cannot see the Kingdom of God (ἐὰν μή γεννηθῇ ἄνωθεν, οὐ δύναται ἰδεῖν τὴν βασιλείαν τοῦ θεοῦ). This reply consists of two elements, *if one is not born from above/again* (ἐὰν μή γεννηθῇ ἄνωθεν) and *one cannot see the Kingdom of God* (οὐ δύναται ἰδεῖν τὴν βασιλείαν τοῦ θεοῦ), which are each taken from different contexts. They are related to each other in a metaphorical[358] way so that they disclose new meaning through the tension between each other as well as through that between Nicodemus' remark and Jesus' reply. As I am going to show in this section,

---

[357] Becker points out (*Johannesevangelium*, 155f) that the evangelist is not only arguing against non-Johannine groups, but also against his own tradition, because the view Nicodemus represents is that of the Signs Source. Hence for Becker the evangelist is actually rejecting the theology of his source. I do not find it very likely that it is possible to reconstruct the Signs Source with sufficient reliability to identify its theological agenda (cf. above, p.62). Becker is very much in danger of constructing a straw-man to fight against.

[358] Cf. above, 'Poetic Language: Metaphor and Symbol' pp.44-47.

Jesus' answer is at first sight cryptic, yet it constitutes a point of contact between Jesus' (or the Johannine) proclamation and the hearer, for both elements can be understood by everyone familiar with contemporary thought. Hence the meaning of the whole metaphor is accessible, provided it is taken as figurative language.[359]

Given that Jesus' reply is metaphorical, it is complete nonsense to take it literally, as Nicodemus' puzzled question in the next verse shows. It has to be seen as figurative language, related to Nicodemus' opening of the discourse in v.2. Jesus rejects Nicodemus' approach to his person and indicates that he has to be understood in a completely different context. He is not merely a teacher, but his real significance can only be seen from within the Kingdom of God. Consequently, the question as to how to enter the Kingdom of God is of great importance for understanding Jesus' person: the entry into the Kingdom of God becomes possible only through being born or begotten ἄνωθεν, which can mean both, 'again' and 'from above.' As we will see in the course of the discussion, this double-meaning is important for the understanding of the whole passage.

The Kingdom of God is a phrase taken from the earliest Christian tradition, probably going back to the proclamation of the historical Jesus, having its roots in Jewish thought. Already in Jesus' proclamation, the concept of the Kingdom of God had undergone significant transformation.[360] It was generally seen as the establishing of God's rule over the world, usually connected with the notions of purity, ritual and Jewish nationalism.[361] Yet Jesus is likely to have proclaimed the Kingdom of God separated from all the ideas of purity, punishment, reward for one's works and the necessity to enforce it as an earthly reality.[362] On the contrary, he saw it as spiritual reality, arriving through his healing-ministry and preaching to the poor.[363] In short, he proclaimed the Kingdom of God as the reinstatement of God's rulership over the world, but he understood it spiritually and with divine love as its ruling principle. In the developing Christian theology the Kingdom of God and Jesus' person are seen in a close relation.[364] In some instances in the gospels, Mark speaks about the Kingdom of God (or a

---

[359] Ibid. In Ricœur's terminology, Jesus' reply to Nicodemus is a root-metaphor, i.e. both elements of the metaphorical utterance refer to a whole system of symbolic and metaphorical language. Cf. above, p.46.

[360] Riches, John; *Jesus and the Transformation of Judaism,* London (Darton, Longaman & Todd) 1980, 87-111.

[361] Ibid. 100.

[362] Ibid. 99f.

[363] Ibid. 105-107.

[364] Cf. Schmidt, Karl-Ludwig; 'βασιλεύς κτλ. E: Die Wortgruppe βασιλεύς im Neuen Nestament' *ThWNT* I 576-593, 590.

synonym),[365] while in the parallels Matthew and Luke use Jesus' person instead of the Kingdom.[366] Here, the Kingdom as the bearer of salvation fulfils the same function as Jesus. At the heart of the language of the kingdom seems to be the new loving relationship between humanity and God that is near or has already arrived in Jesus.[367] Interestingly, the discourse with Nicodemus is the only place in the fourth gospel where the traditional term Kingdom of God can be found. A similar term occurs only in the passion-narrative, where Jesus speaks of my kingdom (ἡ βασιλεία ἡ ἐμή) (18:36). The introduction of a non-Johannine, traditional term must have a particular function in the Nicodemus Discourse,[368] which is to provide a point of contact between Johannine theology and contemporary religious thought, whether non-Christian or Christian.

The familiar concept of the Kingdom of God is paired with the idea of being born or begotten ἄνωθεν, with that of supernatural regeneration. This concept has parallels in Hellenistic religious thought, yet it is not well represented in Judaism or earlier Christianity.[369] A close parallel to this saying can be found in Corpus Hermeticum XIII. Here, the follower of Hermes alienates himself from the world and, when he has prepared himself and is fit, he will be supernaturally regenerated and born again and be of a completely different substance, i.e. he will be divine himself.[370] While C.H. XIII itself is generally considered to be later than John,[371] it is not

---

[365] Cf. Mk 11:10 with Mt 21:9 and Lk 19:38; Mk 10:29 and Lk 18:21 with Mt 19:29; Mk 9:1 and Lk 9:27 with Mt 16:28.

[366] Cf. Schmidt; 'βασιλεύς κτλ.' *ThWNT* I 584, 590f.

[367] Certainly, the Jewish use of the βασιλεία τοῦ θεοῦ continued to be known. Yet in Judaism, the concept of the βασιλεία τοῦ θεοῦ was used quite differently. In Rabbinic thought, in continuation of the Pharisaic conceptuality, it was seen as a sacred realm in which the faithful were separated from the Gentiles and a state of purity in which one could live according to God's will (Cf. Riches; *Jesus and the Transformation of Judaism*, 97f). This is, however, neither the background of the use of the term here not a relevant parallel, because it represents the further development of the use of the concept in another context.

[368] Although it has been argued that the sayings John 3:3,5 are taken from the tradition (Cf. Bultmann; *Johannesevangelium*, 95f, fn.5), the particular function of this term at this place must not be diminished. As the evangelist is not likely to have adopted a tradition without reflection but only purposefully, the reason behind his choice has to be considered.

[369] Cf. Barrett; *John*, 206f; Bultmann; *Johannesevangelium*, 95f.

[370] Cf. Corpus Hermeticum lib.XIII, 1-7, Grese, William C.; *Corpus Hermeticum XIII and Early Christian Literature*, Studia ad Corpus Hellenisticum Novi Testamenti, vol. 5, Leiden (Brill) 1979, 2-15, cf. also pp.72-74.

[371] Cf. Grese, 48f; Barrett, 38.

likely to be dependent on or influenced by John or any other early Christian literature.[372]

> The parallels between C.H. XIII and the NT [...] really only show that C.H. XIII and ECL [i.e. early Christian literature] both made use of similar religious language and that both were part of the same world of Hellenistic religions.[373]

In Hermetic literature, the illuminated person is begotten from God or from the will of God (γεννώμενος θεοῦ or τοῦ θελήματος τοῦ θεοῦ, C.H. XIII, 2). Hermes describes his supernatural regeneration (παλιγγενεσία):

> While seeing in myself a true vision which came from the mercy of God, I came out of myself into an immortal body, and I am not now what I was before, but I have been begotten in Intellect. This thing is not taught, not even by this fabricated element through which comes sight. Therefore the first composite form also does not concern me. I am no longer colored and have neither touch nor measure, but I am different from these. (C.H. XIII, 3)[374]

Here, the concept of supernatural regeneration is used to describe the transition from the worldly state of being into the intellectual or divine. 'The physical body has to be replaced by an intellectual body through a second generation (i.e., regeneration). The individual has to be transformed from existence as man to existence as god.'[375] The language of supernatural regeneration thus means ultimate discontinuity and a transition that is not a human possibility, but happens by the will of God. As Grese points out, this concept of regeneration also occurs in Hellenistic mystery religions.[376] Therefore, it was a familiar concept in Hellenistic religious thought, so the evangelist of John's Gospel could use it as well as the author of C.H. XIII. Consequently, Jesus' statement that one must be born from above was comprehensible to everyone familiar with contemporary religious thought.

These two broadly known concepts, that of the Kingdom of God and that of supernatural regeneration, are combined in a metaphorical way,[377] so that through this saying the evangelist's view of Christian existence is displayed. It is, on the one hand, communion with God and participation in the realm of his love, on the other hand it is ultimate discontinuity, it

---

[372] Cf. Grese, 57f.

[373] Grese, 58. The parallels between C.H. XIII and John's Gospel help the interpreter to understand the religious language used by both. This relevance does not depend on literary dependence of John's Gospel on C.H. XIII. Cf. also the above section on the relevance of parallel text for interpretation, pp.54-56.

[374] Translation from Grese, 9.

[375] Grese, 72.

[376] Ibid.

[377] Cf. above, 'Poetic Language: Metaphor and Symbol' p.44.

comes from above and is outside human possibilities. It means becoming part of the divine realm, but, unlike as in C.H. XIII, it does not mean to cease being human and to become a god.[378]

As response to Nicodemus' opening of the dialogue, Jesus' saying is about his person. Who Jesus is can only be seen from within the Kingdom of God, thus only through supernatural regeneration. On the level of language, to enter the Kingdom of God and to understand who Jesus really is, another language than the 'earthly' one, over which Nicodemus has command, is required. It is not only the perception of his person as a teacher or prophet Jesus is criticising, but the whole conceptuality and language-world of Nicodemus. In order to understand Jesus' significance one has to have joined the world of faith,[379] which entails a completely new perception of reality and thus a new language. This new world can be communicated through language, but it requires a new language, the language of faith, which is able to disclose the world in which Jesus' true significance can be seen, and which is, in this case, figurative language.[380] Thus, in order to communicate who Jesus is, the evangelist has to create a new language by combining elements from different language-worlds in a poetic way and thus discloses the new meaning he wants to express, which is his particular interpretation of the world, centred on the person of Jesus.

Nicodemus, not familiar with the language of faith, takes Jesus' saying literally and understands ἄνωθεν merely as 'again', so that he asks how this new birth is possible in physical terms. In his response, Jesus does not change the mode of his language at all; he explains what he means in strictly figurative language. Jesus explains the meaning of being born ἄνωθεν by combining it with other concepts and pictures rather than by explaining it in non-figurative language. In v.5 he explains that the new birth is not a physical act by connecting it with water and spirit, so that the birth is understood in spiritual terms.

The combination of water and spirit is an allusion to baptism and seems to take up the saying of John the Baptist in John 1:29-34.[381] The baptism

---

378 Cf. Grese, 73.

379 In this context the relation between πιστεύειν and γινώσκειν described by Bultmann (*Theologie*, 425f) can be of importance for understanding the phenomenon of joining the language-world of faith and exploring it.

380 Cf. above, 99, fn.359.

381 Bultmann (*Johannesevangelium*, 98) rules out the phrase ὕδατος καὶ as a later assimilation of this passage to the doctrine of the early catholic church. I agree with Barrett that the ὕδατος καὶ is part of the original gospel. Apart from Barrett's arguments the mentioning of water matches the concept of this whole passage, the enlarging of the horizon of the text by adding new concepts from the sources available to the evangelist. The concept of baptism was certainly known

with water and spirit is, in early Christianity, closely connected to repentance, forgiveness of sins and the death of Jesus.[382] These meanings are
introduced into the language by alluding to baptism. They are, however,
not just taken over, but significantly altered. Only the activity of the spirit
opens the possibility of entering the Kingdom of God, i.e. to become part of
the realm of the spirit (v.6). Hence, the supernatural regeneration, which is
the work of the spirit spirit and completely outside human possibility, is
closely connected with the church's practice of baptism. Baptism is radically spiritualised; it is seen as 'the material sign of the Spirit's spirit
work.'[383] This verse can be seen as a 'warning against a sacramentarian
misapprehension of baptism.'[384] Although baptism is part of the meaning
of this verse, the main focus is still on the work of the spirit, which causes
the transformation from flesh to spirit.

In addition, there is another field of meaning introduced into the discourse by the mentioning of water and spirit. In Jewish tradition, water is
understood as ultimate cleansing, as it is e.g. expressed in Ezek. 36:25-28:

> I will sprinkle new water upon you, and you shall be clean from all your un-
> cleanness [...] A new heart I will give you, and a new spirit I will put within
> you; [...] I will put my spirit within you, and make you follow the statutes and
> be careful to serve my ordinances. [...] and you shall be my people, and I will be
> your God.

Here, water is a sign of cleansing, through which Israel gets a new spirit
and the communion between God and his people is restored. The motif of
cleansing and new spirit is also to be found in Jub. 1:23-25: 'I will create in
them a holy spirit and I will cleanse them [...] I will be their father and they
shall be my children.' A similar thought was also used in the Rule of the
Community from the Qumran texts.

> Meanwhile, God will refine, with his truth, all man's deeds, and will purify for
> himself the configuration of man, ripping out all spirit of injustice from the in-
> nermost part of his flesh, and cleansing him with the spirit of holiness from
> every irreverent deed. He will sprinkle over him the spirit of truth like lustral
> water (in order to cleanse him) from all abhorrences of deceit and defilement of
> the unclean spirit. In this way the upright will understand knowledge of the

---

to the evangelist, since the practice of baptism must be presupposed in all early
Christianity (Cf. Becker; *Johannesevangelium*, 163f) and so it would be only natu-
ral for him to use this concept in creating his language. Cf. also Koester, Craig
R.; *Symbolism in the Fourth Gospel: Meaning, Mystery, Community*, Minneapolis
(Fortress) 1995, 164-166.

[382] Cf. EWNT, 459-469.

[383] Cf. Koester; *Symbolism*, 166.

[384] Barrett, 209.

Most High, and the wisdom of the sons of heaven will teach those of perfect be-
haviour. For these are those selected by God for an everlasting covenant. (1 QS
IV 20-22) [385]

Both the parallel Jub. 1:23-25 and 1QS are likely to be receptions of Ezek.
36:25-28. This shows how the passage from Ezekiel has influenced Jewish
thought of that time and that the concept of sprinkling of water was understood as a sign of ritual cleansing in order to restore the relation between
humankind and God. Thus this concept must have been known to the
community from which John's Gospel evolved, for they were a part of
Jewish religious thought. Therefore, the idea of cleansing and restored
communion with God is introduced to the meaning of this verse. The supernatural regeneration is also ultimate cleansing, and restoration of the
communion between God and his people, which had been destroyed by
human disobedience. The full meaning of the verses about being born
ἄνωθεν is, in my opinion, to be seen in the combination of both the Jewish
and Hellenistic concepts of supernatural regeneration and ultimate cleansing; it combines these concepts in order to disclose what coming to faith
means. The distinction between the realms of flesh (σάρξ) and spirit
(πνεῦμα) is introduced in v.6. Both terms are also known from Paul's epistles and thus they must have been common currency in early Christian
theology. The evangelist, however, uses these terms very differently from
Paul and thus from the early Christian tradition. Paul uses these terms
anthropologically to describe the human condition. Characteristically he
uses *according to the flesh* (κατὰ σάρκα) and *in the flesh* (ἐν σαρκί). Naturally
every human being lives in the flesh, in the sphere of natural life, which
does not necessarily contain a theological judgement.[386] Only if the flesh
determines the human existence, the human being lives according to the
flesh, i.e. in sin.[387] The antonym to flesh is *spirit* (πνεῦμα), which represents
the non-worldly, the invisible.[388] Living *according to the spirit* means to live
in faith, having one's life determined by Christ.[389] Thus, the dualism between flesh and spirit is about how human existence is determined,
whether one lives in obedience or disobedience against God. The evangelist
uses these concepts, yet transforms them by combining them with his particular world-view: he does not use the forms *in the flesh/spirit* (ἐν
σαρκί/πνεύματι) or *according to the flesh/spirit* (κατὰ σάρκα/πνεῦμα), which

---

[385] Translation from Martínez, Florentino García; *The Dead Sea Scrolls Translated: The
Qumran Texts in English*, Leiden (Brill) 1994, 7.
[386] Cf. Bultmann; *Theologie*, 236f.
[387] Cf. Bultmann; *Theologie*, 237f.
[388] Cf. Bultmann; *Theologie*, 336.
[389] Ibid.

are known in Christian tradition, but *from the flesh/spirit* (ἐκ τῆς σαρκὸς/τοῦ πνεύματος). In this usage, they do not describe human existence as either in sin or in faith, as in Paul, but they are used to describe the origin of a human being. The evangelist clearly moves in the direction of the conceptuality of cosmological dualism,[390] which was also current in antiquity. In some respects, the dualism found in Qumran literature forms an interesting parallel to the Johannine. In 1QS III, 13-IV,26, humanity is seen as determined by its origins. There are two groups of human beings, the first is given the spirit of truth, the second the spirit of deceit:[391]

> In these lies the history of all men; in their (two) divisions all their armies have a share by their generations; in their paths they walk; every deed they do falls into their divisions, dependent on what might be the birthright of the man, great or small, for all eternal time. For God has sorted them into equal parts until the last day and has put everlasting loathing between their divisions. (1QS IV, 15-17)[392]

There is, however, an important difference between the dualistic language in the *Rule of the Community* and John 3:1-21. The Qumran dualism is strictly determinist, i.e. every human being is given one of the two spirits and belongs to the respective group 'for all eternal time'; no transition from one division to the other is possible. The Nicodemus Discourse, on the other hand, is about how the transition from the one group to the other is possible. The supernatural regeneration, which is a concept which cannot be found in the Jewish tradition,[393] allows the human being to become part of those born of the spirit. Thus, the Johannine determinism is not a

---

390 Although Johannine thought moves towards a cosmological dualism, it has to be noted that there is no notion of a dualism within the deity, i.e. that a god of light is opposed by a god of darkness. The division in Johannine dualism is between God/being from God and the world/being from the world. It is a radical expression of the creation having turned away from its creator and not of the world being created by an evil force as in Gnosticism.

391 Cf. 1 QS III, 19.

392 Translation from Martínez; *The Dead Sea Scrolls Translated*, 7.

393 Chestnutt points out that in Rabbinic Judaism the language of new birth was known for the conversion to Judaism and being proselytised. Yet the point of this language is not to describe what happens in the conversion, but the legal position of the proselyte, who is seen like a new-born child. It is a transformation of status, not of essence (Chestnutt, Randall D.; *From Death to Life: Conversion in Joseph and Aseneth*, JSPS 16, Sheffield (Academic Press) 1995, 174-176). Thus the imagery may be similar to that of the Nicodemus Discourse, yet it does not contain the idea of supernatural regeneration. In addition, if such a concept of supernatural regeneration had been known in contemporary Judaism, then Nicodemus as representative of the Jewish establishment would have known the imagery and not completely misunderstood Jesus' saying.

determinism strictly speaking, for a human being does not belong to one group or the other 'for all eternal time', because he or she may be born ἄνωθεν and then be from the spirit. Nevertheless, there are important points of contact with the dualism of 1QS, since in both texts the deeds of an individual are determined by his or her origin, an issue which will be made explicit in v.19.[394]

In C.H. XIII a distinction similar to the Johannine juxtaposition of *flesh* and *spirit* (σάρξ and πνεῦμα) is made between *body* and *mind* (σῶμα and voῦς).[395] The supernatural regeneration causes the illuminated to cease bodily existence and start a new being *in the mind* (ἐν νῷ), to which the material realm does not matter, as the real Hermes cannot be found in the body anymore.[396] Only through supernatural regeneration it becomes possible to know (voεῖν) the transcendent god.

> This voεῖν, however, is a possibility only for those who are themselves voῦς, and in becoming voῦς they are made divine and are translated out of human, physical existence. Like God himself, Hermes, who is also voῦς, can be known only by voεῖν, not by sense perceptions.[397]

There are, indeed, some parallels between John's perception of the supernatural regeneration, but there are even more important differences. John, as we have seen above, agrees that the divine, in his case Jesus, cannot be understood by anybody who is not born ἄνωθεν and is thus still part of the realm of the flesh. For John, however, supernatural regeneration does not lead to direct and immediate knowledge of God, but to understanding the person of Jesus, which mediates knowledge of God. In addition, the supernatural regeneration in John 3 is closely connected with the Kingdom of God, which is the realm of a new, loving relationship between humanity and God, in which divine love is the ruling principle. This Kingdom of God, which takes place in the world, although not being part of this world, is the realm of the spirit, into which one enters by the divine gift of understanding Jesus' person. Being taken out of the realm of the flesh means, therefore, not being literally taken out of this world, but being put into a new relation to God and the world, which is opened by the Gospel, in this case as it is proclaimed by John, and which to enter is not a human possibility but the work of the spirit. John combines the early Christian concept of Spirit and Flesh with Hellenistic dualistic thought and thus arrives at a new interpretation of Christianity, which involves a concept of

---

394 Cf, below, p.114.
395 Cf. Grese, 93f.
396 Cf. Grese, 90.
397 Grese, 91.

dualism, which is particular to Johannine thought[398] and a means to express the Johannine interpretation of Christian faith.

In v.8 the work of the spirit is explained in a peculiar way. Playing on the double meaning of πνεῦμα, which can mean 'spirit' as well as 'wind', the *pneuma*, like the wind, can be recognised by its effect, but origin and end are not known. It blows or breathes (πνεῖ) according to its own law,[399] it is completely outside of any kind of human availability, cannot be predicted or domesticated, it is completely external to this world, or, as Barrett points out: 'It breathes into this world from another.'[400] The new birth is a power from outside, that overcomes humanity, and it proves its existence only by its effect, i.e. those that are supernaturally regenerated know that the spirit is at work and therefore exists, but no other evidence for it is available. The evangelist apparently abstains from delivering a doctrine of the Spirit, rather he defines it by its effect and the mystery of its effectiveness only. Therefore he refuses any attempt to make the supernatural regeneration, the coming to faith comprehensible as a worldly phenomenon, but presents it in its otherness from all worldly phenomena and in its unavailability to humanity. It is a divine mystery and, since it is not bound to any condition, it is not a human work but the activity of divine grace.

In this first part of the Nicodemus Discourse, a whole cosmology is opened up. New relations between known concepts are uncovered and thus a new meaning is disclosed. Through the dialectic between the concept of the Kingdom of God and that of supernatural regeneration and the following explanation, the relation between the realm of faith and that of unbelief is outlined. As the whole passage is a response to a remark about Jesus' person, it has to be seen in relation to Jesus' himself. Who he really is can only be understood from within the realm of faith, only through being begotten ἄνωθεν, being taken out of the world and put into a new understanding of the world, which is communicated through the language of faith. This mystery cannot be expressed adequately in direct, objectifying language; the evangelist had to use poetic language, combining known concepts in a new, creative way, in order to communicate his interpretation of the *kerygma*.

Verses 9-12: An Epistemology of Faith

The next part of the dialogue (vv.9-12) is the transition from the more general cosmology of vv.3-8 to the christological discourse of vv.13-20. Its subject is the source of knowledge about faith, it is, as it were, an epistemology

---

[398] Cf. Becker; *Johannesevangelium*, 174-179.
[399] Cf. Schnackenburg; *Johannesevangelium*, I, 387.
[400] Barrett; *John*, 211.

of faith. Jesus responds to Nicodemus' question 'How can this happen?' by presenting himself as the source of knowledge about the spiritual realm. Jesus is the proclaimer in these verses, before he becomes, as the proclaimed, the subject of proclamation in the last part of the discourse.

When Nicodemus asks: 'How can this happen?' he obviously has understood the cosmology of vv.3-8, for he asks not for clarification of that system, but wishes to know how the supernatural regeneration through the spirit is possible. Jesus' answer 'You are a teacher of Israel and do not know that?' is, certainly, ironic. As a Pharisee and Ruler of the Jews (v.1), Nicodemus would have claimed to know the will of God through the revelation of the Torah. The real and ultimate revelation of God's will, however, is Jesus himself, and so Nicodemus' knowledge of scripture cannot be sufficient. The teaching of Israel cannot answer the question as to how salvation is possible, because they do not know Christ as the key to scripture and thus do not understand its real meaning. The mystery of rebirth is completely incomprehensible to natural human beings;[401] it is accessible only through the testimony of Jesus, as the evangelist makes clear in v.11.

In v.11, peculiarly, the person speaking changes, since this verse is completely in plural form. Schnackenburg[402] observes that, by using of the plural, the evangelist departs from the framework of the dialogue. In this setting, Jesus' horizon includes the time in which the disciples take his testimony and make it part of their proclamation. Schnackenburg is certainly right in observing that the evangelist departs from the framework of the dialogue, but one could even go further and say that it is not only Jesus speaking in this verse, but the Johannine community. The perspective of the ministry of Jesus is left and the church is envisaged.[403] And indeed, the distinction between Jesus and the post-Easter Christian community is diffused in this verse; the Church is seen not only as continuing Jesus' ministry, but it is, in a certain way, even identified with him. The church is continuing Jesus' mission in the world by bearing witness to God as Jesus has born witness to him, and the testimony of the church is rejected by the

---

[401] Cf. Bultmann; *Johannesevangelium*, 102f. Schnackenburg (*Johannesevangelium* I, 388) suggests that Nicodemus' question proves his ignorance and not understanding of what Jesus had said before, since he attempts to inquire deeper into that mystery. This perception of the situation is, in my opinion, wrong, since the supernatural regeneration Jesus is talking about is something so alien to human understanding, that it cannot be understood before it is revealed. Nicodemus' question is therefore necessary in order to continue the discourse and to talk about the essential part of the mystery of rebirth, which is Jesus' own person.

[402] Cf. Schnackenburg; *Johannesevangelium*, I, 388f.

[403] Cf. Barrett; *John*, 211f.

world just as Jesus' testimony was rejected. This feature can also be observed in other parts of John's Gospel, e.g. in the Farewell Discourses (cf. 15:18-21), in the 'highpriestly' Prayer of ch.17 and in the resurrection narratives (cf. 20:21). In this verse, the theological point is not made explicit, but it underlies this shift of perspective. The different levels of the narrative are fused and the change in the person speaking signals that this discourse is not only about Jesus, but also about the congregation and their argument with the Jewish community; thus the listeners are taken into the course of the narrative, which is, in turn, applied to their situation.

The contrast *earthly things* (ἐπίγεια) — *heavenly things* (ἐπουράνια) in v.12 refers to the parts before and after this verse. The cosmological background outlined in vv.2-8 are the *earthly things* (ἐπίγεια) and the following passage vv.13-21, which could be titled 'The Johannine *Kerygma*'[404] is referred to by the *heavenly things* (ἐπουράνια). Since I see, unlike Bultmann and Schnackenburg, the passage 3:1-21 as one literary composition, it is not necessary to relate the *heavenly things* to something external to the text, as Schnackenburg suggests.[405] Schnackenburg sees the *heavenly things* as another revelation of heavenly things, which is not contained in the passage, but will follow at a later stage of Jesus' ministry. Barrett,[406] similarly, sees the *heavenly things* as another revelation which Jesus does not give here, because it would be pointless since Nicodemus does not even believe him when he is talking about the *earthly things*. It is certainly questionable whether, in the framework of Johannine theology, a higher revelation than that given in vv.13-21 is possible. Here, the whole *kerygma* is outlined in a very concise way, and the *heavenly things* are revealed in the rest of the passage. Therefore I suggest that the *earthly things* refer to the cosmological background outlined in vv.2-9 and the *heavenly things* to the revelation of the salvation by faith in Christ in vv.13-21. The cosmological background is only an *earthly thing* because it refers to what happens on earth. It is a phenomenological description (by means of a cosmological metaphor) of the distinction between the believers and the non-believers, and of the necessity of supernatural regeneration in order to become part of the believers. That the *earthly things* refer to the cosmological background also explains that Jesus concludes his talking about the *earthly things* with the statement about the Spirit that blows/breathes where it wants, since it points to another level on which the supernatural regeneration has to be seen and leaves it a mystery on the level of the *earthly things*, which is further explained on the level of the *heavenly things* in vv.13-21.

---

404 Cf. Schnackenburg; *Johannesevangelium*, I, 393.
405 Cf. Schnackenburg; *Johannesevangelium*, I, 390-393.
406 Cf. Barrett; *John*, 212.

Verses 13-21: Jesus as the heavenly Son of Man

In the section vv.13-21, the mode of discourse changes from a dialogue between Jesus and Nicodemus to a speech given by Jesus. This change in the mode of discourse correlates with the content of the second half of the passage, because there is no point of contact between natural human understanding and what Jesus is about to reveal about the *heavenly things*. In the first section of the discourse, which is about the cosmological background for an understanding of Jesus' person, and in the second section, which discusses the source of knowledge about God and Jesus, a dialogue could take place between the positions of Nicodemus and Jesus. Yet the third section explains the true significance of Jesus' person, which is utterly incomprehensible in human terms. In fact, this proclamation that Jesus is the heavenly Son of Man and truly sent by God, is the Johannine *kerygma* and thus the call to faith. Believing understanding of this section of the discourse can only take place from within the Kingdom of God, thus through supernatural regeneration. Faith in Jesus' testimony about himself is not a natural human possibility, but an act of God's love.

The uniqueness of Jesus' revelation is emphasised in v.13, and the reason for this is given: he is the only one who has ever been in heaven and thus is able to reveal the ἐπουράνια. The ἐπουράνια are, in turn, that Jesus is the one who came down from heaven and who makes the new birth from the spirit possible. Nobody else brings salvation than the one who came down from heaven. It is impossible to ascend to heaven by human power, e.g. by means of mysticism; it is only possible through Jesus' mediation. Only through him authentic knowledge of God, i.e. that God is the one who sent Jesus into the world, is possible.

In this verse, Jesus is identified with the Son of Man, which was a common Christian description of Jesus. Earliest Christianity, possibly even Jesus himself, had connected the figure of the Son of Man from Dan 7:13 with Jesus' person.[407] This meant a far-reaching reinterpretation of that text, for this text had not commonly been interpreted as referring to an individual before.[408] In earlier Christian theology, this image was used to express 'the belief that Jesus had been vindicated after death and would soon "come with the clouds of heaven".'[409] Jesus Christ was expected to come again in final triumph and judge the world.[410] This interpretation of Jesus as the Son of Man is radically transformed in this passage. First, in earlier

---

[407] Cf. Dunn, James D.G.; *Christology in the Making: A New Testament Inquiry into the Doctrine of the Incarnation*, London (SCM) 1980, 82-95, esp. 87.
[408] Ibid. 67-82, esp. 81f.
[409] Ibid. 87.
[410] Ibid. 96.

Christianity, the Son of Man was not usually seen as a pre-existent figure before. It was the future coming of Christ which was understood in terms of the coming of the Son of Man in Dan 7:13. In John 3:13, however, the Son of Man is connected with the Johannine concept of Christ's pre-existence, which stems from the early stages of Johannine Christology, as it can be seen in the *logos*-hymn in John 1.[411] Secondly, the reference to Dan 7:13 was, in pre-Johannine Christianity, an expression of the expectation of Jesus' future coming, not a retrospective understanding of his earthly ministry. In John, however, Jesus in his earthly ministry is given the title Son of Man. Thirdly, the Son of Man was seen as Christ coming back in triumph and judgement. While, in pre-Johannine Christianity, the lowliness of Jesus' earthly ministry was contrasted with the glory of his second coming, the evangelist does not differentiate between these anymore; the earthly Jesus possesses his full heavenly glory (cf. John 1:14) already during his earthly ministry. Moreover, to describe Jesus as the Son of Man before his exaltation means that his first coming into the world, his earthly ministry, is his coming to judge the world. In the encounter with Jesus' proclamation the judgement takes place; either one accepts it believing and thus is rescued or rejects it and is judged. This aspect is further explored in v.18f.[412] To sum up, through the combination of the reference to Dan 7:13 with Jesus' earthly ministry, the latter is understood in a completely different way. The distinction between his first and second coming collapses, and already Jesus' earthly ministry is understood as the ultimate eschatological event. In the encounter with his person the final judgement takes place.

The motif of ascent and descent in John's Gospel is closely connected with the Johannine messenger-Christology.[413] This understanding of his ministry sees Jesus as being sent by the Father, thus coming down from heaven into the world (cf. v.17), and returning to the Father by his ascent to heaven through his exaltation. This scheme of mission and return is not fully elaborated in this passage, but the ascent and descent motif is used to understand the outline of Jesus' ministry. It will be taken up again in v.17, where Jesus' coming into the world is described as his mission.[414]

In vv.14 and 15 the Son of Man image is altered by connecting it with the image of the serpent on the pole from Num. 21:8, a way of understanding the crucifixion for which no earlier example is known.[415] Just as the serpent was lifted up by Moses, the Son of Man must be lifted up. By relating these concepts to each other, a new meaning is added to the picture

---

[411] Cf. the section 'The Prologue: John 1:1-18' pp.69-93, esp. 79-84.
[412] Cf. below p.114.
[413] Cf. Becker; *Johannesevangelium*, 178, 487-494.
[414] Cf. below, p.113.
[415] Cf. Becker; *Johannesevangelium*, 170 and Schnackenburg; *Johannesevangelium*, 408.

of Jesus that is presented here. The eschatological Son of Man, the one who bears the ultimate witness to God and whose appearance on earth is the final judgement, is the one who will be lifted up on the pole as the serpent was in Num. 21:8. In Num. 21:8, the bronze serpent is lifted up to heal everybody who looks at it from the bites of the fiery serpents which have occurred as a punishment of Israel's disobedience. In the second half of the sentence (v.15), this picture is altered even more by changing the *seeing* of the bronze serpent (ὁράω, Num. 21:8 (LXX)) into *believing* (πιστεύω) and the 'he will live' (ζήσεται) into 'he may have eternal life' (ἔχῃ ζωὴν αἰώνιον). Through the introduction of the bronze serpent in vv.14 and 15, a new element is added to the description of what Jesus is. First, the tradition of the bronze serpent is a story about Israel's disobedience. The fiery serpents are sent to punish Israel for its disobedience, by biting and killing many Israelites. Because of Israel's repentance, the bronze serpent is lifted up and those who see it survive. Barrett remarks that ancient Jewish exegesis related the healing through seeing the serpent not to the serpent itself but to faith in God, who caused the healing.[416] In a similar way, the eternal Son of God has become incarnate because of human disobedience towards God, to open the possibility of a positive relation between God and humanity, and to rescue humankind from death. However, salvation does not merely consist in physical survival, as in Num. 21:8, but in eternal life. Secondly, the task of the heavenly Son of Man, which is to reveal God's nature and to judge the world, is fulfilled only through his being lifted up, i.e. through the crucifixion, which is, at the same time, the exaltation (ὑψόω = *to lift up* and *to exalt*). The image of being lifted up illustrates the motif of the ascent in v.13. The Son of Man has to ascend into heaven (v.13), and so he has to be lifted up and thus to be exalted.[417] Thirdly, salvation, which is brought by the eternal Son of God incarnate, is only possible through faith in the crucified and exalted one. As the healing from the bite of the serpents took place, as it was understood in ancient Judaism, through faith in God, mediated by the bronze serpent, so salvation from death and eternal life happens through faith in Jesus the crucified one because God becomes visible in him.

In order to define more clearly the meaning of the picture outlined in the previous verse, the metaphorical speech is explained in v.16 by a direct statement about Jesus' mission in the world. Jesus' coming into the world is an act of God's love; the Son of Man is also the eternal Son of God, who is given in order to save humankind and open the possibility of eternal life.

---

[416] Cf. Barrett 213f and Strack, Herrmann L. and Billerbeck, Paul; *Kommentar zum Neuen Testament aus Talmud und Midrasch*, München (C.H.Beck), 5 vols., 1922-1961, vol.2, 425f.

[417] Cf. Becker; *Johannesevangelium*, 171.

The term only-begotten (μονογενής), in connection with Jesus as the Son of God, occurs only in the fourth gospel. It must be part of the Johannine tradition, since it already occurs in the hymn underlying the prologue (1:14) and describes the unique relationship between God and Jesus.[418] The term ἔδωκεν (he gave) contains an element of giving away or sacrifice. As the 'believing in him' takes up the comparison with the serpent on the pole of the previous verses, this verse means that the Father is giving away his only Son to be lifted up like the serpent. The crucifixion is alluded to here, although not explicitly mentioned. The pair 'believing' and 'having eternal life' of v.15 is supplemented with its opposition, which is 'being lost.' Without faith in the Son of God, which is only possible because of the Son's being given, the world is in a state of perdition. Because of God's love towards the world, one of the most important motifs in Johannine theology (cf. 1 John 4:8-10), God gives away his only Son so that the world may have the possibility of leaving the state of perdition and have eternal life. The language of this verse is strongly dualistic, for the world is seen as lost, and life is only possible for those who believe in the Son. This is, in fact, the subject of this whole passage and only possible through supernatural regeneration.

The same point is made again in v.17, yet from another angle. Jesus' coming into the world is understood in terms of the messenger-Christology.[419] As in antiquity all communication and trade depended on messengers, universally recognised and standardised rules for the tasks of messengers developed, which were used also in religious thought to describe the exchange of heavenly and earthly beings.[420] If the evangelist uses the messenger-terminology in order to understand Jesus' earthly ministry, the whole institution of messengers in antiquity resonates. Jesus is God's own messenger, who is sent into the world to bring eternal life. Before the concept of judgement (κρίσις) is elaborated in v.18, it is emphasised again that the purpose of the Son's mission, part of which is the judgement, is the salvation of the world. Therefore, the whole concept of judgement is preceded by that of God's love towards the *kosmos*, and the judgement is seen as subordinate to it, i.e. it is but a function of God's love, though a necessary one.[421]

---

[418] Cf. Fitzmeyer, J.A.; 'μονογενής' EWNT, 1082-1083.

[419] Cf. Becker; *Johannesevangelium*, 488 and above p.111.

[420] Cf. Becker; *Johannesevangelium*, 488.

[421] Cf. also John 12:47. The idea of judgement as a function of God's love and prerequisite for salvation is already found in the Old Testament. Cf. Herntrich, V.; 'κρίνω κτλ., B. Der at.liche Begriff מִשְׁפָּט' ThWNT III, 922-933, 929-932 and Liedke, G.; 'שפט' THAT II, 999-1009, 1007-1009. Note that in the Qumran-texts the term is used the same way, Liedke, 'שפט' 1009.

In v.18, the concept of judgement, an important aspect of Jesus' person which has not been elaborated yet, is unfolded. The concept has, indirectly, been introduced through the concept of the Son of Man, yet only in the final part of this passage is it carried out explicitly. The concept of judgement is transformed radically here. Judgement is seen not just as a future event that the world is waiting for, but as taking place in the encounter with the only Son of God, a term that carries now all the meaning that has been connected with it in the previous verses. In the encounter with Jesus as the only Son of God it is decided whether someone belongs to the realm of the flesh or to that of the spirit. In this encounter the supernatural regeneration takes place if Jesus is accepted as what he is, i.e. as God's authentic messenger, the ultimate expression of God's love towards humankind. If one belongs to the realm of the spirit, he or she will not be judged, one has already eternal life. Not accepting Jesus as the one he is, not having faith in him, means belonging to the realm of the flesh and thus already being judged and condemned.

In v.19, dualistic language is used again, though this time it is not the dualism of *flesh* and *spirit*, but that of *light* and *darkness*, a language that connects to the prologue, where this imagery is used as part of the great cosmological narrative (John 1:4f, 9). In v.19, it is said explicitly that the judgement is the light's coming into the world, and since humanity belongs to the other part of that cosmological dualism, to the darkness and the flesh, the light is rejected. Consequently, those rejecting the light are judged by their staying in the darkness and in the flesh. By taking up the cosmological dualism again in the end of this passage, the second part about the *heavenly things* is linked with the first one about the *earthly things*, and thus it is expressed that the second part is the answer to Nicodemus' question how the supernatural regeneration can happen. The dualism of light and darkness is also linked with human works. As the judgement takes place in the encounter with Jesus, human works do not have direct implications for salvation, since the works do not bear a consequence for judgement, which take place only on the ground of faith or unbelief in Jesus. Therefore, doing evil or truth is apparently not a merely moral matter, but a matter of having faith in Jesus. Everything that is done through faith in Jesus is truth, and everything that is done without that faith is evil. The sentence vv.20,21 expresses this in a paradox way: those that do evil hate the light and keep away from it, whereas those that do the truth come to the light so that it may be shown that their deeds have been done in God. This sentence seems to contradict what has been said before, that the decision, whether someone is saved and being supernaturally regenerated, is taken in the encounter with Jesus. This tension between these statements leads to an altered understanding of morality.

The concept that the moral quality of human deeds is determined by the origin of the human being is known from the kind of dualism which is represented by the *Rule of the Community* of the Qumran-texts.[422] In 1QS III, 13-IV,26, for example, the deeds of human beings are determined by the spirit which has been given to them. Those that have the spirit of injustice hate truth and vice versa,[423] just as those who do evil hate the light. An important difference is however, that, as pointed out above,[424] in the dualism as it is expressed in the *Rule of the Community* no transition from one state of being to the other is possible. One has either the spirit of truth or that of deceit for ever and thus belongs to those loved by God or hated by him for all time. Yet Johannine dualism allows the transition from one state of being to another, from the realm of the flesh to that of the spirit, by means of supernatural regeneration, which leads to a new existence in Christ. A new loving relationship, in which the human individual is loved by God on the grounds of his or her faith in Christ, is opened through the mission of the Son. Therefore, in this new relation between God and humanity the believer lives by grace alone. Thus, the person does not act in order to define his or her personality, in order to gain reward from God, for the person in Christ is part of the loving communion with God because of his or her faith in the divine love. Being part of this communion has, certainly moral implications (cf., e.g. John 13:34), but they do not constitute the membership in that communion. Everybody who is part of this loving communion, can, therefore, come to the light regardless of his or her works, since one does not have to trust, i.e. have faith in them anymore. Those living in the flesh, however, trust in what they are doing in order to define themselves, in human as well as in divine terms. Therefore they cannot be part of the simply loving communion, and they cannot persist before God, because human works are generally seen as evil (cf. v.19). In this way it is possible to talk about works in the context of the belief in being accepted by God through divine grace as it is presented in this passage. The introduction of human works into the argument fulfils also another function, because it excludes libertinism, which could result from the teaching of the sole work of divine love in this text. The decision whether one belongs to the realm of the light or the darkness comes about in the encounter with Jesus, resulting in faith or unbelief in his person. Yet human action is not irrelevant but those who are part of the realm of the light act in accordance with their being in loving communion with God.

---

[422] Cf. above, p.105.

[423] 1QS IV, 17.

[424] Cf. above p.105.

Conclusion

As we have seen in this chapter, creation of language takes place in the dialogue between Jesus and Nicodemus. This creation of language does not happen by creating a language out of nothing, but existing human language is taken up and transformed so that it opens up a new language-world. The evangelist takes up elements from the religious languages of different traditions, which he combines in a new, creative way, so that new meaning is brought about.

New meaning is brought out by the combination of known terms and concepts, which still carry their old meaning with them. In fact, the new meaning of language does not mean the extinction of former meanings of the elements of language, but they are put together in a poetic way so that they mean more than merely the sum of the single elements. Programmatically this is shown in v.3, where the evangelist sets the agenda for the whole discourse by introducing a strong metaphor: 'no one can see the Kingdom of God without being born from above.' Both elements can be understood by everybody familiar with religious language of that time, so the metaphor is comprehensible, provided that the hearer knows that the mode of speech is metaphorical. Starting from this metaphor, the evangelist introduces more and more known concepts, which he combines with the initial metaphor, thus unfolding ever new meaning until he arrives at his theology in a nutshell, which is expressed only in figurative language.

As Heidegger suggested, language gathers up things, i.e. it collects the whole world of that what is said.[425] Thus, the content of meaning remains with the language when languages are combined into a new one, and the new language entails the worlds of the old languages. Therefore, the creative and gathering language of the passage which I studied here is essentially open to other language-worlds and has the ability to transform them. This openness is an important feature that has to be brought out by exegesis. If this general openness of the text is recognised, one sees that the text is not open only to the worlds from which its language is taken, but it is open to different languages in general, and it can relate to the different worlds of these languages. Nevertheless, to make possible an encounter between the modern interpreter and biblical texts, the texts need to be translated, so that they are able to speak into today's world and transform it by adding new meaning to it.

---

[425] Cf. above, p. 36 and Thiselton; *Two Horizons*, 337-340.

Chapter 8

The Final Prayer: John 17

Introduction

The great final prayer in John 17 lends itself as the third of our textual studies. The first text we interpreted, the hymn which is contained in the prologue to John's Gospel, represents, as I have shown, a very early stage of Johannine theology. The hymn was embedded in the Gospel, the main body of which displays a distinctive theology again. A fine example of this stage of the development of Johannine thought is the Nicodemus Discourse, which we discussed in the second case-study. The final prayer, or the 'High-Priestly-Prayer', as it is traditionally called, not only represents the last stage of theological reflection to be found in John's Gospel, but it also contains a remarkably comprehensive and distinguished theological approach, which is arguably one of the most fascinating of all that can be found in the New Testament. In John 17, a highly condensed language is developed to express the Johannine circle's interpretation of Christianity, or, in other words, what the presence of the living Christ means for the life of the community and, not least, for the church through all generations.

We have seen that the hymn is strongly influenced by Philonic or similar thought.[426] In the Nicodemus Discourse the main influences were traditional Christian thought, apocalyptic thought — especially embodied in the Son of Man concept — and a strong element of Gnostic thought, which we have found in the Hermetic parallels to the concept of supernatural regeneration.[427] In this chapter, I am going to establish the particular interpretation of Christian faith which John 17 offers and to ascertain how Johannine thought developed the language of faith which it had taken over from its forebears. As we will see, certain strands of Johannine thought, namely the Gnostic current, gained more influence, whereas other strands disappeared. Furthermore, I shall analyse the influences on Johannine thought which helped to shape the particular language of John 17, identifying parallels in its contemporary religious thought, which will help to explain the particularities of the language of John 17. This will show how a developing

---

[426] Cf. above, pp.80f and 85f.
[427] Cf. above, pp.101f.

understanding of Christ leads to the further development of a language for faith within the Johannine community and Johannine theology.

Setting

It is broadly agreed among Johannine scholars that John 17 was inserted into the Gospel at a late stage,[428] and there is much evidence for this assumption. First, the whole Farewell Discourses after John 14:31 seem to be a later addition in different stages. John 18 connects perfectly with 14:31 ('Rise, let us be on our way'. 'After Jesus had spoken these words, he went out with his disciples across the Kidron valley…'), and chs15-17 interrupts the plausible flow of the narrative, so that chs15-17 are likely to be an insertion.[429] We can then discern different layers of redaction in the Farewell Discourses. However, I am not going to discuss the genesis of the Farewell Discourses here, but restrict myself to discuss the position of ch.17 within the Farewell Discourses and the Gospel.[430]

Within John's Gospel, and even as within the Farewell Discourses, John 17 stands out quite remarkably. As we will see, there are important theological differences between the main body of the Gospel and the Farewell Discourses on the one hand and the final prayer on the other. John 17 cannot have been part of the Gospel before the addition to the Farewell Discourses chs15-16, because ch.17 does not at all connect with 14:31, but it connects relatively smoothly with 16:33. Therefore, John 17 must have been inserted either together with the Farewell Discourses or afterwards.[431] There is also a certain development of theological thinking, which can be traced from the main body of the gospel to the Farewell Discourses. The final prayer represents an even later stage of this development. Thus it is likely that, after the composition of the main body of John's Gospel, the Farewell Discourses have been inserted and then, in a final stage, the final prayer of John 17, which represents the last stage of distinctive Johannine theology (before the ecclesiastical redaction) known to us.

---

[428] Cf. Becker, Jürgen; 'Aufbau, Schichtung und theologiegeschichtliche Stellung des Gebetes in Johannes 17' *ZNW* 60, 1969, 56-83; Brown; *John 2*, 582-588; Painter, John; 'The Farewell Discourses and the History of Johannine Christianity' *NTS* 27 (1980-81) 525-543, Schnackenburg, Rudolf; *Das Johannesevangelium*, Vol.3, HTKNT 4/3, Freiburg (Herder) 1976, 190, 230f.

[429] Cf. Becker, Jürgen; 'Die Abschiedsreden Jesu im Johannesevangelium' *ZNW* 61, 1970, 215-246.

[430] For this question cf. Becker; 'Abschiedsreden' and Painter; 'Farewell Discourses'.

[431] Cf. Dietzfelbinger, Christian; *Der Abschied des Kommenden: Eine Auslegung der johanneischen Abschiedreden*, WUNT 95, Tübingen (Mohr-Siebeck) 1997, 12-16.

An important question for the understanding of the prayer in John 17 is its setting. The situation described in the prayer is that of departure. Jesus is praying in front of his disciples when the *hour*, the time of his passion and glorification, has arrived. The place of the prayer within the gospel underlines this setting; just after the Farewell Discourses and before the Passion-narrative. There are, however, indications that this fictional setting of the prayer is not carried out consistently. In this passage, Jesus does not speak as the earthly Jesus anymore, but already as the glorified Christ.[432] Verse 4, for example, expresses that Jesus has already fulfilled his task, yet he can only say 'τετέλεσται', 'it is finished', when he dies after his suffering (19:30). In addition, the glorification of Christ in the church, as it is mentioned in v.10, is only possible after the resurrection, when the disciples really understand who Jesus is. Furthermore, vv.11 and 12a describe Jesus as already having left the world, although he is still talking to his disciples. Finally, the mission of the church in v.18, which is expressed in the Aorist, can take place only after Easter. This leads us to the assumption that it is not only the Johannine Jesus speaking here, but also the Johannine church at the end of the first century. Their experiences and context are dealt with by this prayer, which is a prayer of Christ, who is present with and in his church and intercedes for it at the Father's throne. The horizons between the pre-Easter Jesus and the post-Easter Christ are completely fused, a feature which is common in John's Gospel.[433] Therefore, we cannot interpret this prayer as really spoken in the situation of departure or as intended to be read as such, as this would lead to grave misinterpretations. It is meant to be spoken by the already glorified Christ who is interceding for his church, as well as by the earthly Jesus just before his passion. The Johannine church gained the authority to fuse the horizons between the earthly Jesus and the glorified Christ, and to insert their context and concerns into the gospel by the presence of the Paraclete in the church, which authorised them to speak in the name of the glorified Christ.[434]

---

[432] Cf. Dietzfelbinger; *Der Abschied des Kommenden*, 258-261.

[433] Cf. Onuki, Takashi; *Gemeinde und Welt im Johannesevangelium*, WMANT 56, Neukirchen-Vluyn (Neukirchener Verlag) 1984, 167-173 and Käsemann, Ernst; *Jesu letzter Wille nach Johannes 17*, Tübingen (Mohr-Siebeck) ⁴1980, 16-20.

[434] Cf. Dietzfelbinger, Christian; 'Paraklet und theologischer Anspruch im Johannesevangelium' *ZTK* 82 (1985), 389-408, 402-408. Cf. also above, pp.77f.

Structure

The structure of John 17 has always been seen as a problem, and so a multitude of different structures has been suggested.[435] However, the attempts to find a coherent outline in John 17 have shown that it is virtually impossible to achieve a consistent structure of this text without violating the text by too many literary-critical operations. The major obstacle to finding a coherent structure in this passage is that the different motifs in this prayer are interwoven and cross-linked, so that they cannot be separated clearly. Dietzfelbinger suggested that the prayer lacks a clear structure, but consists of four motif-'circles', which are situated around central imperatives.[436] These motif-'circles' are not closed against each other, but they may overlap and allow anticipation of later or recurrence of earlier motifs. This structure of the passage enables the interpreter to take seriously the particular form of this text whilst, at least partly, satisfying the interpreter's desire for structured exegesis.

> The first 'circle' extends from vv.1-5 and is situated around the imperative 'glorify!' (δόξασον; v.1b,5). The Subject of this 'circle' is the mutual glorification of Father and Son after the Son has finished his task.
>
> The second 'circle' includes vv.6-13. It surrounds the imperative 'protect!' (τήρησον; v.11) and deals, mainly, with the preservation of the church in the *name* (ὄνομα) of the Father.
>
> The third 'circle' stretches from vv.14-19 and focuses on the imperative 'sanctify!' (ἁγίασον; v.17). It addresses the subject of the sanctification of the church in the *word* (λόγος) and the *truth* (ἀλήθεια).
>
> The fourth 'circle' consists of the vv.20-26 with the imperative-like form 'I want that...' (θέλω ἵνα; v.24) as its centre. Its topic is the unity and perfection of the church.

These four circles are not, however, proper sections, but loose gatherings of thought around key motifs, in which anticipation and repetition is possible. For example, the term ὄνομα (name) is connected with the τήρησον (protect!) of v.11 and occurs again in v.26. The term λόγος (word) dominates the third circle around the imperative ἁγίασον (sanctify! v.17), yet it is used already in v.6.[437] In addition, what is said about the *name* and the *logos* 'penetrates and supplements each other.'[438] This particular outline of the prayer John 17, which does not show any clear structure, underlines

---

435 For a good summary cf. Becker; 'Aufbau' 56-61.
436 Cf. Dietzfelbinger; *Der Abschied des Kommenden*, 266-269.
437 Ibid.
438 Ibid. 9.

the overall meditative character of the piece and its particular use of language.

Interpretation

Prayer for Glorification (17:1-5)

After the introduction to the prayer (v.1a), Jesus declares that the *hour* has arrived. He prays that the Father may glorify him, so that he may glorify the Father. Without much introduction, Jesus goes directly *in medias res* and asks for what is the central point of this prayer: glorification. The first petition is, in fact, so central to the whole prayer, that one can assume that it is the main petition and the following are its expositions.[439] Although the motif of glorification is familiar in John's Gospel, it is never systematised the way it is in the final prayer. The motif of Jesus being glorified by the Father occurs in 7:39, 12:16,23, and John 13:31 knows of a mutual glorification of Father and Son. However, the motif is not explored in such a comprehensive way as in ch.17.

The glorification of the Son, through which the Father is glorified, takes place in 'the hour', which is the time of Jesus' passion. The hour is introduced and explained in 12:23-25: 'The hour has come for the Son of Man to be glorified. Very truly, I tell you, unless a grain of wheat falls into the earth and dies, it remains just a single grain; but if it dies, it bears much fruit [...].' It is the time when Jesus will be glorified through his passion and death. This thought is presupposed and further developed in this passage. The hour is the time when Jesus has fulfilled the task which has been given to him by the Father (v.4), which is the time when he can say 'it is finished' and die (19:30) . Through the fulfilment of Jesus' task Father and Son are glorified in one another. In the first circle of the prayer in John 17, the understanding of Jesus' ministry up to his crucifixion is established: Jesus is the messenger, who has been sent by the Father and who has been given the Father's *authority* (ἐξουσία), the right of disposal of God's own rights, in order to fulfil the task that has been given to him (cf. v.2).[440] Interestingly, in John 17, Jesus' task is different from that in the main body of the gospel. In this passage, his task is to give eternal life to those given to him by the Father. The universal perspective, which we have seen in the Nicodemus Discourse, where Jesus has come for the judgement of the world, has gone out of the focus here. In the dialogue with Nicodemus,

---

[439] Cf. Becker; 'Aufbau' 69 and Becker; *Johannesevangelium*, 617f.

[440] Cf. Bühner, Jan-Adolf; *Der Gesandte und sein Weg im 4. Evangelium*, WUNT 2/2, Tübingen (Mohr-Siebeck), 1977, 194.

Jesus is described as coming into the world as the *light*, so that in the encounter with him the world must decide for or against him, and thus is
judged. This whole event is an expression of God's love to the world
(cf.3:16f, 12:47). In John 17, however, Jesus seems only to be in the world to
gather those that belong to him, those who have been given to him by the
Father. A certain shift in the significance of Jesus takes place here. This
becomes particularly clear in v.2. Though Jesus has the authority over all
flesh, his task is only to gather his own and bring them eternal life. The
universal *krisis* makes space for the collecting of his own. This shift is also a
shift towards a more radical doctrine of predestination.

In the main body of the gospel, there is a certain tension between predestination and the decision between belief and unbelief. In the *krisis*,
which is the self-revelation of Jesus, the decision between acceptance and
rejection, belief and unbelief takes place.[441] Certainly, this decision is not a
human possibility, as the language of the supernatural regeneration in
chapter 3 suggests. In John 17, however, the decision does not take place in
the *krisis*, but only by the will of the Father, who has given a part of all flesh
to the Son, who gives, in turn, eternal life to this group. We will have to
return to this question later, after having established the wider cosmological framework of John 17.

The term ἐξουσία (authority) is used in the same way as in the main
body of the gospel. It is used twice before in connection with Jesus: on the
first occasion (5:27), the Father has given the Son authority to judge the
world. The second time it occurs in 10:18, Jesus has authority to lay down
his life and to take it again. Both instances are God's very own right, which
has been handed over to Jesus, in order to enable him to fulfil his task as
God's messenger. The giving of authority over all flesh is consistent with
this understanding. There is, however, an enormous development from the
view of the authority of the earthly Jesus in Mark's gospel. Here, Jesus has
the authority to teach, to perform healings and exorcisms and to forgive
sins. Matthew attributes the full divine authority only to the risen Christ.[442]
The full divine ἐξουσία, however, is attributed to the earthly Jesus nowhere
else in the New Testament but in John's Gospel. Thus, a much deeper understanding of Jesus Christ is achieved in Johannine theology. The first
traces of this can be found in the prologue, where the church is able to see
the divine glory (δόξα) in the incarnate Word through the flesh. This insight has been carried out and, in the main body of the gospel, the full divine δόξα and ἐξουσία apply to the earthly Jesus.

---

441 Cf. Becker; *Johannesevangelium*, 620.
442 Cf. Broer, Ingo; 'ἐξουσία' EWNT II, 23-29, 25f.

Verse 3 is a later, redactional insertion into the prayer,[443] which explains the meaning of αἰώνιος ζωή (eternal life) and is designed to guard against misinterpretations. Eternal life consists of the recognition that Jesus Christ is sent by the Father. The direct connection of the name 'Jesus' and the title 'Christ' occurs only three times in John's Gospel, the first time in the redactional addition to the prologue 1:17, then at this place 17:3, and, finally, in the first ending of the gospel, 20:31, where the purpose of the gospel is given and described as 'so you may believe that Jesus is the Christ.' The connection of 'Jesus' and 'Christ' seems to have become the core of the christological argument, which is addressed in 1 John 2:18-25. The dissenters from the Johannine community seem to deny the identity of the Christ with Jesus, and thus the title Jesus Christ occurs six times in 1 John. It is possible that the insertion of v.3 is a result of this christological argument, inserted to guard the right understanding of the concept of eternal life against the opponents of 1 John.

Prayer for Preservation (17:6-13)

The revelation of the name *and the* word *(vv.6-8)* The second petition of the final prayer can be divided into three groups: Revelation of the *name* (ὄνομα) and the *logos* (v.6-8); distinction of and reason for the petition (v.9-11a); content of and another reason for the petition (v.11b-13).[444] The first group describes how the glorification of the Father, which had been the subject of v.4, takes place. The Son has revealed the Father's name to the people whom the Father has given to him. The most striking feature v.6 is that Jesus has revealed the Father's name only to those who have been given to him. In the main body of the gospel, the Son reveals himself as the divine messenger to all the world, and in this revelation the *krisis*, the judgement takes place. Thus while, in the main body of the gospel, the revelation is to the whole cosmos, here, in John 17, it is restricted to a certain group out of the cosmos which has been given to the Son. The rest of the world is not addressed by the revelation at all. In a way, the universal significance of Jesus is played down in John 17; he has not come into the world for the *krisis* of the world, but to reveal the divine name to those who belong to him.

The *name* of the Father is God as he can be perceived and understood by humanity.[445] The name of the Father is revealed by Jesus through his

---

443 Cf. Becker; *Johannesevangelium*, 615, 621; Brown; *John 2*, 741.

444 Cf. Dietzfelbinger; *Der Abschied des Kommenden*, 292.

445 Cf. Bietenhard, H.; 'ὄνομακτλ.' *ThWNT* V, 242-283, 271 and Untergassmair, Franz-Georg; *Im Namen Jesu: Der Namensbegriff im Johannesevangelium*, FB 13,

proclamation (ῥήματα, v.8+9) and through the fulfilment of his task as the messenger, which is his earthly ministry up to his death on the cross. Through these elements of revelation, those who are given to Jesus can see who God really is and live in communion with him. An important element of the divine name is the *oneness* of the Son with the Father, the fact that Jesus, who revealed God's will and died on the cross, is sent by the Father and is one with him. As we will see later in the discussion of the Prayer for Unity and Perfection (17:20-end), this oneness between the Father and the Son is extended to those belonging to the Son.

It is interesting to observe that there are important parallels between the use of the concept ὄνομα (name) in John 17 and in the Gnostic *Gospel of Truth* (*Evangelium Veritatis*, EvVer).[446]

> When, therefore, it pleased him that his name which is loved should be his Son, and he gave the name to him, that is, him who came forth from the depth, he spoke about his secret things, knowing that the Father is without evil. For that very reason he brought him forth in order to speak about the place and his restingplace from which he had come forth.[447]
>
> [...] teach those who will receive teaching. But those who are to receive teaching [are] the living who are inscibed in the book of the living.[6-10] Then, if one has knowledge, he receives what are his own and draws them to himself.[448]

These parallels become even more significant if we consider that, in John 17, the revelation is only to those given to Jesus by the Father, not the whole world as in the main body of the gospel. This is not to say that John 17 is a Gnostic text, as there are too many important differences from the EvVer for John 17 to be fully Gnostic. However, the author of John 17 takes up patterns of thought in order to develop his understanding Christianity which come close to Gnosticism. Already in our discussion of the Nicodemus Discourse we have seen that there are affinities between Johannine thought and Gnosticism,[449] and this influence increases to the level we find in John 17. Struggling for language to understand Christian faith in its own spiritual and social environment led Johannine Christianity into this dangerous closeness to Gnosticism. As 1 John illustrates, this closeness to Gnostic thought contributed to the Gnostic dissent from the Johannine community.

Stuttgart (Katholisches Bibelwerk) 1974, 79f. Cf. also Hartmann, Lars; 'ὄνομα' EWNT II, 1268-1278, 1271.

[446] Cf. Untergassmair: *Im Namen Jesu*, 291-305.

[447] EvVer 40:23-29: (Translation from Robinson, James M. (ed.); *The Nag Hammadi Library in English*, San Francisco (Harper & Row) [3]1988, 50).

[448] EvVer 21:1-5, 11-14.

[449] Cf. above, p.101.

There is, however, one most important difference between Gnostic and Johannine thought. Whilst EvVer knows only of a mythological revealer without real existence, John 17 uses Gnosticising cosmology and understanding of revelation in relation to a historical figure, Jesus, and uses Gnostic concepts to understand the historical event of Jesus' crucifixion. If the connection between the historical figure of Jesus and the heavenly Christ is broken, then this theology becomes truly Gnostic. As long as this link is kept, however, the appropriation of this kind of thought can be understood as an extremely daring approach to understanding the truth of Jesus Christ more deeply and more fully.

Another important difference between EvVer and John 17 is that the teaching in EvVer is actually about the human self. 'It is about themselves that they receive instruction, receiving it from the Father, turning again to him.'[450] EvVer teaches about the true heavenly origin of the human soul, which has to return there, whereas John 17 is talking about redemption of the chosen from a radically fallen world. It must be noted that John 17 is placed within John's Gospel, which contains the notion about the world being divine creation and its fallenness.[451] Jesus is the redeemer who comes into a fallen world in order to bring salvation, which is outside the human self and brought about through faith in him, rather than to bring knowledge about the heavenly origin of the human soul and the way back to this original state. John 17 is about faith in Jesus as the one who is sent by the Father rather than about knowledge about human nature.

Verse 6 returns to the motif of the Father giving a group out of the world to the Son. The Father, equipping the Son for his task as the messenger, gives him some people out of his own property. Again, it is interesting to notice that only those who have held God's word, which is Jesus' proclamation of himself being the Father's messenger, are given to the Son. The rest are ignored and belong somewhere else. The *logos*, the proclamation those belonging to the Son have held, is explained in v.7: everything Jesus has said and done is from the Father, thus that he is really sent by the Father. Verse 8b.c. makes the same point. The subject of Christian faith, as John 17 understands it, is to recognise that Jesus came from the Father and to believe that he has really been sent. Only Jesus' proclamation, his ῥήματα, is mentioned explicitly here. However, it is important to note that Jesus is not seen only as an authoritative teacher, as he proclaims *himself* and his relation to the Father. To accept his words therefore means to accept him as the true messenger. In addition, we must not forget that the whole prayer John 17 is set in the *hour*. The hour of Jesus' suffering and

---

450 EvVer 21:5-8.
451 Cf. above, p.76.

death is among what the Son is given by the Father. To lose sight of this connection leads, inevitably, to the Gnostic misunderstanding of Johannine Christology. Faith means, for John 17 as well as for the rest of John's Gospel, that Jesus, the teacher who ended his career on the cross and died there, is the Christ, the divine messenger with all authority given to him. As this motif is repeated again and again in John 17, it must be a major concern of the author and, probably his community.

Distinction of the Petition and its Reason (vv.9-11a) Verse 9 distinguishes the object of the petition; Jesus does not pray for the world, but only for those the Father has given to him. The reason is given in the ὅτι-clause: because they are his (i.e. God's) own. This idea seems, at first glance, inconsistent with the rest of the gospel and also with v.2 of ch.17 ('...since you have given him authority over all flesh...'). Verse 9 can be read so that only those belonging to the church belong to the Father, while the rest of the world does not belong to him but somewhere else, which is not elaborated here. This would imply a metaphysical dualism between those belonging to God and those who do not, which is unlikely to be part of Johannine thought. In fact, v.2 as well as the whole development of Johannine theology make this interpretation impossible. Thus, the 'ὅτι σοί εἰσιν' (because they are yours) refers to the positive relation between God and the church and not to the negative relation between him and the world. The church belongs to God and to Christ in the sense of v.2, i.e. that the Son has authority over the whole world, so that he may give eternal life to his own.

It is surprising that a church can pray or a theologian can let Jesus pray only for the church and not for the world, especially in such an eminent position as in the final prayer in John 17. This rejection of the world can only be explained by the growth of a dualistic world-view. We recall that, in John 3:16, Jesus' coming into the world is seen as an act of God's love for the world, whereas here, in John 17, the world is completely rejected and not even worth intercession. This development of thought, and in this context the use of the concept of the ὄνομα (name) and its revelation to the church, suggests an important step toward Gnosticism. Statements such as v.9, in particular, including the clause 'because they are yours' (ὅτι σοί εἰσιν), are very close to that school of thought which the church will rule out as heretical later in its struggle against Gnosticism. The Johannine *Struggle for Language* has reached a critical stage, and 1 John bears witness to the dangers involved in this kind of language.

Verse 10 concludes the sentence and qualifies the ὅτι σοί εἰσιν-clause. Since everything that belongs to Jesus belongs to the Father, and vice versa, the special relation between Jesus and the church, which is that its members were given to him by the Father, extends also to the church's relation to the Father. It is a new aspect in Johannine theology that Jesus is glorified in the church. Is has been assumed that Jesus is glorified in the church because it is the visible evidence that he has fulfilled his task.[452] This is certainly an important element of Jesus' glorification in the church, although v.10b must be read in the light of v.18, which speaks of the sending of the church into the world to continue Jesus' task. As Jesus proclaimed himself and as in the encounter with his proclamation the world is judged, so the church proclaims Jesus as God's Son and messenger, and so continues Jesus' ministry. Thus in the encounter with the risen Christ through the proclamation of the church, those who belong to God are gathered. In this respect Jesus is present in the church, his glory is perceived and proclaimed only here, so that he is glorified within and through the church.[453]

The prayer continues with the reason why the prayer is so urgent. Jesus is leaving the world and the church will be left behind. Yet the church is not part of the world and is alien to it, as Jesus was an alien in the world. While Jesus' ministry ends with his return to the Father, to the place where he belongs, he leaves the church behind, as the place where he is glorified and as the successor to his mission. This leaves the church in a dangerous position, and the prayer for its preservation is urgent.

Verse 11a ('And now I am no longer in the world...') is important as a connection between the introduction to the petition in v.9f and the petition itself (v.11b), and constitutes a climax in the description of the background of the petition. Verse 11a produces an additional tension which is resolved by the petition: the church is founded on Jesus' revelation of the Father's *logos* and *name* (v.6) and it is an alien in a hostile world (v.9, expanded in v.16). The situation of the church in the world is contrasted by the close relation between Father and Son as well as by the glorification of the Son in the church; the church is Jesus' foundation in a hostile world. As a response, v.11a introduces the urgent demand for the petition: Jesus is going back where he belongs and leaves the church in the world. Thus the author builds up a tension between the heavenly foundation of the church in a hostile world on the one hand and the going away of its founder on the other. Therefore it is urgent and necessary to take measures to preserve the church in the world. The action Jesus takes is to pray to the Father for the preservation of the church.

---

452 Cf. Becker; *Johannesevangelium*, 624. Similar Schnackenburg; *Johannesevangelium III*, 203.

453 Cf. Bultmann; *Johannesevangelium*, 383f, and Dietzfelbinger; *Der Abschied des Kommenden*, 298.

Content of and another Reason for the Petition (vv.11b-13) After this introduction, the petition itself is vital for the church. The church cannot survive in the world on its own, because it is not of the world, left behind by its founder, JesusChrist. It is remarkable that the church is to be protected in the *name* of the Father rather than through the Paraclete, who has this task in the rest of the Farewell Discourses (Cf. 14:16+26; 15:26; 16:7+13). Here, the preservation of the church in the *name* of the Father seems to take over the function of the assistance and preservation through the spirit. Here, an important shift in the language about the preservation of the church takes place. While, in the main body of the gospel and in the Farewell Discourses, the church saw itself protected and assisted through a divine helper, who inspired them to act as a church and mediated the presence of Christ in the church,[454] this task is now fulfilled by the possession of God's name. This does not exclude divine guidance, but this does not happen through inspiration anymore, but through knowledge of the divine nature, which is *oneness*. The more dynamic concept of the inspiration through the Paraclete has been replaced by the static concept of the possession of God's name.

Verse 12 reflects further on the subject of preservation in the Father's name. Because Jesus is not physically present amongst his own anymore, he cannot preserve them in the Father's name as he did while he was amongst them. The church has to be guarded against leaving the communion with the Father and the Son in the Father's name, hence against its becoming a part of the world again. The fear, against which this petition is a reaction, is not the fear of persecution or failure in the church's mission, but that of not living according to God's name anymore, that of becoming worldly again. Thus, the focus of the petition is, like that of the whole prayer, inward looking; the global perspective of the main body of the gospel and the Farewell Discourses has been lost. The church seems only concerned with its own salvation. Certainly, through the insertion of ch.17 into the gospel, the connection to the more outward-looking language of the main body of John's Gospel has been made, but this notion seems not to be an issue for the Johannine community anymore. The community is mainly concerned with what is happening inside, it is not afraid of the world as a persecutor anymore, but it sees it as an ensnaring and seductive power, which may lead the church astray, so that it becomes like the world and thus ceases to be the church.

Another important difference to the rest of John's Gospel is that, after Jesus' departure, the church is alone in the world and needs to be protected by the Father because the Son is not present anymore. It seems that for the

---

[454] Cf. Becker; *Johannesevangelium*, 625.

author of John 17, Jesus' mission to the church ends with his departure to the Father, and the Father has to care for the orphaned church, while, in the main body of the gospel, the glorification of Christ is the coincidence of Easter, Pentecost and Parousia, through which Christ is eternally present in and for his church.[455] In the final prayer, Jesus' mission seems to be to reveal his oneness with the Father and to draw the church into it. After he has fulfilled it, the church is commissioned to continue this mission and gains the necessary protection from the Father. The focal point of thought has shifted from Christology to the doctrine of God. The result of Jesus' departure to the Father is, that the church lives in the perfect joy (χαρά) of being part of the oneness between the Father and the Son (v.13). This joy is given to the church by the revelation Jesus has given, this joy is now part of the church's being, and thus it needs to be maintained in this state of joy. To have joy apparently means to be the final state of salvation, in which the church has to be maintained. This type of language is paralleled by the concept of *rest* in the EvVer,[456] where the aim of revelation is to give *rest* to its recipients. Through the revelation of the divine *name* the recipient receives *gnosis* (knowledge) and *rest*. In turn, being in the state of *rest* is having *gnosis* and thus salvation. Again, John 17 has developed a language very similar to that of Gnostic writings, although it is definitely Christian and not Gnostic. The author of John 17 uses this language in order to describe what Christ means to him and his community in their particular surroundings, and the possibilities of this language for expressing Christian faith are explored.

Verse 12b is a likely redactional insertion. The expression Son of Perdition (ὁ υἱὸς τῆς ἀπωλείας) is a Semitism[457] and a *hapax legomenon* in the Johannine writings.[458] In addition, the whole of v.12b disturbs the order and structure of the prayer; it explains something to the reader rather than being part of the reason for the petition.[459] The phrase 'and guard' (καὶ ἐφύλαξα) is a superfluous double-expression to 'protect' (ἐτήρουν). There is no other expression of one point through two synonymous verbs in John 17. In addition, there is no other allusion to a perspective of salvation history in this prayer, as it is expressed in the remark 'so that the scripture may be fulfilled' (ἵνα ἡ γραφὴ πληρωθῇ). Thus there is much evidence that 12b is a later insertion, trying to deal with the problem of Judas, the one who has been lost despite Jesus preserving his church during his earthly ministry. It is not impossible that this insertion reflects the problem of

---

455 Cf. Becker; *Johannesevangelium*, 625.
456 Cf. Untergassmair; *Im Namen Jesu*, 270-275.
457 Cf. Brown; *John 2*, 760; Barrett; *John*, 508f.
458 Cf. Becker; 'Aufbau' 74.
459 Cf. Becker; 'Aufbau' 73f.

people leaving or betraying the church, which must be a significant theological problem for a community which sees itself in such a close relation
to God as the Johannine does. Possibly, the division of the Johannine
church, which is subject of 1 John, is already at the horizon here.

Prayer for Sanctification (17:14-19)

Verse 14 continues the motif of vv.6-8, of Jesus giving the divine *logos*. The
church has been given the *logos*, and therefore is not of the world anymore.
Since the church is not of the world, but embodies the word and mission of
Christ, it is a challenge to the world, just as Jesus was a challenge, and the
world must hate it. As the church has been described as left orphaned in
the world in the previous petition, it is now addressed as threatened by the
world. The natural reaction to being hated and threatened by the world,
and really belonging elsewhere, would be to go away or to be taken away
to the place where the church belongs, which is in unity with the Father
and the Son. But this possibility is explicitly rejected. The church must stay
in the world, although it sees itself as a stranger here, and must continue
the mission of Jesus to bear witness to the unity of the Son with the Father
and to testify that the Son is truly sent by the Father. What the church
therefore needs is protection within the world. Next, Jesus asks for protection against the evil or the evil one. Although the genitive τοῦ πονηροῦ can
be understood as a neuter, meaning 'from evil' it is likely that it is gram-
matically masculine and thus means the evil one, the devil.[460] In the context
of John 17, the devil cannot be a mythological figure, but it must be the
metaphorical personification of evil, and a breaking away from the truth in
particular. The church is not to be protected against the hatred of the
world, but from falling into perdition because of the world's hatred. God is
asked to preserve those he has chosen and given to the Son, so that they do
not break away from the truth in face of the world. This general understanding of the church within the world is repeated in v.16, which is a
quotation of v.14b. It could be a secondary insertion as a doublet to v.14b,
but it could also be that 14b and 16 form an inclusion around v.15 in order
to underline the relevance of the rejection of taking the church out of the
world but letting it stay in the world though protected from the evil.

The petition itself follows in v.17. It explains also what the protection of
the church from the evil means: holiness. Ἁγιάζω can mean 'to sanctify' as
well as 'to consecrate' and 'to purify.' It is closely linked with v.19, where
Jesus states that he sanctifies/consecrates himself so that the church will be
sanctified/consecrated. In the context of this petition, this term must mean
separation from the world, belonging to God rather than to the world. It is

---

[460] Cf. Becker; *Johannesevangelium*, 625f. Cf. also Brown; *John 2*, 761.

connected with being in the truth, because the sanctification/consecration takes place in the truth (v.17), which is God's word. Therefore, being *holy* is living in the word rather than in the world. The cause for holiness is Jesus' departure from the world and return to the Father. As Jesus is speaking in the context of the *hour*, which is given in v.1b, the sanctification and consecration of Jesus can only refer to his following Passion and return to the Father.[461] The church is founded by his departure, which is, at the same time, his sanctification/consecration, because it causes the church to be holy, i.e. not to be of the world, separated from it and to be one with the Father and the Son. Therefore, the petition aims at the church being maintained in its state of otherworldliness, in its opposition to the world and being hated by the world, yet living in a state of divine joy.

In this state of holiness, the church continues Jesus' mission (v.18). As the Son has been sent by the Father, so the church is sent by the Son. Thus it bears witness to the unity of the Father and the Son and to its own unity with the Father and the Son. As Jesus drew those people to himself who were given to him by the Father and, by means of the divine *logos*, enabled them to live out of the world in a state of joy and oneness, the church is now the divine messenger. It constitutes a scandal to the world, and thus it must be rejected. Only those who have been given to Christ by the Father, will listen to the church proclaiming the unity of the Father and the Son and the sonship of Jesus, and accept the church's word, which is the same as the word of Jesus. It is important to recognise that, in John 17, the church is not sent to the world, but it exists only to continue Jesus' mission, which is to gather those belonging to him and give them the name of the Father, so that they can participate in the communion with God and the state of joy.[462] Similarly, the coming of Jesus Christ into the world has a different significance in John 17 than elsewhere in the gospel. The mission of the church means something different in the final prayer than in the rest of the gospel. In the Johannine writing earlier than John 17, the Christian mission is to make faith possible in the world through the church's proclamation. Jesus came into the world to proclaim the judgement of the whole world, so that the decision of belief and unbelief may take place in the event. The theological thrust of the main body of the gospel is, on the whole, positive toward mission.[463] John 17, however, does not display such a positive concept of mission; the church appears to be more closed up in itself. Accordingly, the world is not the whole of humanity anymore, which is to be addressed, so that the κρίσις takes place; rather, it is just the crowd, from

---

[461] Cf. Becker; *Johannesevangelium*, 626-628.

[462] Cf. Becker; 'Aufbau' 79f.

[463] Cf. Becker; *Johannesevangelium*, 216-221.

which the elect have to be gathered. The emphasis in the concept of mission has significantly changed toward a more dualistic perception of the world. Or, in other words, the world is only the place where the gathering of the elect happens and is not the object of divine love.[464]

Although I have emphasised the differences between John 17 and the rest of John's Gospel, it must not be forgotten that John 17 is a part of John's Gospel and has been inserted into it purposefully. Therefore, it would be wrong to say that it contradicts the theology of gospel, but it definitely sets a different accent. We can see how Johannine thought developed in a direction that brought it dangerously close to Gnosticism, and in the process many aspects of Johannine theology were treated rather differently. Nevertheless, these new viewpoints are all a legitimate part of the Johannine tradition. Therefore, they can be inserted into John's Gospel, and produce a tension between the different approaches. The placing of John 17 within John's Gospel produces a tension within the gospel, a tension which shows that Christian proclamation and theology is not anything static, but a dynamic development, a living voice, which speaks anew to each generation and is challenged by previous ways of speaking. No generation of Christians can see itself and its theology as absolute and binding for previous and later generations, but only as a particular attempt, on the grounds of its tradition, to understand the Christian Gospel for its own context. Each generation is thus part of the *Struggle for Language*, which continues throughout Christian history. The theologian has to cope with the tension of the different approaches towards Christianity, be challenged by them and define his or her own position without merely repeating what earlier generations have said, but to struggle for a language through which to express the Christian truth in his or her own world and context.

'What you have inherited from your fathers, acquire it to own it!'[465]

Prayer for Unity and Perfection (17:20-end)

The final prayer continues with the fourth and final petition, that for the unity and perfection of the church. The subject of the unity of the church through the generations (v.20f) connects very well with my previous reflections. Nevertheless, I suppose that something different is envisaged

---

[464] Cf. EvVer 21f (Robinson, *The Nag-Hammadi Library*, 42) Cf. Becker; *Johannesevangelium*, 627, who implicitly argues against Schottroff, Luise; *Der Glaubende und die feindliche Welt: Beobachtungen zum gnostischen Dualismus und seiner Bedeutung für Paulus und das Johannesevangelium*, WMANT 37, Neukirchen-Vluyn (Neukirchener Verlag) 1970, 283. Cf. also Käsemann, Ernst; *Jesu letzter Wille nach Johannes 17*, Tübingen (Mohr-Siebeck) ⁴1980, 135.

[465] Goethe, Faust, 1. Scene: Night, vv.682f.

here. The first four verses of the fourth petition (vv.20-23) deal with the unity of the church, both with the horizontal and the vertical unity, i.e. the unity of the church within one generation and through the generations. These verses are structured in complex parallelisms. Vv.20f and 22f consist of one sentence each, which is divided into a main clause and three ἵνα- (so that-) clauses. The first ἵνα-clause is expanded by a comparative καθώς-clause, the final one is supplemented by complementary ὅτι-clauses. The structure becomes more clear through a synopsis of the two sentences: [466]

20f.:	22f.:
Οὐ περὶ τούτων δὲ ἐρωτῶ μόνον, ἀλλὰ καὶ περὶ τῶν πιστευόντων διὰ τοῦ λόγου αὐτῶν εἰς ἐμέ, <u>ἵνα</u> πάντες ἓν ὦσιν, <u>καθὼς</u> σύ, πάτερ, ἐν ἐμοὶ κἀγὼ ἐν σοί, <u>ἵνα</u> καὶ αὐτοὶ ἐν ἡμῖν ὦσιν, <u>ἵνα</u> ὁ κόσμος πιστεύῃ <u>ὅτι</u> σύ με ἀπέστειλας.	Κἀγὼ τὴν δόξαν ἣν δέδωκάς μοι δέδωκα αὐτοῖς, <u>ἵνα</u> ὦσιν ἓν <u>καθὼς</u> ἡμεῖς ἕν· ἐγὼ ἐν αὐτοῖς καὶ σὺ ἐν ἐμοί, <u>ἵνα</u> ὦσιν τετελειωμένοι εἰς ἕν, <u>ἵνα</u> γινώσκῃ ὁ κόσμος <u>ὅτι</u> σύ με ἀπέστειλας καὶ ἠγάπησας αὐτοὺς καθὼς ἐμὲ ἠγάπησας.
I ask not only on behalf these, but also on behalf of those who will believe in me through their word, <u>so that</u> they all may be one, <u>as</u> you, Father, are in me and I in them, <u>so that</u> they may also be in us, <u>so that</u> the world may believe <u>that</u> you have sent me.	And the glory which you have given me I give to them <u>so that</u> they may be one <u>as</u> we are one; I in them and you in me <u>so that</u> they may be completely one <u>so that</u> the world may know <u>that</u> you have sent me and have loved them as you have loved me.

Some have suggested that vv.20f is a later, redactional insertion and a doublet to 22f.[467] Yet the elaborate parallelism of vv.20f and 22f makes this unlikely. In my opinion, the very complex structure of a *parallelismus membrorum*, enlarged by paralleling not two short sentences, but enlarging the format into paralleling entire structures of thought,[468] points at a very careful composition. It is unique among the redactional insertions into John 17. In fact, there is no other doublet to be found in the whole of John's Gospel, which indicates that this is a careful and elaborate composition.[469] It is therefore more likely that vv.20-23 is an original composition of the author of ch.17. Even though the proclamation of the church is called *logos* nowhere else in John's Gospel, this unique use of *logos* for the church's

---

[466] Cf. Appold, Mark L.; *The Oneness Motif in the Fourth Gospel*, WUNT 2/1, Tübingen (Mohr-Siebeck) 1976, 157.

[467] Cf. Becker; *Johannesevangelium*, 617 and 'Aufbau' 74f. Cf. Also Schnackenburg; *Johannesevangelium III*, 214-216.

[468] Cf. Appold; *Oneness*, 158.

[469] Cf. Becker; *Johannesevangelium*, 617 and 'Aufbau' 74f.

proclamation has to be seen in the light of v.18. Since the church continues Jesus' mission, it is possible to identify the church's proclamation with that of Jesus; it is essentially the same. Therefore v.18 introduces an extraordinary thought, which is carried out in vv.20f. Finally, we have to consider, that nowhere else in John 17 is the second generation of disciples, those that come to faith, or better, those who are gathered by the proclamation of Jesus' direct disciples, addressed.[470] As a matter of fact, already in v.18 the coming to faith through the church's proclamation is envisaged, and v.20f carry out this motif. The aspect of unity of the church is addressed with respect to both those that are present in the fictional setting of John 17 and those who will be part of the church. True unity is horizontal and vertical, and so vv.20f are necessary. Thus, the unity, of which vv.22f speak, is the unity of all Christians of one generation and that of the church through the generations, from the first disciples to the Johannine community, to the church of the early twenty-first century, of which we are a part, and, finally, of the church of all generations to come. This is the universal perspective in which the language of unity in John 17 is meant to be seen.

Jesus asks for the unity of the church, of the present and of the future church. The unity is not just the being-together and accepting-each-other of the church, but has a metaphysical quality. Unity, or better, as Appold translates, *oneness*, is caused by the glory (δόξα), which the Father has given to the Son and the Son, in turn, has given to the church. Oneness of the church means to participate in the oneness of the Father and the Son, and this is perfection. Both sentences, 20f and 22f, address the main aspects of the proclamation within John 17; *oneness* of the Son with the Father and faith and understanding that the Son is truly sent by the Father. Therefore, to believe and to have understood that the Son is sent by the Father means to be one in and with Father and Son, which is *oneness* beyond loving communion, being metaphysical rather than sociological; it is the state of salvation rather than the loving communion of the church (cf. 13:34f).

Appold points out the Gnostic parallels to this concept of oneness.[471] He sums up his findings through an assessment of Gnostic literature:

> In the Gnostic context, however, the language of oneness receives its fullest and most specific function as the basic structural element intrinsic to a cosmological and soteriological interpretation of man and the world. Here oneness is explicated not as an abstract principle or in terms of personal transformation but as a soteriological state of being in separation from the world and in awareness of a given identity with the transcendent world.[472]

---

[470] Cf. Becker; 'Aufbau' 74f.

[471] Cf. Appold; *Oneness*, 166-174, 189-193.

[472] Appold; *Oneness*, 174.

This view of oneness in Gnostic literature is, in fact, very close to the concept of oneness in John 17. In both cases salvation is a state of being, which can be expressed through the language of oneness.[473] This is paralleled by the concept of joy (χαρά) in v.13, which is also seen as a soteriological state of the believer, in which to be is the aim of salvation. We have seen in the discussion of v.13, that this concept of soteriological joy is close to the Gnostic concept of calmness.[474] Through these parallels we can begin to understand the soteriology of John 17. Through having come to believe and having understood that Jesus is truly sent by the Father, and that the Father and the Son are one, which is only possible to those given to the Son by the Father, the believer reaches a state of salvation, which can be expressed through the language of *oneness* or that of *joy*. Thus, there is an important shift in the concept of salvation and the perception of the being of the believer. In the main body of the gospel, the κρίσις is the main element of the ministry of Jesus, and having faith in him, as the one who is lifted up at the cross (3:14f), leads to salvation and true faith in God (cf.12:44f). This faith is possible through the work of the Holy Spirit (3:6-8), which opens a loving communion between God and the believer (cf. 14:21) as well as within the church (cf. 13:34f). The Spirit also teaches the church (16:13) and is the agent of Christ's glorification (16:14). All these elements are not entirely excluded by the author of John 17, but his emphasis is completely different; John 17 sees Jesus as the one who gathers his own by proclaiming that he is truly sent by the Father and that the Father and he are one. Believing and having understood this, the believer is in the state of salvation and in metaphysical communion, which is a very different concept from that of the main body of the gospel, where the believer is not judged, but loved by God and guided by the Spirit. This is an important further development of the Gnostic elements which we have found already in the discussion of the Nicodemus Discourse. The other elements of Johannine theology are left in the background and are not further developed, but they make space for the full development of the Gnostic elements in Johannine theology.

How can we understand the Gnostic development of Johannine theology? Certainly, there was no such thing as a homogenous Gnostic movement, but there is a certain way of thinking which can be found in different appearances.[475] This particular way of thinking was not fully developed at the time when John's Gospel was written. Yet the different Gnostic traditions were evolving, and the main elements and concepts of Gnostic

---

[473] Cf. EvVer 24f+29 (Robinson, *The Nag-Hammadi Library*, 43f, 45).
[474] Cf. above, p.129.
[475] Cf. above, pp.65ff.

thought developed. Similarly, Christianity was not a unified movement at that time. The church as a defined group and discipline came about only after the Gnostic crisis. Before, we must assume that there were many cross-links between Gnosticising and Christian thought.[476] Partly, both movements developed in a parallel way and took up elements from each other. In order to understand Christianity in their own context, the Johannine 'theologians' took up elements from the developing Gnosis and interpreted their faith in these terms. That Johannine thought, as it is expressed in John 17, is still distinctly Christian has, I hope, become clear through the present considerations. Through the acceptance of earlier Johannine tradition and the linking of the final prayer with the Passion of Christ by setting it in the *hour*, John 17 can clearly be identified as interpreting Jesus' cross and resurrection and as struggling for a language to understand it, although it is pushing forward the boundaries in Christian thought and finds a radical solution to the Christian *Struggle for Language*.

In vv.21+23, the author lets Jesus say that the church is to be one as the Father and the Son, so the world may believe (v.21) and understand (v.23) that Jesus is sent by the Father. This may mean either that the author of John 17 is trying to regain a universal perspective of Jesus' and the church's mission, or that the world is merely the place where the evidence that the Son is sent by the Father is displayed. Are these clauses to be interpreted in the light of v.2 and v.9, or do they create a tension with the impetus of the rest of the prayer? It has been noted that it is hardly possible to harmonise the statements about the world in vv.21+23 with the view of the world expressed in the rest of the prayer.[477] In the rest of the prayer, the world is the world that rejects Christ and the church, whereas in vv.21+23 the Johannine community has not given up the hope for successful mission, despite its distance to the world and its dualistic understanding of the world. I suppose that a solution to the problem suggested by Ernst Käsemann is acceptable: the Johannine community has to continue the mission in the world in order to find those who are given to the Son by the Father, those who are elected to believe.[478] But the community cannot know who they are and how many, and therefore the church is sent into the world but not to the world. It aims, however, only at those who belong to Christ, yet everybody must be addressed in order to find out whether or not he or she actually belongs to Christ. Therefore, the community must show to the world that it is one, so that those who can understand, but are scattered all

---

476 Cf. Appold; *Oneness*, 190.
477 Schnackenburg; *Johannesevangelium III*, 218.
478 Käsemann; *Jesu letzter Wille*, 135f.

over the world, may see and join the church in its joy and oneness with the Father and the Son.

The prayer is concluded with the final section vv.24-26. That it comes to its conclusion is indicated by the invocation 'Father' at the beginning of v.24. Here we find the fourth petition itself, expressed not through an imperative like the previous three, but through the phrase 'I want that...' (θέλω ἵνα), which is an 'extremely bold expression.'[479] Jesus is *demanding* from the Father; now he is openly speaking as the glorified Lord, and the fictional setting of the prayer is left behind. Jesus already speaks in the authority of his divine glory. Most interpreters see the petition of v.24 as referring to the union with Christ after the physical death of the believer.[480] After the previous considerations about the view of faith and unity with Christ the author of John 17 presents, it is unlikely that the destiny of the believers after their death is envisaged here. According to John 17, the believers are already in a state of salvation, they are one with the Father and the Son and in a state of joy. In these expressions, it is implied that the believer already sees the divine glory of Christ; it is part of the state of salvation, of oneness and joy, to see the glory, which, in turn, includes oneness and joy. Thus the vision of the divine glory in oneness with God is the state in which the church finds itself already in this earthly life. It is the expression that it is not from the world but belongs to the divine realm. The mystical oneness or union with the Father and the Son leads to the vision of the glory, which leads to joy.

Finally, the interaction with Gnostic thought has led Johannine theology into a kind of mysticism, where salvation consists of oneness with the divine (20-23), of the vision of the divine glory (v.24) and of participation in it (v.22), as well as living in a state of supernatural joy or, to use the parallel term, rest. Having said that, it must not be forgotten, that the theology of John 17 is still distinctly Christian and not Gnostic. The oneness with God can only be achieved through faith in the Son, only through believing that Jesus is truly sent by the Father, and that his death on the cross is part of his mission. In fact, for the author of John 17 the crucifixion is the fulfilment of Jesus' mission and his return to the Father. The glory which the church sees, is, in fact, a particularly christological glory, it is that of Jesus Christ, which has been given to him by the Father, before the creation of the world as an expression of his love. It must not be forgotten that this Jesus Christ is saying this prayer in the hour facing his passion. Although close to Gnosticism, this keeps the theology of John 17 firmly within Christianity.

---

479 Bultmann; *Johannesevangelium*, 397, fn.5.
480 Cf. Becker; *Johannesevangelium*, 630; Bultmann; *Johannesevangelium*, 397-399; Schnackenburg; *Johannesevangelium III*, 222f.

The last sentence (v.25f) starts again with an invocation of the Father, this time addressing him as 'righteous Father.' Now, in the end of the whole text, the epistemology of John 17 is described. It is not that the Holy Spirit or Paraclete makes the church understand Christ and the Father; rather it is Jesus' revelatory ministry and task as the messenger. The world cannot understand or get to know God; this is, before the background of Hellenistic religious thought, not surprising. God is entirely transcendent and inaccessible to human minds. This is, in fact, one of the most basic presuppositions of the whole Gospel. It can first be observed in the prologue, where the Philonic *logos*-concept is introduced, which bridges God's transcendence and the immanence of world and humanity. For the author of John 17, and presumably also for the community in which he was writing, Jesus has understood God, he knows God, and he is sent to make him known to the church. The church is the church by the very fact that it recognises and believes that Jesus is God's messenger, and that what he reveals about God is true. Through Jesus' revelation the church has been given God's name. In v.26 a parallel structure between these two elements, the Aorist ἐγνώρισα αὐτοῖς τὸ ὄνομά σου ('I made your name known to them') and the future γνωρίσω, ἵνα ἡ ἀγάπη ἣν ἠγάπησάς με ἐν αὐτοῖς ᾖ κἀγὼ ἐν αὐτοῖς ('I will make it [i.e. God's name] known, so that the love with which you have loved me may be in them, and I in them') can be observed. Through this parallelism Jesus says that the name which he has given to his disciples is, as they will see in his passion, that they are included in the love with which the Father loved the Son from the beginning. Through their union with Christ they are loved by God, and through Christ's passion they, and the whole church throughout all generations with them, are the object of God's love. Humanity cannot achieve this love by any means. It is a free gift which God gives to those who do not deserve it. And so the author of John 17 arrives at the focal point of all Johannine theology: God is love.

Conclusion

In the analysis of John 17, we have seen how the author used the language which is was in the Johannine community, and combined it with language he could take from his environment in order to express the Christian *kerygma* for the particular situation of the Johannine church at the end of the first century. The approach he took is, without doubt, extremely daring. The author takes up many elements from an inceptive Gnosticism and combines them with Johannine thought, so achieving a new understanding of what Christ means for the church in its particular historical and spiritual environment. In doing so, he makes the Christian *kerygma* relevant for his fellow-Christians in their world. He does not change the essence of the Christian proclamation, but translates the *kerygma* in order to make it heard and understood by his contemporaries. He gains the legitimacy for this theological work from the presence of the Spirit, who interprets and mediates the word of God to the church.

The author is, however, not only writing for his community. His language is comprehensible to the whole church, as it has been proven by the 'canonisation' of John's Gospel including John 17, although the fact that it was highly appreciated by Gnostics shows that it is on the borderline between orthodox Christianity and heresy.[481] What John 17 offers to the church is a view of the Gospel, shaped by the particular environment and circumstances in which its author wrote. In his situation, he developed a particular language to understand the Gospel for himself and his community, a language which eventually was accepted by the wider church as an authentic interpretation of Christianity. Today, the interpreter's task is to understand the particularities of this language which grew out of the author's environment and is an offering to the whole church. Or, as Rudolf Bultmann puts it, 'the main task of exegesis is to identify the ways of talking which are possible for the author within the tradition in which he finds himself.'[482] Another way of talking is not possible for the author, and therefore we have, in order to take him seriously, to accept that he is writing from a certain perspective and envisaging a particular audience. Then, however, we can truly understand this text in its context and appreciate his particular contribution to the Christian *Struggle for Language*. Only then can the particular text help us to find a language by means of which to proclaim the same truth as the author of the great prayer of John 17.

---

[481] The final canonisation of John's Gospel indeed shows that its language was acceptable to main stream Christianity.

[482] Cf. Bultmann; *Johannesevangelium*, 6 (own translation).

Chapter 9

From Theological Hermeneutics to Hermeneutical Theology

In the course of this study I have developed a hermeneutic of the New Testament, which takes seriously that the New Testament is both a historical document and the sacred scripture of Christianity. This approach has been developed starting with a discussion of Karl Barth and Rudolf Bultmann's respective presuppositions which led them to their different positions. In the discussion of the Barth-Bultmann debate, usually only the differences on the surface are recognised, so that Barth's approach is described as 'theological', and Bultmann's either as 'existentialist' or even as merely 'technical'. Yet at the heart of this argument lies a fundamental disagreement about the relation between the transcendent and the immanent with important implications for their distinct hermeneutical approaches. In short, Karl Barth assumes that the text cannot contain the meaning to which it refers; the text can only point at its meaning. Thus the interpreter has to reach to the meaning through the text, in order to arrive at 'the Word behind the words.' Rudolf Bultmann, on the contrary, holds that the text itself can carry the meaning, which is thus to be found in the words of the text rather than behind them. Further, we have discussed the epistemological foundations of the existentialist interpretation and have seen that Bultmann's hermeneutical approach does not dissolve theology into anthropology but that it is a possible way of understanding the world without turning it into an object.

On the grounds of the critical evaluation of both positions, I chose to follow the approach proposed by Rudolf Bultmann, yet only to embark on a critical discussion of his hermeneutics. Although Bultmann's existentialist interpretation provides, in my opinion, an indispensable basis for biblical interpretation, it is necessary to address two main problems of his theology. First, Bultmann does not take seriously that language is the bearer of meaning. Therefore, contrary to his assumptions, it is not possible to find the *kerygma* in the New Testament and then reformulate it in another, presumably innocent language, without loss of meaning. Second, Bultmann reduces the subject of theology, and thus the meaning of the *kerygma*, to the isolated human self before God. He does not consider that humanity is always part of the world, part of creation, so that a perception of the world as fallen and redeemed creation must fall within the perspective of theological hermeneutics as well.

Having considered these points we set out on 'The long Path to Language' in order to find a theory of language which takes seriously the insights of Bultmann's existentialist interpretation and yet solves the two main problems of this approach. In the course of the conversation with the later Heidegger, Hans-Georg Gadamer and Paul Ricœur we arrived at the concept of the *Struggle for Language*, which fulfils these demands. It consists basically of understanding the New Testament as a reflection of the early Christian development of a language of faith. Earliest Christianity, as well as every successive generation of Christians, had to find a language through which the new faith could be understood and communicated. Taking up terms and concepts from other religious languages and transforming their meaning, Christianity developed a language of faith. Yet as the earliest church before the Gnostic crisis was not a monolithic organisation but a heterogeneous group of churches with hardly any overarching organisation,[483] many different approaches towards Christianity developed and led to different writings each having its distinct character. Thus, the different currents within early Christianity led to a plurality of theologies within the canon of the New Testament. Therefore, I agreed with Käsemann's famous statement that the New Testament does not found the unity of the church but a plurality of denominations.[484] It is the interpreter's task to understand the processes through which the authors of the New Testament adopted and transformed elements from other religious languages and so used them for their understanding of the Christian *euangelion*. Having understood how the early church struggled for a language to understand the Christian faith, it is the interpreter's task to find a language to understand and communicate the truth of Christianity. The interpreter's endeavours to formulate the Christian *kerygma* for his or her own situation and environment must then be based on the interaction with the same movement in the canonical (and non-canonical) writings, and with that within the tradition of the church. In order to understand the text, the interpreter must make the subject matter of the text relevant for him- or herself in the framework of his or her environment.

This perception of the task of biblical interpretation crosses the traditional borderline between the different theological disciplines. The study of

---

483 Cf. above pp.65ff.
484 Käsemann, Ernst; 'Begründet der neutestamentliche Kanon die Einheit der Kirche?' 221.

the New Testament is not a merely descriptive task, but part of the theological process of understanding Christianity and formulating it responsibly in the present context. In order to make the text relevant for the presence, the interpreter has to be part of the debate taking place in contemporary theology, history of doctrine and church-history as well as of the discourse taking place with the neighbouring subjects like philosophy, sociology, history, politics etc. Yet, unfortunately, this is too voluminous a task for one person, so that a practical division between biblical studies and contemporary theology will be unavoidable. The ideal is, however, that there is *one* process of understanding, which embraces the biblical text and the contemporary debate. In this process, the Christian heritage is received through the dialogue with scripture and tradition, translated so that it is a meaningful contribution to the present discourse. Taken seriously, this will make the borders between the theological subjects open to the participation of students of a particular theological discipline in the discourse taking place in other disciplines and subjects.

In the second part of the study I have applied the hermeneutical insights gained in the first part to selected passages from John's Gospel. Here we have seen that the concept of the *Struggle for Language* is a useful tool to understand the New Testament, in this instance John's Gospel, as sacred scripture as well as a historical document. At the same time we have taken seriously the demand that the literary dimension of the New Testament has to be recognised.[485] Yet alien literary theories have not been applied to the text; rather it has been read as ancient literature, the type of literature from which it originates. Taking seriously the antiquity of the New Testament implies that it is necessary to see it within its contemporary context. Therefore the usage and meaning of a term in antiquity, for example, needs to be considered in order to establish the particular way in which the author used the term and so the meaning which it carries. The same applies to the concepts underlying the thoughts which are developed in the text. We can sum up in Bultmann's words: 'The main task of exegesis is to identify the ways of talking which are possible for the author within the tradition in which he finds himself.'[486]

The importance of the exegetical part of this study lies not in new exegetical insights into John's Gospel, which may or may not be found here, but in the application of the methodology which follows from the concept of the *Struggle for Language*. It shows how the integrity of the biblical text as a piece of ancient literature can be maintained and, at the same time, the New Testament can be understood as sacred scripture of Christianity. As

---

[485] Cf. above, p. 9.
[486] Cf. Bultmann; *Johannesevangelium*, 6 (own translation).

this study is concerned mainly with hermeneutical questions, the guiding principles of the interpretation of the texts from John's Gospel were hermeneutical considerations. Yet the texts can speak in a much wider range of contexts. The way John's Gospel has been approached from a hermeneutical viewpoint in this study, it can also be interpreted in the light of any other theological question. Yet it is crucial that there is no pretended immediate understanding, but that readers distance themselves from the text and discover its otherness by exploring its horizon and world. Then, in the tension between text and interpreter, understanding may take place. Different biblical texts have different views of every kind of issues. Already within John's Gospel we have seen that some questions are approached in different ways. Hence, in order to understand a theological issue, the interpreter has to interact not only with one biblical text, but with a whole range of different texts. Understanding them within their own context then leads to a theological understanding of the issue. There will always be more than one possible answer, for the New Testament itself offers a multitude of approaches. Based on the insights, gained in interaction with the Bible, however, the interpreter can partake in the discussion of this issue. A struggle of conflicting interpretation cannot be avoided and replaced by any kind of orthodoxy prescribed by a *Church Dogmatic*.

The approach to the New Testament proposed in this study has far-reaching implications. If the notion is taken seriously that the authors of the New Testament were struggling to understand the Christian faith through language and the interpreter is to take part in that struggle for language in order to understand Christian faith through the language of the Bible and then formulate it in a way that it is relevant for the present situation, the relation between interpretation and theology must be reconsidered. The task of theology is then to understand Christian faith through language and to formulate in a way that it is relevant in the present situation. The step is made from theological hermeneutics to a hermeneutical theology. This type of theology is not restricted to the church or the theological faculty, but it can take part in the interdisciplinary discourse and in the inter-faith dialogue from a distinctly Christian position. New Testament scholarship, for instance, can enter into and profit from a discussion with classicists and historians of antiquity, for all these subjects are involved in the study and interpretation of ancient texts. Yet the student of the New Testament is likely to share the faith which finds its expression in the biblical writings. Yet this does not influence directly the methods of exegesis. The theologian involved in systematic or contemporary theology, to present another example, will have to engage in a dialogue with philosophy and social sciences, for he or she will have to respond to questions which are raised in these disciplines and find a way to formulate a position which expresses the same faith as the authors of the New Testament in the contemporary context. In order to do so, the theologian will have to take up terms and concepts from languages of other disciplines but transform them in a way that what they say is distinctly Christian and represents at the same time a contribution to the interdisciplinary discourse. In sum, theology understood as hermeneutical theology can and must participate in the interdisciplinary discourse as a critical participant and partake in the conflict of the different interpretations of the world.

This perception of theology meets the criticism Watson directs against historical-critical scholarship. Watson's criticism is that theology and biblical scholarship are, as he perceives it, separated and that there is no theological interest in biblical interpretation.[487] Yet as I have already pointed out in the Prolegomena, Watson's solution to this problem is, in my opinion, not satisfying, for it makes theology rule over against *exegesis* which, as a servant, easily becomes *eisegesis*. Therefore I prefer the approach proposed in this study which fulfils Watson's demands, yet turns around Watson's approach by defining the whole task of theology as hermeneutics and making the hermeneutical question the key-question of theology. This approach takes up Ebeling's demand, made as early as 1950, that the insights of the historical-critical method must be radically applied in the whole theological discourse and not only in biblical scholarship.[488] In fact, the recent attempts like Watson's to make dogmatic theology rule biblical interpretation affirm, even more than half a century after his analysis, Gerhard Ebeling's depressing verdict:

> The critical historical method is certainly recognized in principle, except by a few outsiders. But in practice it is widely felt in ecclesiastical and theological circles to be really a tedious nuisance. Its results may perhaps be noted, but then they are left aside after all instead of being worked through. And where the critical historical method is seriously applied today, it remains a matter for the individual historical disciplines, and does not have an effect on theology as a whole, still less on the church — or when there is any visible sign of consequences of such a kind, it is pronounced to be rationalism and liberalism, or even rouses the cry of heresy. The path which theology has to tread in this situation for the church's sake is certainly full of unsolved problem, but there is no doubt as to the direction it must take.[489]

---

[487] Cf. Watson; *Text, Church and World*, 1f.

[488] Cf. Ebeling, Gerhard; 'Die Bedeutung der historisch-kritischen Mehode for die protestantische Theologie und Kirche' in: *Wort und Glaube*, Tübingen (Mohr-Siebeck) ³1967, 1-49, 46-49 (English: 'The Significance of the critical historical Method for Church and Theology in Protestantism' in: Ebeling, Gerhard; *Word and Faith*, London (SCM) 1963, 17-61, 57-61).

[489] Ibid. 49 (Engl. 61).

This study is only a first stage on the path onto which Ebeling has led us. It shows, however, that it is possible to take seriously the insights of historical-critical research and understand the New Testament as sacred scripture of Christianity, to accept the integrity of the text as an ancient document and yet read it with theological concern. This path leads theology out of self-inflicted isolation and the ghetto protected by the *Church Dogmatics* into a position from which it can partake in the struggle of the conflicting interpretations of the world and enter the interdisciplinary discourse and ecumenical dialogue as an equal partner.

Bibliography

Appold, Mark L.; *The Oneness Motif in the Fourth Gospel*, WUNT 2/1, Tübingen (Mohr-Siebeck) 1976.

Argyle, A.W.; 'Philo and the Fourth Gospel' *ExpTim* LXIII (1951), 385-386.

Aristotle; *Poetics*, ed. and trans. by Stephen Halliwell, in: Loeb Classical Library 199, Cambridge, Massachusetts, London (Harvard University Press) 1995.

Ashton, John (ed.); *The Interpretation of John*, Issues of Religion and Theology 9, Philadelphia (Fortress) and London (SPCK) 1986.

Ashton, John; *Studying John: Approaches to the Fourth Gospel*, Oxford (Clarendon) 1994.

Ashton, John; *Understanding the Fourth Gospel*, Oxford (Clarendon) 1990.

Barrett, Charles K.; *The Gospel according to St. John*, London (SPCK) [2]1978.

Barth, Gerhard; *Der Tod Jesu im Verständnis des Neuen Testaments*, Neukirchen-Vluyn (Neukirchener Verlag) 1992

Barth, Karl — Bultmann, Rudolf; *Briefwechsel 1922-1966* (ed. by Bernd Jaspert), Karl Barth, Gesamtausgabe, V. Briefe, vol.1, Zürich (TVZ) 1971.

Barth, Karl; *Der Römerbrief*, Zürich (TVZ) [15]1989.

Barth, Karl; *Die kirchliche Dogmatik*, Zürich (TVZ) 1932ff.

Barth, Karl; *Einführung in die evangelische Theologie*, Zürich (TVZ) [3]1985.

Barth, Karl; *Erklärung des Johannes-Evangeliums (Kapitel 1-8)* (ed. by Walther Fürst), Karl Barth, Gesamtausgabe, II. Akademische Werke, 1925/26, Zürich (TVZ) 1976.

Barth, Karl; *Fides quaerens intellectum: Anselms Beweis der Existenz Gottes im Zusammenhang seines theologischen Programms* (ed. by E. Jüngel and I.U. Dalferth), Karl Barth, Gesamtausgabe, II. Akademische Werke, 1931, Zürich (TVZ) 1981.

Barth, Karl; *Rudolf Bultmann: Ein Versuch, ihn zu verstehen - Christus und Adam nach Röm. 5: Zwei theologische Studien*, Zürich (EVZ) [3/2(respectively)]1964.

Barton, Stephen C.; 'Early Christianity and the Sociology of the Sect' in: Watson, Francis (ed.); *The Open Text: New Directions for Biblical Studies?*, London (SCM) 1993, 140-162.

Bauckham, Richard (ed.); *The Gospels for All Christians: Rethinking the Gospel Audiences*, Edinburgh (T&T Clark) 1998.

Bauckham, Richard; *For whom where the Gospels written?* in: Bauckham, Richard (ed.); *The Gospels for All Christians: Rethinking the Gospel Audiences*, Edinburgh (T&T Clark) 1998, 9-48.

Bauer, Walter; *Orthodoxy and Heresy in Earliest Christianity*, in: The New Testament Library, London (SCM) 1972.

Bayer, Oswald; 'Entmythologisierung?' *NZSTh* 34, 1992, 109-124.

Bayer, Oswald; *Autorität und Kritik: Zu Hermeneutik und Wissenschaftstheorie*; Tübingen (Mohr-Siebeck) 1991.

Bayer, Oswald; *Theologie*, Handbuch Systematischer Theologie Vol.1, Gütersloh (Gütersloher Verlagshaus) 1994.

Becker, Jürgen; 'Aufbau, Schichtung und theologiegeschichtliche Stellung des Gebetes in Johannes 17' *ZNW* 60, 1969, 56-83

Becker, Jürgen; 'Aus der Literatur zum Johannesevangelium (1978-1980)' *TRu* 47, 1982, 279-301, 305-347.

Becker, Jürgen; 'Das Johannesevangelium im Streit der Methoden (1980-1984)' *TRu* 51, 1986, 1-78.

Becker, Jürgen; 'Die Abschiedsreden Jesu im Johannesevangelium' *ZNW* 61, 1970, 215-246.

Becker, Jürgen; *Das Evangelium nach Johannes*,

Vol.1, ÖTK 4/1, Gütersloh (Mohn) [3]1991

Vol.2, ÖTK 4/2, Gütersloh (Mohn) [3]1991.

Bible and Culture Collective, The; *The Postmodern Bible*, New Haven and London (Yale University Press) 1995.

Bietenhard, H.; ὄνομα κτλ., *ThWNT* V, 242-283.

Borsch, F.H.; 'Further Reflections on the "Son of Man": The Origins and Development of the Title' in: Charlesworth, James H.(ed.): *The Messiah: Developments in Earliest Christianity (the first Princeton Symposium on Judaism and Christian Origins)*, Minneapolis (Augsburg Fortress) 1992, 130-144.

Broer, Ingo; ἐξουσία, *EWNT* II, 23-29.

Brown, Raymond E.; *The Community of the Beloved Disciple: The Life, Loves, and Hates of an Individual Church in New Testament Times*, New York, Mahwah (Paulist Press) 1979.

Brown, Raymond E.; *The Gospel according to John*

Vol.1, The Anchor Bible 29, New York (Doubleday) 1966.

Vol.2, The Anchor Bible 29A, New York (Doubleday) 1970.

Bühner, Jan-Adolf; *Der Gesandte und sein Weg im 4. Evangelium*, WUNT 2/2, Tübingen (Mohr-Siebeck), 1977.

Bultmann, R.; 'ζάω κτλ. D.: Der Lebensbegriff des Judentums', *ThWNT* II 856-862.

Bultmann, Rudolf; 'Das Problem der Hermeneutik' in: *Glauben und Verstehen* vol.2, Tübingen (Mohr-Siebeck) [6]1993, pp. 211-235.

Bultmann, Rudolf; 'Zu J. Schniewinds Thesen', *K&M* I, 122-138.

Bultmann, Rudolf; 'Zum Problem der Entmythologisierung', *K&M* II, 179-208.

Bultmann, Rudolf; 'Zum Problem der Entmythologisierung', *K&M* IV, 20-27.

Bultmann, Rudolf; *Das Evangelium des Johannes*, Kritisch-exegetischer Kommentar über das Neue Testament, Vol.2, Göttingen (Vandenhoek und Ruprecht) [21]1986.

Bultmann, Rudolf; *Jesus Christ and Mythology*, London (SCM) 1960.

Bultmann, Rudolf; *Neues Testament und Mythologie: Das Problem der Entmythologisierung der neutestamentlichen Verkündigung* (ed. by Eberhard Jüngel), Beiträge zur evangelischen Theologie vol.96, München (Kaiser) [3]1988.

Bultmann, Rudolf; *Theologie des Neuen Testamentes*, Tübingen (Mohr-Siebeck) [9]1984.

Charlesworth, James H.(ed.): *The Messiah: Developments in Earliest Christianity (the first Princeton Symposium on Judaism and Christian Origins)*, Minneapolis (Augsburg Fortress) 1992.

Chestnutt, Randall D.; *From Death to Life: Conversion in Joseph and Aseneth*, JSPS 16, Sheffield (Academic Press) 1995.

Childs, Brevard S.; *Biblical Theology of the Old and New Testaments: Theological Reflection on the Christian Bible*, London (SCM) 1992

Childs, Brevard S.; *The New Testament as Canon: An Introduction*, London (SCM) 1984.

Conzelmann, H.; 'σκότος κτλ.' *ThWNT* VII, 424-446.

Conzelmann, H.; 'φῶς κτλ.' *ThWNT* IX, 302-349.

Cunningham, Mary Kathleen; *What is Theological Exegesis?: Interpretation and Use of Scripture in Barth's Doctrine of Election*, Valley Forge (Trinity Press) 1995.

Demke, Christian; 'Der sogenannte Logos-Hymnus im johanneischen Prolog', *ZNW* 58, 1967, 45-68.

Dietzfelbinger, Christian; 'Paraklet und theologischer Anspruch im Johannesevangelium', *ZTK* 82 (1985), 389-408.

Dietzfelbinger, Christian; *Der Abschied des Kommenden: Eine Auslegung der johanneischen Abschiedreden*, WUNT 95, Tübingen (Mohr-Siebeck) 1997.

Dodd, C.H.; *Historical Tradition in the Fourth Gospel*, Cambridge (University Press) 1963.

Dodd, C.H.; *The Interpretation of the Fourth Gospel*, Cambridge (University Press) 1953.

Duff, J.Wight; *A Literary History of Rome: From the Origins to the Close of the Golden Age*, London (T. Fisher Uwin) [5]1923.

Dunn, James D.G.; 'Let John be John' in: Stuhlmacher, Peter (ed.); *Das Evangelium und die Evangelien*, WUNT 28, Tübingen (Mohr-Siebeck) 1983, 309-339.

Dunn, James D.G.; *Christology in the Making: A New Testament Inquiry into the Doctrine of the Incarnation*, London (SCM) 1980.

Ebeling, Gerhard; 'Word of God and Hermeneutics' in: Ebeling, Gerhard; *Word and Faith*, London (SCM) 1963, 305-332.

Ebeling, Gerhard; 'Wort Gottes und Hermeneutik' in: *Wort und Glaube*, Tübingen (Mohr-Siebeck) [3]1967, 319-348.

Ebeling, Gerhard; 'Die Bedeutung der historisch-kritischen Mehode for die protestantische Theologie und Kirche' in: *Wort und Glaube*, Tübingen (Mohr-Siebeck) [3]1967, 1-49.

Ebeling, Gerhard; 'The Significance of the critical historical Method for Church and Theology in Protestantism' in: Ebeling, Gerhard; *Word and Faith*, London (SCM) 1963, 17 –61.

Ebeling, Gerhard; *Word and Faith*, London (SCM) 1963.

Ebeling, Gerhard; *Wort und Glaube*, Tübingen (Mohr-Siebeck) [3]1967.

Fischer, Hermann; *Systematische Theologie: Konzeptionen und Probleme im 20. Jahrhundert*, Stuttgart, Berlin, Köln (Kohlhammer) 1992.

Fitzmyer, J.A.; 'μονογενής' *EWNT* II 1082-1083.

Fuchs, Ernst; *Hermeneutik*, Tübingen (Mohr-Siebeck) [4]1970.

Fuchs, Ernst; *Zum hermeneutischen Problem in der Theologie: Die existentiale Interpretation*; Tübingen (Mohr-Siebeck) [2]1965.

Gadamer, Hans-Georg; *Wahrheit und Methode*, in: Gadamer, Hans-Georg; *Gesammelte Werke*, vol.1: *Hermeneutik: Wahrheit und Methode: Grundzüge einer philosophischen Hermeneutik*, Tübingen (Mohr-Siebeck) ⁶1990.

Gadamer, Hans-Georg; *Truth and Method*, London (Sheed and Ward) ²1979.

Goodenough, Erwin R.; *An Introduction to Philo Judaeus*, Oxford (Blackwell) ²1962.

Grese, William C.; *Corpus Hermeticum XIII and Early Christian Literature*, Studia ad Corpus Hellenisticum Novi Testamenti, vol.5, Leiden (Brill) 1979.

Grondin, Jean; *Einführung in die philosophische Hermeneutik*, Darmstadt (Wissenschaftliche Buchgesellschaft) 1991.

Haenchen, Ernst; *Das Johannesevangelium*, Tübingen (Mohr-Siebeck) 1980.

Harrisville, Roy A. and Sundberg, Walter; *The Bible in modern Culture: Theology and historical-critical Method from Spinoza to Käsemann*, Grand Rapids (Eerdmans) 1995.

Heidegger, Martin; *Einführung in die Metaphysik*, Tübingen (Niemeyer) ³1987.

Heidegger, Martin; *Holzwege*, Frankfurt (Klostermann) ⁷1994.

Heidegger, Martin; *Sein und Zeit*, Tübingen (Niemeyer) ¹⁷1993.

Heidegger, Martin; *Unterwegs zur Sprache*, Stuttgart (Neske) ¹⁰1993.

Hengel, Martin; *Der Sohn Gottes*, Tübingen (Mohr-Siebeck) 1975.

Hengel, Martin; *Die johanneische Frage*, WUNT 67, Tübingen (Mohr-Siebeck) 1993.

Herntrich, V.; 'κρίνω κτλ., B. Der at.liche Begriff מִשְׁפָּט' *ThWNT* III 922-933.

Hofius, Otfried; 'Struktur und Gedankengang des Logos-Hymnus in Joh 1:1-18' ZNW 78, 1987, 1-25.

Hunsinger, George; *How to read Karl Barth: The Shape of his Theology*, New York and Oxford (Oxford University Press) 1991.

Hurtado, Larry W.; *One God, One Lord: Early Christian Devotion and Ancient Monotheism*, London (SCM) 1988.

Jaeger, Hans; *Heidegger und die Sprache*, Bern (Franke) 1971.

Jeanrond, Werner; *Theological Hermeneutics: Development and Significance*, London (SCM) 1991.

Käsemann, Ernst; 'Aufbau und Anliegen des johanneischen Prologs' in: *Exegetische Versuche und Besinnungen*, vol.2, Göttingen (Vandenhoek und Ruprecht) 1964, 155-181.

Käsemann, Ernst; 'Begründet der neutestamentliche Kanon die Einheit der Kirche?' in: *Exegetische Versuche und Besinnungen*, vol.1, Göttingen (Vandenhoek und Ruprecht) 1960, 214-223.

Käsemann, Ernst; *Exegetische Versuche und Besinnungen*, 2 vols, Göttingen (Vandenhoek und Ruprecht) 1960 and 1964.

Käsemann, Ernst; *Jesu letzter Wille nach Johannes 17*, Tübingen (Mohr-Siebeck) ⁴1980.

Kearny, Richard; *Modern Movements in European Philosophy*, Manchester and New York (Manchester University Press) ²1994.

Kleinknecht, H.; 'λέγω B: Der Logos in Griechentum und Hellenismus' *ThWNT* IV, 76-89.

Koester, Craig R.; *Symbolism in the Fourth Gospel: Meaning, Mystery, Community*, Minneapolis (Fortress) 1995.

Körtner, Ulrich; 'Arbeit am Mythos? Zum Verhältnis von Christentum und mythischem Denken bei Rudolf Bultmann' *NZSTh* 34, 1992, 163-181.

Köster, Helmut; 'The History-of-Religion School, Gnosis and Gospel of John' ST 40 (1986), 115-136.

Köster, Helmut; *Einführung in das Neue Testament: im Rahmen der Religionsgeschichte und Kulturgeschichte der hellenistischen und römischen Zeit*, Berlin-New York (de Gruyter) 1980.

Kümmel, Werner Georg; *Einleitung in das Neue Testament*, Heidelberg (Quelle & Meyer) [21]1983.

Liedke, G.; 'שׁפט' *THAT* II 999-1009.

Logan, A.H.B. and Wedderburn, A.J.M. (eds.); *The New Testament and Gnosis: Essays in honour of Robert McL. Wilson*, Edinburgh (T&T Clark) 1983.

Lohse, Eduard; *Die Entstehung des Neuen Testaments*, Theologische Wissenschaft Vol. IV, Stuttgart, Berlin, Köln (Kohlhammer) [5]1991.

Luther, Martin; *Kritische Gesamtausgabe*, Weimar 1883ff.

Martínez, Florentino García; *The Dead Sea Scrolls Translated: The Qumran Texts in English*, Leiden (Brill) 1994.

Martyn, J. Louis; *History and Theology in the Fourth Gospel*, Nashville, Tennessee (Abington) [2]1979.

McCormack, Bruce L.: *Karl Barth's Critically Realistic Dialectical Theology: Its Genesis and Development 1909-1936*, Oxford (Clarendon) 1995.

Meeks, Wayne A.; 'The Man from Heaven in Johannine Sectarianism' in: Ashton, John (ed.); *The Interpretation of John*, Issues of Religion and Theology 9, Philadelphia (Fortress) and London (SPCK) 1986, 1401-173.

Melanchthon, Philipp; *Loci Communes, 1521*, Latin and German, ed. Lutherisches Kirchenamt der Vereinigten Evangelisch-Lutherischen Kirche Deutschlands, transl. and annotated by H.G. Pöhlmann, Gütersloh (Mohn) 1993.

Moberly, R.W.L.; 'The Church's Use of the Bible; The Work of Brevard Childs' *ExpTim* 99/4 (1988), 104-109.

Onuki, Takashi; *Gemeinde und Welt im Johannesevangelium*, WMANT 56, Neukirchen-Vluyn (Neukirchener Verlag) 1984.

Ovidius Naso, Publius; *Tristia Epistulas Ex Ponto,* Latine et Germanice, ed. by Georg Luck, Zürich (Artemis) 1963.

Painter, John; 'Glimpses of the Johannine Community in the Farewell Discourses' *ABR* 28 (1980) 22-38.

Painter, John; 'The Farewell Discourses and the History of Johannine Christianity' *NTS* 27 (1980-81) 525-543.

Pannenberg, Wolfgang; 'Christologie II: Dogmengeschichtlich' in: RGG[3], 1762-1777.

Perkins, Pheme; *Gnosticism and the New Testament*, Minneapolis (Fortress) 1993.

Philo; *Works in Ten Volumes*, ed. and trans. by F.H. Colson and G.H. Whitaker, in: Loeb Classical Library, Cambridge, Massachusetts, London (Harvard University Press) 1929ff.

Pöhlmann, Horst Georg, *Abriß der Dogmatik: Ein Kompendium*, Gütersloh (Mohn) [5]1990.

Riches, John; *Jesus and the Transformation of Judaism*, London (Darton, Longman & Todd) 1980.

Richter, Georg; 'Die Fleischwerdung des Logos im Johannesevangelium' *NovT* 13, 1971, 81-126.

Ricœur, Paul; 'Erzählung, Metapher und Interpretationstheorie' *ZTK* 84 (1987), 232-253.

Ricœur, Paul; 'Preface to Bultmann' in: Ricœur, Paul; *Essays on Biblical Interpretation*, Philadelphia 1980, 49-72.

Ricœur, Paul; 'The Metaphorical Process as Cognition, Imagination, and Feeling' *Critical Inquiry* 5, 1978, 143-160.

Ricœur, Paul; *Biblical Hermeneutics*, Semeia 4, 1975, 29-148.

Ricœur, Paul; *Essays on Biblical Interpretation*, Philadelphia (Fortress) 1980.

Ricœur, Paul; *InterpretationTheory: Discourse and the Surplus of Meaning*, Fort Worth (Texas University Press) 1976.

Ricœur, Paul; *The Rule of Metaphor: Multi-disciplinary Studies of the Creation of Meaning in Language*, London (Routledge) 1986.

Ricœur, Paul; *Time and Narrative* (3 vols.), Chicago and London (Chicago University Press) 1984-88.

Robinson, James M. (ed.); *The Nag Hammadi Library in English*, San Francisco (Harper & Row) ³1988.

Robinson, James M. and Cobb, John B. Jr. (ed.); *The Later Heidegger and Theology*, in: *New Frontiers in Theology: Discussions among German and American Theologians*, New York, Evanston and London (Harper & Row) 1963.

Sandmel, Samuel; 'Parallelomania' *JBL* 81, 1962, 1-13.

Sandmel, Samuel; *Philo of Alexandria: An Introduction*, New York and Oxford (Oxford University Press) 1979.

Sasse, H.; 'κόσμος κτλ.' *ThWNT* III, 867-898.

Schmidt, Karl-Ludwig; 'βασιλεύς κτλ. E: Die Wortgruppe βασιλεύς im Neuen Nestament' *ThWNT* I 576-593.

Schmithals, Walter; 'Der Prolog des Johannesevangeliums' *ZNW* 70, 1979, 16-43.

Schmithals, Walter; *An Introduction to the Theology of Rudolf Bultmann*, London (SCM) 1968.

Schmithals, Walter; *Neues Testament und Gnosis*, in: Erträge der Forschung 208, Darmstadt (Wissenschaftliche Buchgesellschaft) 1984.

Schnackenburg, Rudolf; *Das Johannesevangelium*,
Vol.1, HTKNT 4/1, Freiburg (Herder) 1965
Vol.2, HTKNT 4/2, Freiburg (Herder) 1971
Vol.3, HTKNT 4/3, Freiburg (Herder) 1976
Vol.4, HTKNT 4/4, Freiburg (Herder) 1984.

Schneiders, Sandra M.; *The Revelatory Text: Interpreting the New Testament as sacred scripture*, San Francisco (HarperSanFrancisco) 1991.

Schniewind, Julius; 'Antwort an Rudolf Bultmann. Thesen zum Problem der Entmythologisierung' *K&M* II, 77-121.

Schottroff, Luise; *Der Glaubende und die feindliche Welt: Beobachtungen zum gnostischen Dualismus und seiner Bedeutung für Paulus und das Johannesevangelium*, WMANT 37, Neukirchen-Vluyn (Neukirchener Verlag) 1970.

Smith, D. Moody; *The Composition and Order of the Fourth Gospel: Bultmann's Literary Theory*, New Haven and London (Yale University Press) 1965.

Smith, D. Moody; *The Theology of the Gospel of John*, in: *New Testament Theology*, ed. by J.D.G. Dunn, Cambridge (Cambridge University Press) 1995.

Strack, Herrmann L. and Billerbeck, Paul; *Kommentar zum Neuen Testament aus Talmud und Midrasch*, München (C.H. Beck) , 5 vols., 1922-1961.

Stuhlmacher, Peter (ed.); *Das Evangelium und die Evangelien*, WUNT 28, Tübingen (Mohr-Siebeck) 1983.

Thiselton, Anthony C.; *The two Horizons: New Testament Hermeneutics and Philosophical description with special reference to Heidegger, Bultmann, Gadamer, and Wittgenstein*, Grand Rapids (Eerdmans) and Carlile (Paternoster) 1980.

Thyen, Hartwig; 'Aus der Literatur zum Johannesevangelium' *TRu* 39, 1979, 1-69, 222-252- 289-330; 42, 1977, 211-270; 43, 1978, 328-590; 44, 1979, 97-134.

Troeltsch, Ernst; *Die Soziallehren der christlichen Kirchen und Gruppen*, Tübingen (Mohr-Siebeck) 1912.

Untergaßmair, Franz; *Im Namen Jesu: Der Namensbegriff im Johannesevangelium*, FB 13, Stuttgart (Katholisches Bibelwerk) 1974.

Watson, Francis (ed.); *The Open Text: New Directions for Biblical Studies?*, London (SCM) 1993.

Watson, Francis; *Text and Truth: Redefining Biblical Theology*, Edinburgh (T&T Clark) 1997.

Watson, Francis; *Text, Church and World: Biblical Interpretation in Theological Perspective*, Edinburgh (T&T Clark) 1994.

Wilson, Robert McLachlen; 'Philo and the Fourth Gospel' *ExpTim* LXV, 1953, 47-49.

Wisse, Frederik; 'Prolegomena to the Study of the Testament and Gnosis' in: Logan, A.H.B. and Wedderburn, A.J.M. (eds.); *The New Testament and Gnosis: Essays in honour of Robert McL. Wilson*, Edinburgh (T&T Clark) 1983, 138-145.

Witherington, III, Ben; *John's Wisdom: A Commentary on the Fourth Gospel*, Luisville, Kentucky (Westminster John Knox Press) 1995.

Yamauchi, Edwin; *Pre-Christian Gnosticism: A Survey of the Proposed Evidences*, London (Tyndale Press) 1973.

Index